Gender, Space and City Bankers

Gendered processes of globalisation, transnationalisation and urbanisation are increasing local and global inequalities and widening the gap between the rich and the poor. The global finance industry plays a key role in these processes, directing its operations from local command points in global cities such as London. Drawing on empirical data collected after the 2008 financial crisis – in depth interviews with male City of London bankers who are also fathers, in depth interviews with the bankers' wives, observational data of work and family spaces, and banks' promotional online material – this book explores the day-to-day individual and institutional social practices of wealthy City bankers and banks. The book's analysis offers insight into how the spaces of work and home are integrally linked in ways that mutually shape, support and sustain the gendered dominance of the industry and its highly paid workers.

This book will appeal to postgraduate students, researchers and academics interested in the fields of gender studies, critical studies of men and masculinities, urban and metropolitan studies, sociology, studies of globalisation and transnationalisation, anthropology, cultural studies and business management. It will also be interesting for those concerned about the role of the finance industry and neoliberal capitalist ideologies, values and practices in ever-widening local and global inequalities.

Dr Helen Longlands is a lecturer in Education and International Development at UCL Institute of Education, University College London. Her research interests are interdisciplinary and centre on issues relating to gender, inequalities and social justice, particularly men, masculinities and transnational relationships and structures of power.

Routledge Advances in Feminist Studies and Intersectionality

Routledge Advances in Feminist Studies and Intersectionality is committed to the development of new feminist and pro-feminist perspectives on changing gender relations, with special attention to:

- Intersections between gender and power differentials based on age, class, dis/abilities, ethnicity, nationality, racialisation, sexuality, violence and other social divisions.
- Intersections of societal dimensions and processes of continuity and change: culture, economy, generativity, polity, sexuality, science and technology;
- Embodiment: Intersections of discourse and materiality, and of sex and gender.
- Transdisciplinarity: intersections of humanities, social sciences, medical, technical and natural sciences.
- Intersections of different branches of feminist theorising, including: historical materialist feminisms, postcolonial and anti-racist feminisms, radical feminisms, sexual difference feminisms, queer feminisms, cyber feminisms, post-human feminisms, critical studies on men and masculinities.
- A critical analysis of the travelling of ideas, theories and concepts.
- A politics of location, reflexivity and transnational contextualising that reflects the basis of the Series framed within European diversity and transnational power relations.

Gendered Power and Mobile Technology
Intersections in the Global South
Edited by Caroline Wamala Larsson and Laura Stark

The Reproductive Body at Work
The South African Bioeconomy of Egg Donation
Verena Namberger

Gender, Space and City Bankers
Helen Longlands

Gender, Space and City Bankers

Helen Longlands

Routledge
Taylor & Francis Group
LONDON AND NEW YORK

First published 2020
by Routledge
2 Park Square, Milton Park, Abingdon, Oxon OX14 4RN

and by Routledge
605 Third Avenue, New York, NY 10017

First issued in paperback 2021

Routledge is an imprint of the Taylor & Francis Group, an informa business

British Library Cataloguing-in-Publication Data
A catalogue record for this book is available from the British Library

Library of Congress Cataloging-in-Publication Data
Names: Longlands, Helen, author.
Title: Gender, space and city bankers / Helen Longlands.
Description: Abingdon, Oxon ; New York, NY : Routledge, 2020. | Series: Routledge advances in feminist studies and intersectionality | Includes bibliographical references and index.
Identifiers: LCCN 2019015323| ISBN 9781138092853 (hardback) | ISBN 9781315107226 (ebook)
Subjects: LCSH: Banks and banking—Social aspects—England—London. | Financial institutions—Social aspects—England—London. | Sociology, Urban. | Elite. | Social stratification.
Classification: LCC HG3000.L82 L66 2020 | DDC 332.1082/09421—dc23
LC record available at https://lccn.loc.gov/2019015323

ISBN 13: 978-0-367-78505-5 (pbk)
ISBN 13: 978-1-138-09285-3 (hbk)

Typeset in Times New Roman
by codeMantra

In memory of my father
James Thomas Longlands 1938–1988
For his love, kindness and compassion

Contents

Acknowledgements

A number of institutions and individuals have helped me bring this book to fruition, and I am very grateful for their support, advice and kindness along the way.

My gratitude goes particularly to the ESRC for funding my initial research study, and to the Library of Congress in association with the AHRC/ESRC for awarding me a scholarship to conduct research at the Kluge Academic Center, Library of Congress, Washington, DC, which was a valuable and enriching experience. I am also enormously grateful for the opportunity I was given to be part of the inspiring, collaborative and hugely supportive GEXcel (Joint University Centre of Gender Excellence) fellowship programme, *Research Theme 9 on Gendered Sexualed Transnationalisations, Deconstructing the Dominant: Transforming Men, "Centres" and Knowledge/Policy/Practice*, at Linköping University, Sweden, funded by the Swedish Research Council. And I am incredibly thankful to Emily Briggs and Elena Chiu at Routledge/Taylor & Francis for working so considerately with me in the production of this book, as well as the Series Editors Jeff Hearn and Nina Lykke.

In addition, I am very grateful for all the support from and discussions with colleagues, students and friends at UCL Institute of Education that helped me develop, question, revisit, extend and clarify my thinking. I would particularly like to thank Elaine Unterhalter, Amy North, Jon Swain, Jenny Parkes, Ivette Hernandez Santibañez, Rosie Peppin Vaughan, Jo Heslop, Alexandra Lewis, Miriam David and my other colleagues at the UCL Centre for Education and International Development. I have been enormously fortunate to present and discuss my work in seminars and at conferences in different parts of the world, and I offer special thanks to Richard Collier, Winnie Poster, Sebastián Madrid, Raewyn Connell and Anika Thym for their insightful and encouraging comments on my research.

My heartfelt thanks go also to my other wonderful friends and my lovely family.

Finally, and perhaps most importantly of all, I am sincerely grateful to the men and women who so kindly and generously gave up their time to participate in my research and discuss their lives with me.

Introduction

Global finance and the inequality of hegemony

The aim of this book is to explore ways the everyday gendered social processes and spatial practices of the finance industry based in the City of London combine to sustain, normalise and naturalise a local and global dominance of the finance industry today. Embedded within the premise of this study is my concern to interrogate assumptions about gender and men's power and dominance in relation to global finance and local and global forms of inequality.

The research for this book was situated in a particular geographical place at a particular historical time – a time when the world was still reeling from the collapse of the US subprime mortgage market in 2007 and the ensuing global financial crisis. The reverberations of the 2008 financial crisis were felt not only in key centres of banking, including the City of London[1] and Wall Street, but around the world, as businesses collapsed, and people lost jobs, homes and livelihoods. Yet wider shifts in social forces towards a more just society that many academics, politicians and other social commentators hoped at the time could emerge from the wake of the crisis (see, for example, Toynbee and Walker 2008; Sassen 2009a; Sen 2009; Massey 2010; Harvey 2011) have to date proved elusive. Practices in the financial sector are a central component of this problem. For what the financial crisis did make clear is the relationship between the structures, practices and cultures of modern neoliberal capitalism – epitomised and embodied by the financial services industry – and the development and perpetuation of social inequalities, including gender inequalities, both in the countries in which financial institutions are based and elsewhere in the world (see also Hanieh 2009; Sassen 2009a; Sen 2009; Massey 2010; Griffin 2012).

It is at a personal level that the enormity and effects of crises are felt most acutely. While many wealthy individuals lost considerable sums of money during the 2008 financial crisis (see, for example, Clark 2009), the people who have been most affected by the adverse consequences of the crisis, including increased levels of unemployment, the ongoing slashing of public services and welfare provisions, and the ever-rising costs of essential goods and services, are not the wealthy few of the world, they are those who were already the most poorly off (Sen 2009: 1) – those who have few, if any, spare resources to fall back on in times of need. In contrast, people with more social, political, economic and/or educational resources to draw on are more insulated and more likely than others to be able to cope with the consequences of crises; some may even exploit them – creatively or not – for their own advantage by generating large profits from the misfortunes of others, for example, or pushing through extreme political agendas (for more discussion, see Klein 2007, 2017; Berman 2010; Harvey 2012; Lanchester 2016).

In 2008, Wall Street and the City controlled $160 trillion financial assets, a sum 3.5 times global GDP (Sassen 2009a). By 2013, UK banks were said to control assets worth four times UK GDP (Hughes and Wassall 2013) despite the financial crisis, during which the UK government reportedly allocated £66 billion bailout to the Royal Bank of Scotland and Lloyd's Banking Group – a sum equal to 80% of the subsequent coalition government's £81 billion programme of public spending cuts (Treanor 2012; Wintour and Elliot 2012). By 2014, the head of Lloyd's Banking Group reportedly enjoyed a 50% pay increase as Lloyd's saw a return to profits despite at the time not having paid back any of the government bailout it received (Treanor 2015; Verlaine and Choudhury 2015); by 2016, Lloyd's CEO was the sixth highest paid CEO in the UK, receiving £11.54 million (more than 418 times the average UK salary) (Treanor and Farrell 2016). In 2016, it was also reported that, in 2014, the UK had more than three times the number of high earners than the rest of the European Union combined, with the majority working in investment banking, nearly 3,000 of whom were paid over £800,000 (Kollewe and Davies 2016). In 2017, analysis by Emolument[2] – a salary comparison website – showed that banking was still London's best paying sector.

Such figures are important for raising awareness about levels of inequality associated with global finance, but they do not speak for themselves (Griffin 2012: 16). They do not provide us with knowledge about how and why processes of privilege work, and how they are legitimised, justified and perpetuated. As Katharina Hecht has argued, for example, in her 2017 relational analysis of very highly paid workers in the UK – those defined as in the top 1%[3] of the income distribution (Piketty 2014) – incomes and wealth are socially constructed and evaluated in a process that reproduces and justifies inequalities (see also Wilkinson and Pickett 2019). In particular, very highly paid workers have a tendency to defend income inequality by drawing on market values including rationality and merit, suggesting that those who receive huge salaries "earn" their wealth through hard work, talent and market contribution (Hecht 2017).

As Hecht explains, this is not to say that many very highly paid workers do not understand that they are advantaged compared with the general population, but that the majority, on the one hand, normalise their wealth because they tend to work and socialise with people who receive the same or higher salaries than them, yet, on the other hand, still feel relatively disadvantaged.

Income differences among those at the top are vast (i.e., between the top 1% and the top 0.1%), and people often work with those who receive more money than them and have a tendency to compare upwards and aspire to the lifestyles of people who are richer than them (Hecht 2017: 6; see also Ho 2009; Toynbee and Walker 2008).

In banking and other high-status professions, such as law, men's continued dominance is unequivocal, particularly in the very highly paid upper echelons, despite increasing rhetorical commitment towards gender equality and a growing array of diversity and inclusion policies (Headworth et al. 2016). Figures compiled by the *Financial Times* (2017), using data from 25 of the world's largest banks, found women comprised just 23.4% of senior board members in 2017 despite comprising over 50% of the banking workforce in general. A 2016 report commissioned by the UK government, meanwhile, highlights how such figures mask the even greater under-representation of women with executive as opposed to non-executive directorships, which in the UK in 2015 stood at just 7% versus 27%, with the majority of women not progressing beyond middle management levels (HM Treasury and Virgin Money 2017). As a 2018 report by The Treasury Committee stated:

> There is clearly an underrepresentation of women in senior positions in the financial services sector. The gender distribution of financial firms typically follows a "pyramid" model where the number of women diminishes in line with seniority. Furthermore, women are generally better represented in firms' support functions rather than profit generating functions.
>
> (HoC 2018: 6)

Given the central positioning of global finance transnationally and the gendered nature of elite finance, where men significantly outnumber women among those employees receiving the largest remuneration payments in the sector and working in the more high-status positions, it is therefore important to develop better understanding of the gendered intricacies of social practices and divisions of power within the industry.

In the years since the 2008 financial crisis, there have been ongoing rumblings of discontent, some significant eruptions of social protest, and other notable events in the UK and elsewhere in the world that relate to local or global social inequalities and reflect deep social divisions. These include the Arab Spring in 2010, the Occupy Movement which began in 2011, the London riots of 2011, the 2016 Brexit vote[4] in the UK, the 2016 presidential election of Donald Trump in the USA, the catastrophic fire of 2017 that killed 72 residents in Grenfell Tower – a high-rise, low-cost, social housing block situated in one of London's wealthiest districts – and the growing momentum of movements and campaigns promoting gender equality and women's rights, including the high profile #MeToo movement. Collectively, such events may, or may not, signal the beginnings of more profound longer-term destabilisation and the eventual unravelling of the current global neoliberal[5] socio-economic and sociopolitical fabric, with global finance at its core (see further Fraser 2019). Likewise, an unravelling of the current system, if it were to occur, may or may not result in an alternative system built on the principles of equality and social justice.

While it is a challenge to imagine a different future, however, and even more of a challenge to realise one, it is not impossible. Understanding the ways in which the social processes that underpin the perpetuation of ever-widening inequalities function is as necessary for the present moment as it was a decade ago. These are complex processes, which to undermine as opposed to unsettle first require recognition and understanding of how they are constituted and embedded, and then require collective radical rethinking and a letting go of deeply entrenched ideas and practices (Klein 2017; Wilkinson and Pickett 2019). This book aims to contribute to this understanding.

As many scholars have pointed out, financial and economic systems are not new, nor are they static; rather they are in a constant, endless state of transformation (Ho 2009; Berman 2010; Massey 2010; Sassen 2014; Klein 2017). Likewise, periods of financial and/or political instability or crisis do not necessarily signal decline, but instead may inherently characterise a deliberate strategy and culture associated with neoliberalism (see Klein 2007, 2017; Ho 2009; Griffin 2012). Modern life under the current era of capitalism demands constant development, reinvention and "modernisation" – or in the words of Marshall Berman (2010: 99):

> All that is solid … [is] made to be broken tomorrow, smashed or shredded or pulverised or dissolved, so [it] can be recycled or replaced next week, and the whole process can go on again and again, hopefully forever, in ever more profitable forms.

This is "the thrill and dread of the modern world in which 'all that is solid melts into air'" (Berman 2010: 13).

Sassen (2014) has argued that the current period of capitalism has witnessed the ascendance of global finance. It is a period marked by extraction and destruction, operating through an increasingly complex global system combining persons, networks and machines. While this system has no obvious centre, there are places, such as global cities (including London, New York and Hong Kong), where "power becomes concrete and can be engaged, and where the oppressed are part of the social infrastructure for power" (pp. 10–11). What we now see, explains Sassen, are "predatory 'formations', a mix of elites and systemic capacities [including government support] with finance a key enabler" (p. 13). This is significant, not least because these predatory formations have brought about ever-acute concentrations of wealth for particular individuals and global firms located in particular places, such as global cities. As a consequence, these global cities become the command point for ever-powerful groups of global elites who, through their daily social practices, both deliberately and by default shape the space of the city for their own advantage (Massey 2010: 45–47), and in the process squeeze out businesses and individuals who cannot afford the rising costs of living.

The widening socio-economic gulf between high- and low-income workers in global cities, highlighted by Sassen and a number of other scholars (e.g., McDowell et al. 2005; Harvey 2006; Perrons 2015; Perrons et al. 2016), remains a fundamental social justice concern. It results in a dual process of exclusion comprising, first, the forceful expulsion of poorer members of society from many forms of social participation (through, for example, the rising costs of essential and non-essential goods and services) and, second, the self-exclusion by rich individuals from forms of social responsibility, such as organising their finances in order to pay minimal tax (Sassen 2014). This dual process of forced and voluntary exclusion has both material and metaphorical dimensions, embedded in institutions, social structures and everyday discourses, and experienced in people's everyday lives and social interactions in both the public and private realm. Moreover, as Wilkinson and Pickett (2019) have compellingly argued, while " it is at the bottom of the social ladder where inequality does most damage" (p. 173), the effects of living in unequal societies are damaging for everyone and for the environment, negatively impacting on social relations, health and well-being, with the effects ever more acute the more unequal a society becomes.

Hegemony, space and gender

This book connects with scholarship on global cities and the material and metaphorical dimensions of gender inequality and crisis that mark the contemporary period through its concern with processes of hegemony linked with global finance. My discussion draws on the theorising of Antonio Gramsci (1971) who commented on the dynamics of large-scale historical change comprising material, economic, political, cultural and discursive dimensions. For Gramsci (1971: 7–8), hegemony is a process associated with the bourgeoisie – a way of organising "experience through an esprit de corps" by drawing on economic authority and asserting intellectual and moral leadership. In other words, as Mike Donaldson (1993: 645) has written, hegemony is about "the ways in which the ruling class establishes and maintains its domination", whereby the "ruling class" refers not to a homogenous or harmonious group of people, but rather to a collective of those people who have direct or indirect access to power, wealth and privilege and can respond to social and economic constraints (Donaldson and Poynting 2007; Madrid 2017; see also Wright 1985).

This does not mean, however, that hegemony is constituted and perpetuated through domination. Rather, hegemony attends to the relations of power and ideology, and the authority of what is "taken for granted", and thus largely unquestioned, in the normative and naturalising definitions of any given situation (Hearn 2012: 590). Hegemony primarily depends on consent, both provisional and contingent. Its legitimacy comes not only from those who hold power but also from those who do not. While consent is occasionally backed by force or the potential for coercion, hegemony is more about compliance and seduction, for hegemony often functions to make relationships of power seem not what they are, but rather soft, sweet, natural or beneficial (Connell 2005a; Hearn 2012). Hegemony is a process of historical continuity, and precisely because it is always ongoing, it is never complete (Gramsci 1971; Connell 2005). And herein lie both the strength and weakness of hegemony: its ability to absorb new elements, and to rearticulate and reassert itself, as well as its vulnerability to contestation and collapse.

Hegemony, as explored in this book, is a dynamic, multidimensional social process relating to ways in which individuals working as bankers in the City of London become compromised, and how change, although possible, is difficult; people's biographies, experiences and everyday social practices[6] at work and home feed into processes of hegemony linked with global finance. My focus on hegemony is concerned particularly with the dimensions of gender and space. Hegemony brings together elites and systems of power (Sassen 2014) and is a process wherein one must consider how socio-spatial relations constitute authority (Featherstone 2012). Likewise, socio-spatial relations and systems of power relating to global finance are interlaced with ideas and practices relating to gender.

A growing body of scholarship exploring gendered dynamics of globalisation, neoliberal capitalism and transnational processes increasingly presents strong arguments for understanding gender relations and structures of power in transnational arenas because of the complexity of a growing number of transnational processes and their bearing on local, national and global policies and inequalities (see, for example, Acker 2004; Massey 2010; Griffin 2012; Hearn et al. 2013; Connell 2013b, 2014; Hearn 2014; Perrons et al. 2016). Research also highlights the active collective and individual role of elites in maintaining hegemonic structures and practices that serve their own interests (Massey 2010; Jones 2014; Sassen 2014). To date, however, the subjectivities of world elites, particularly elite men, have been frequently overlooked in the global city literature in favour of economic and urban structures and functions, along with a prioritisation of global space over and above local space (see Hopkins and Noble 2009), in part, perhaps, due to the general difficulty of gaining access to elite groups of people (Connell 2012; Madrid 2013).[7] The normalisation of men's relationship with power in the elite, high-status workplaces of global finance, however, suggests cultural ideals about gender are connected with institutional power structures, thus constituting a form of hegemony that Raewyn Connell (2005a: 77) has termed "hegemonic masculinity".

Hegemonic masculinity

The concept "hegemonic masculinity" was first proposed by Carrigan, Connell and Lee (1985) in relation to a study of social inequality in Australian high schools, which revealed the existence of hierarchical relations based on gender and class, as well as active constructions of gender (Messerschmidt 2010: 4). Since then, Connell has developed and positioned the concept within a broader theory of gender, explaining hegemonic masculinity as "the configuration of gender practice which embodies the currently accepted answer to the problem of the legitimacy of patriarchy, which guarantees (or is taken to guarantee) the dominant position of men and the subordination of women" (Connell 2005a: 77). Hegemonic masculinity is therefore linked with the interests of all men while at the same time embracing recognition of the diversity and heterogeneity of men's lives (Collier 2012: 456).

James Messerschmidt (2010: 20) has explained how hegemonic masculinity is constituted through social action and, as such, is both situational and able to change historically. Masculinities[8] are unavoidably related to gender, but they are not entirely defined by it; they are also the products of other markers of difference, including race, ethnicity, age and social class (Connell et al. 2005: 3), which contribute to the constitution of hierarchies. Crucial to Connell's concept of hegemonic masculinity is her recognition that masculinity – hegemonic or otherwise – "as an object of knowledge is always masculinity-in-relation" (Connell 2005a: 44). As Messerschmidt (2010: 6) expands, hegemonic masculinity arguably "has no meaning outside its relationship to emphasised femininity – and to nonhegemonic masculinities – or to those forms of femininity that are practised in a complementary, compliant and accommodating subordinate relationship with hegemonic masculinity". Such recognitions are central in this book to its exploration of hegemonic masculinity as it relates to men working in City banking through drawing on the narratives of both men and women. Of particular note, and in accordance with Gramsci's notion of hegemony, is the understanding that it is through the *process* of the legitimisation of the relationship between power and accepted or quiescent subordination that the "meaning and essence" of hegemonic masculinity are exposed (Messerschmidt 2010: 6). Of course, it is also here that they can be contested.

Connell (1995: 77) initially positioned hegemonic masculinity at the top of a global gender hierarchy – a singular, overarching form of masculinity that individuals did not embody, but which operated as a gender ideal on a global scale. In a more recent reframing of the concept, however, Connell and Messerschmidt (2005: 849) acknowledge the possibility of local, regional and global gender hierarchies, and hegemonic masculinities that may be shaped somewhat differently to one another. In this latter framework, local hegemonic masculinities are constructed in the context of the family or small communities, regional hegemonic masculinities are developed at the level of the nation state and global hegemonic masculinities are formed in international arenas such as large transnational corporations (Messerschmidt 2010: 3).

Connell (2009: 115) has argued that this stratification should be considered in the context of the interdependency of individual men and masculinities to national, transnational and global economies, ideologies, politics, global markets, media and the international state, alongside recognition that power is unevenly distributed at local, national and global levels. These different spaces, in other words, overlap and intertwine and are not discrete from one another. As Connell (2009: 83) has also noted, masculinities "bear the traces of the social processes by which they were made". These ideas are central to my consideration of the ways in which the processes of hegemony relating to global finance in the City are linked with the socio-spatial relations and practices of elite City bankers in local sites (particularly in individual family spaces, communities and workplaces) and in global sites (most notably the global city and global finance).

Given the ubiquitous use of hegemonic masculinity in research on men and masculinities, the concept has inevitably come under close critique (see, for example, Donaldson 1993; Whitehead 2002; Beasley 2008). Messerschmidt (2010) and Hearn (2012) have suggested that this is largely a consequence of the ways in which the concept has been misapplied or ambiguously applied, rather than a problem with the concept itself. For example, a number of scholars have argued that the concept's essentialising potential can impose a false unity on men, as well as particular groups of men, and mask the fluid, complex reality of men's lives (see, for example, Beasley 2008; Holter 2009; Aboim 2010). Jeff Hearn (2006: 45), however, has proposed that this perhaps merely reflects the strength of hegemonic masculinity: that one of the "subtleties of the hegemonic may be its very elusiveness and the difficulty of reducing it to a set of fixed positions and practices". Certainly, if hegemony is viewed as an ongoing process, as Gramsci suggested, then fluidity is integral to its constitution.

The essentialising critique has often been applied with particular reference to Connell's (1995/2005a: 263) concept "transnational business masculinity", which she proposed as a possible global variance of hegemonic masculinity that develops specifically through corporate sectors. Connell (2009: 129) introduced this variation with recognition that "new arenas" of institutions, including global markets and transnational corporations, which operate on a world scale, do so in gendered ways despite the overriding gender-neutral discourse of globalisation.[9] Given the economic and political power of these institutions in global contexts, Connell (2009, 2005b: 77) has emphasised the importance of examining the masculinities associated with the overwhelmingly predominant numbers of men, rather than women, who control the major institutions of the global economy, including those working in global finance.

Initially, Connell (1995: 263) proposed that transnational business masculinity was a new form of hegemonic masculinity emerging from the changing and increasingly transient, fluid and transnational nature of corporate business, and marked by "increasing egocentrism, conditional loyalties and a declining sense of responsibility for others". Over time, studies by Connell and other scholars (see, for example, Reis 2002; Hearn and Piekkari 2005; Holgersson 2006; Tienari et al. 2010; Connell 2010, 2012; Collier 2013; Madrid 2017) suggest instead that there are varied and complex gendered practices among corporate managers. Moreover, findings also suggest a persistent attachment (in practice if not in rhetoric) among many men in corporate management positions in a range of country contexts, especially those in higher-status positions, to more traditional ideals of masculinity and gender relations at work and home centred on notions of breadwinning (even in Scandinavian countries with a more gender aware cultural reputation). In line with this empirical research, Connell (2008: 67; 2010) has refined her concept, suggesting more recently that transnational business masculinity can, therefore, perhaps be more accurately understood as a contemporary variation of an already familiar, traditional bourgeois ideal, with high-status corporate managers favouring conventional leisure tastes, breadwinning notions of masculinity, the control of emotions and the exercise of authoritative forms of masculinity in the workplace.

Connell's suggestion that it might be possible to conceive of an overarching form of global hegemonic masculinity that relates to corporate business, however, has been queried by some transnational masculinities scholars, not least because of potential for competing cross-cultural ideals regarding masculinities and forms of employment (see, for example, Hearn 2009: 7–8; Poster 2013). Yet, as Connell (2005b: 77–78) has noted, "a certain common ground is inevitably created by processes of globalisation". She further argues that the global gender order rests on a set of gender relations that are "partially integrated, highly unequal and turbulent", with global reach but uneven impact (Connell 2000: 42).

Global finance is a key sector in which these uneven local and global dynamics can be explored. Because of the specific local and global positioning of the finance industry in London, the social, cultural and political positioning of highly paid bankers working in the City is significant at both local and global levels. Individual practices of bankers, and gender regimes of wealthy banks based in London, while strongly connected to the local context are also globally connected – which is not to say that they are representative at a global scale (see Hearn 2015). But it is to recognise that the daily practices of global finance, however (i.e., those of both banks and bankers), feed into global processes and help shape the constitution of hegemonic masculinities associated with global finance.

The discussion in this book is mindful of the contested scope of hegemonic masculinities. Yet in contrast to the majority of empirical research on hegemonic masculinities to date, the book shifts the discussion away from thinking about the *form* of hegemonic masculinity to an analysis of the dynamic, multidimensional *process* of hegemony, more in line with Gramsci's original theorising on hegemony. It also focuses on men as much as it focuses on masculinities, along with their relationship to the spaces of global finance linked with the global city of London, in recognition that men are central to the socially structured world of global finance (Griffin 2012; Hearn 2015; Longlands and Collier 2018). As such, this book seeks to uncover processes by which the dominance of men in global finance and the patriarchal relationships of gendered power relating to City banks and bankers are masked behind an authoritative ideology that promotes the current system as seductive, soft, sweet, beneficial and natural.

Seven lives, one City

The fieldwork for this book took place in London and its surrounding counties in South East England between 2008 and 2013. During this time, I conducted seven in-depth case studies of men who were fathers and who worked in management in banking in the City of London.

I have never worked in City finance or in any other capacity in the City apart from one day's temping work as a receptionist in a large, wealthy investment bank many years ago. I have, however, lived, studied and worked in London for most of the past 24 years. My social world is intertwined with others who live and work in London, including the elite workers of City finance, business and law firms, some of whom are my friends and relatives. Over the years, I have walked extensively around the streets, squares and plazas of the City. I have socialised in its cafés, restaurants and bars. On occasion, I have frequented its exclusive hotels to drink or eat with friends from out of town. I have seen businesses come and go. And I have witnessed numerous new buildings increasingly crowd its skyline – for building work persists in the area despite the fluctuating financial and economic fortunes of global finance, London and/or the UK. I feel at once both a sense of familiarity with and a sense of alienation from this space and all it encompasses and represents – a somewhat disembodied state that seems one at the same time disorientating and normal. A state encapsulated, perhaps, in Berman's (2010: 13) observation that "to be modern is to live a life of paradox and contradiction".

My research approach drew on ethnographic techniques, including in-depth, face-to-face semi-structured interviews, field notes and observations of the City, work and family spaces. This approach was designed to capture some of the diversity and complexity of people's everyday lives in order to gain greater understanding of the ways in which the spatial and gendered hegemonies of global finance operate as a social process. It involved a small number of cases so that I could explore complex, interwoven issues in detail. While my research does not pretend to provide definitive conclusions, distinctive and situated events are able to reveal a good deal about the bigger picture (Blommaert and Dong 2010: 16). It is in the small and everyday that the constitution and peculiarities of the hegemonies of global finance are grounded (Ho 2009: 42; see also Griffin 2012).

Researching the elite of City finance

There is a delicate line to tread between, on the one hand, researching powerful groups of people in ways that privilege them further by providing yet more space to the social practices they help shape, voice and perpetuate, and, on the other hand, researching the elite in order to help expose the ways in which systems of inequality and stratification are constructed and perpetuated (Conti and O'Neill 2007; Connell 2012; Nyström et al. 2018). As Connell (2012: 2) has argued, there is an urgent need to understand how the processes of the hegemonies of global finance are constituted because of the gendered issues of social justice that arise from them – this necessarily requires researching the banking elite.

The seven men at the centre of my case studies all worked in management positions in banking in the City of London. This meant they were part of what Connell (2012) has defined "the elite financial class", which is not to dismiss the heterogeneity of either this class of people or the world of banking. It is to recognise, however, that these were men who were members of an elite socio-economic class of people who collectively, through the status and power associated with their jobs, have the ability (or potential ability) to assert significant social, cultural, economic and political influence (Madrid 2017; see also Donaldson and Poynting 2007; Hecht 2017). The men did not need to be CEOs of powerful banks in order to be part of this class of people. Yet because of their privileged positioning, they were men who could help shape or contest processes of cultural and global hegemony relating to global finance.

Gaining access to potential participants is a well-documented problem in much research on elite people, including corporate men who generally work long hours and may often travel overseas for work (Connell 2011: 1; see also Kezar 2003; Donaldson and Poynting 2007). As Odendahl and Shaw (2002: 306) have suggested, gaining access "typically requires extensive preparation, homework, creativity on the part of the researcher, as well as the right credentials and contacts". In keeping with other research on elite groups, I experienced a few difficulties gaining access, despite my personal contacts as well as assurances from potential respondents that they would participate. Nevertheless, difficulty gaining access is part of most ethnographic-style fieldwork, not only research that involves elites, and practices associated with gaining access – emails, phone calls and so forth – are integral to the process of building relationships and rapport between researchers and participants (Nadar 1972: 302; Denscombe 2014).

I drew on my personal contacts – men and women – in order to gain access to men working in City banking. I was lucky in that, due to the social networks I am part of, most of the people I approached agreed straightaway to talk with me. My existing relationship with my "gatekeepers", along with the relationships these gatekeepers had with respective participants (as friends, colleagues or relatives), undoubtedly helped enormously, for it brought elements of trust, familiarity and legitimacy to the research process that would have been harder to establish otherwise. The main issue I encountered, therefore, was not so much one of gaining in-person access to the people themselves, but the time it actually took from initial email contact to actually meeting, which was several months in each case due to people's timetables and availability.

The men at the centre of my case studies had certain shared characteristics in order for me to explore cultural practices and behaviours in depth (Druckman 2005: 209). Limiting the variables was important because lines of privilege are often heavily masked (Laclau and Mouffe 1985; Hills et al. 2010) and may be even more difficult to identify with too many variables to consider. Similarities between the men were important also because hegemony is configured in particular situations, and through particular social practices and relations and their interrelationship with one another. Closely matched comparative cases thus allowed for similarities and differences in social practices to become visible.

I deliberately interviewed men of different ages in order to better consider how bankers at different stages of their career and life course may interrelate differently with processes of hegemony linked with global finance in the City of London. Other studies of men and fatherhood have shown, for example, how ideas and practices relating to work and family can shift over time (see, for example, Dermott 2008; Miller 2011; Collier 2013). Such shifts can potentially allow for the identification of weak spots or contradictions in processes of hegemony because of the impact the life course may have on not only what an individual values in life, but also the relationship between his or her working life and home life, as well as his or her identity and sense of being (Longlands and Collier 2018).

An additional sampling criterion related to forms of education. While all of the men were educated in the UK, I purposely interviewed some men who had been educated in the private sector and some who had been educated in the state sector. It was a requirement for my study that the men had all been educated in the UK in order to limit social and cultural variables that may have shaped different forms of social practice and affected the men's understandings of and engagement with different processes of hegemony. For example, it was important that they had experienced similar sociocultural exposure to norms relating to work and family structures and lifestyles as well as contemporary ideals of masculinity and fatherhood. Nevertheless, the different forms of education they had received was an important variable because I wanted to explore the ways school and university study as well as schooling choices as social practices interrelate with other social practices relating to the hegemonies of global finance. This is because of the identified link in the UK between forms of privileged education and both entry to high-status careers and enhanced career prospects in high-status forms of employment (de Vries 2014) as well as an identified link in other contexts (e.g., the USA) between high-status universities and elite jobs in global finance (see Ho's 2009 study of Wall Street bankers; see also Navidi 2017: 82). It is also because of the understanding that education is a means through which elite groups look to sustain and strengthen their social and economic position and is imbued with notions of worth and value (Maxwell and Aggleton 2015: 1).

A further shared characteristic was that the men were all fathers with children of school-going age or younger, and all lived with their children and with the mother of their children. I sought out such men in order to more easily explore, from the perspectives of both men and women, how gendered power relations and social practices relating to family may be negotiated in ways that support, shape, comply with or contest forms of hegemony relating to global finance. As such, it was necessary also for the women – the men's partners – to agree to talk with me. I interviewed the women in addition to, but separately from, the men (on different days and in different places) in order to maintain each individual's confidentiality.

I was mindful of the fact that including the voices of these particular women in this study alongside those of the men was important for a number of reasons. First, women and femininities are fundamental components of gender regimes and contribute to the processes of constituting masculinities, hegemonic or otherwise (Connell 2005a: 44; Messerschmidt 2012: 6). Second, the mobilising and seductive force of the patriarchal dividend[10] (see Connell 2009: 142) means that women, like those in this study, may (whether happily or not) actively demonstrate support for existing processes of hegemony in global finance because of the benefits they and/or their children get from the fact their partners or husbands work in certain kinds of City banking jobs. Third, historical patterns of change, which include processes of hegemony, are lived and expressed in the ways individual family relations are negotiated within wider cultural dynamics (Kehily and Thomson 2011: 3.1; see also Silva 2010). People's lives, their personal, intimate relationships and ways that couples develop and maintain a sense of togetherness are important areas of study (Letherby 2003: 73); they are key to understanding how forms of hegemony and inequalities that stem from them (whether local or global forms) are stable or unstable, and thus the extent to and ways in which they are contestable and changeable (Jamieson 2011: 7.7). Fourth, by talking with the women as well as the men, I was able to explore ways the iterative character of narrative reflects and sustains processes of hegemony in different circumstances – through narrative, men and women make sense of their experiences in ways which connect them to and reflect their situation, and which position them in the dynamics of family and the wider environment (Kehily and Thomson 2011: 54, see also Flyvbjerg 2006). As Connell (2005a: 72) has observed, "social practice is creative and inventive but not inchoate": it occurs in and is shaped by particular situations and is constituted within particular structures of social relations. The social and spatial practices relating to the contingent hegemonies of the finance sector need to be understood as part of complex and dynamic everyday realities and relationships in both public and private realms. Finally, men and/or women can contest the dominance gained through hegemony of any group (Connell 2005a: 77).

Any other similarities between the men were, for the purposes of selection for this study at least, incidental. Nevertheless, it is worth highlighting that the men were all white and they were all married to their partner – reflecting, in some respects perhaps, the general lack of diversity among what have often been termed the "pale, male and stale" managers of male-dominated professions such as City banking, particularly at elite levels (see, for example, HoC 2010; Sealy et al. 2016). I introduce the men and the women in the following chapters of the book. Their participation in this study was entirely voluntary, all of their names have been changed, and key identifying features have been masked.

Ideally, I wanted a mixture of interview sites – work-related and home-related – in order to develop a better picture of the kinds of conditions in which high-status City bankers work and live. In this regard, I was fortunate that some of the men chose to be interviewed at work and some in or near to their homes, and most of the women chose to be interviewed at home. I interviewed four of the men in the workplace, one of the men in a local café near to where he lived, and two of the men in their homes. I interviewed two of the women in local cafés and five of the women in their homes. Each of the interviews lasted between 50 minutes and 2¼ hours.

Elite interviews are often discussed in terms of "studying up". Researchers have highlighted difficulties, such as powerful people controlling the interview situation through manipulating questions to address topics on their own terms and to their own advantage, or controlling the timing or pacing of the interview (Charmaz 2006: 27; see also Odendahl and Shaw 2002; Kezar 2003). Describing elite interviews as "studying up" and/or problematic, however, ignores the contradictory complexity, interconnectedness and fluctuating nature of power relations (Conti and O'Neill 2007: 67; see also Gilding 2010). It also overlooks what for me was the important insight that such demonstrations of power could provide to the processes of constituting hegemony in global finance. As Richard Collier (2012: 459) has argued, it does not automatically follow that values associated with hegemony will be experienced in any uniform way. Recognising differences, as well as similarities, in ways hegemony is experienced not only offers insight into the complexity and permeability of hegemonic processes, but can also provide potential to identify where hegemony might be contested. Interview narratives, like any other form of narrative, are socially constructed – the interview narratives of the men and women in this study represent a retrospective view of their lives through their own storytelling (Chase 2008).

Language used, including body language, and spatial practices engaged in by the men during their interviews, offered interesting insight into power dynamics within City banks as well as power dynamics between the men and me. For example, Dan, a 43-year-old banker working for a European bank, sat with his back to the wall in his office so that he maintained a clear view of the adjacent open plan office behind me. As we talked, I frequently caught his eyes sweeping the office, seemingly checking up on the people working in it, and he sometimes asked me to repeat questions, suggesting a level of distraction. He also repeatedly spoke about issues in the third person, thus abstracting his feelings and avoiding directly addressing many of the issues I was asking him about – a tactic that, as Charmaz (2006: 29) has noted, is often used by men who mask their emotions.

Intensive interviews, meanwhile, especially those on sensitive or personal topics, can upset power relations, as people – particularly men – may feel uncomfortable sharing aspects of their lives they do not normally talk about or would not reflect on or describe to others, particularly in an interview situation and/or in certain contexts such as a workplace (Charmaz 2006). I was mindful of such issues and careful to remain respectful throughout all contact with respondents, both email correspondence and face-to-face encounters. While I encouraged the men and women to talk or give more detail when appropriate, I was also careful not to probe unduly or sound as though I was interrogating them. I reassured all respondents at the start of the interviews (and during whenever necessary) that they did not have to answer a question if they felt uncomfortable doing so, although, as it turns out, this did not actually happen. Rather, on the whole, the men and women talked at some length, and many of the questions I had prepared were answered incidentally within the course of our conversations.

I recorded all of the interviews with permission from the participants, and transcribed each of them word for word, including pauses, silences and vocal inflections, in order to preserve the narrative as much as possible. I was aware that all of these features and nuances of spoken language are potentially significant in terms of narrative structuring (Blommaert and Dong 2010: 72) and, as such, may contribute to and/or stem from the process of shaping and conferring hegemonies relating to global finance. Nevertheless, I realised it was not enough to rely on transcription, for it is just one among many ways of representing an extremely complex situation. I also, therefore, made detailed field notes before and as soon as possible after each interview in an attempt to capture more of the complexity of the interview situation and context, and in order to develop better understanding of the lived realities of the men and women in the study (Coffey 1999: 127).In addition, I conducted five separate observations in the City between May and June 2013, each lasting between one and two hours. These observations took place at different times of day and on different days of the week, including one at the weekend, in order to develop deeper and more rounded understanding of the interdependence of spatiality and sociality in the City and the relationship of this to the authority and dominance of global finance. During these observations, I tried to capture the immediacy and dynamic nature of City space, both in terms of my place in it and in terms of my emotional and sensual reactions to it. I walked around as well as stood still watching and making notes in different locations in the City. I recorded the sounds of the City on my phone in addition to making rough but detailed notes about the smells of the City and the things I saw, including people, buildings, transport and amenities. I also made notes about how these different aspects and my experiences of being part of the different configurations and social relations of the City space made me feel.

In the following chapters, I have developed some of these field notes and observation notes into more refined passages of descriptive text, each representing one of the three primary spaces explored in this book: the City of London, the workplace (City banks) and the family. These passages, together with extracts from the interviews and banks' promotional literature, help to illustrate the complexity and multidimensionality of hegemonic processes and to reflect the dynamic, relational nature of space. They help me to share my experiences of briefly being part of the lives of these men and women and the everyday spaces they inhabited.

As a final form of data, extracts from the official online promotional literature of wealthy City-based banks are used in order to offer insight into ways in which official discourse feeds into processes of hegemony linked with global finance. Banks' promotional material is designed to attract new recruits at any stage of their career as well as potential clients. It is carefully crafted to present a particular institutional and sector-wide image and is thus an important element in both the constitution and conferring of notions of hegemony linked with global finance.

In the process of analysing the different forms of data, I combined aspects of grounded theory and critical discourse analysis (see Fairclough and Wodak 1997; Charmaz 2006). These methods highlight the need to maintain the link between data and analysis. This required the analysis to be ongoing and fluid, starting from the beginning of the research process and continuing throughout the fieldwork and the writing up of the study. The process of analysis was iterative, which allowed me to become intimate with the different kinds of data (Coffey 1999). It involved reading and rereading data – interacting with and making sense of data over and over again, allowing new ideas to emerge and understandings to adjust and develop (Charmaz 2006: 46). This approach required close observation of different forms of language and communication (verbal and non-verbal) and the ways these interrelate with gender, as well as consideration of different possible interpretations (Fairclough and Wodak 1997; Ramazanoğlu and Holland 2002; Charmaz 2006). This approach helped me to keep the analytical focus on social problems and political issues, and the ways in which social processes of discursive and structural power relating to forms of dominance and discrimination, inclusion and exclusion, are shaped and perpetuated in both opaque and transparent ways (Wodak and Meyer 2009: 32). It also helped me keep focus on the ways in which power relations occur in different contexts, whether contrasting or comparable (e.g., family spaces, workplaces, the City), and how discourse has ideological, cultural, historical, social and political dimensions (Fairclough and Wodak 1997: 271–280; Van Dijk 2011). As such, my analytical approach helped maintain my focus throughout this research on the discursive means through which social inequalities relating to the processes of hegemony linked with global finance are expressed, constituted, normalised and legitimised by City banks, male City bankers and women closely related to these men. Although analysis was ongoing, it was during the process of drafting and redrafting the book that some of the deepest levels of analysis and critical reflection occurred, and where my repeated interrogation of and reinterpretation of data and analysis crystallised into text.

Structure of the book

The book is organised around three spaces within which the gendered dominance of global finance is shaped and sustained: the City of London, the workplaces of City banking, and the private family and community spaces of City bankers. The first two chapters centre on the public realm of global finance, in particular the indoor and outdoor spaces of the City that help constitute the gendered social fabric of global finance and City banking. The next two chapters shift the focus to the private realm to better understand how processes of hegemony linked with global finance are constituted, confirmed and conferred through the day-to-day social practices and relationships of City bankers who are also fathers. The fifth chapter then returns to the City to explore the men's narratives of the 2008 financial crisis and associated processes of redundancy in City banking. Within these chapters, two potential sites of contestation for processes of hegemony are explored in particular. The first of these sites is fatherhood because of contemporary shifting sociocultural ideals of fatherhood away from breadwinning towards more present, hands-on parenting. The second site of contestation is the 2008 financial crisis because of the potential such a severe moment of crisis presents for disrupting the status quo. Finally, the conclusion considers the insights to processes of hegemony linked with global finance explored in this book and reflects on the ways these insights might allow us to reframe the present and consider alternative future possibilities.

Notes

1 The City of London is London's main financial and business district, commonly known as the City (see Chapter 2 for more detail).
2 See www.emolument.com/career_advice/bank_bonus_2017.
3 Those who were paid about £267k in 2010.
4 On 23 June 2016, a majority of the UK public voted to leave the European Union – a process of withdrawal that has come to be known as Brexit.
5 Raewyn Connell (2013a: 100) provides a useful definition of neoliberalism, explaining that it broadly refers to "the agenda of economic and social transformation under the sign of the free market, as well as the institutional arrangements to implement this project", she explains that neoliberalism is not just a matter of political economy but it is also an agenda for the transformation of everyday life.
6 Social practice is a pattern of social organisation that may be spontaneous or embedded in everyday life and involves the dynamics of social agency, structural elements of symbolic interaction and the interrelationship of the two (Castellani and Hafferty 2009: 37–38).
7 Two notable exceptions that connect with the themes of this book include Karen Ho's 2009 ethnographic insight into the workings of elite finance on Wall Street in the mid- to late 1990s – a time of economic prosperity, when banking was perhaps more glamorous than it has been post the 2008 financial crisis. While working on Wall Street, Ho observed the day-to-day peculiarities of investment banking and interviewed young recruits to banking, primarily young women. Owen Jones 2014 book on Britain's wealthy elite, meanwhile, offers an important commentary on the persuasive and pervasive ideology of capitalist neoliberalism, although it does not focus specifically on gender or the finance industry.
8 Connell's theory of gender concurs with almost universal contemporary agreement among social scientists that masculinity is a social construction, that there are multiple forms of masculinity, and that masculinities vary historically (Messner 1992; Gutmann 1996; Hearn 2004; Connell 2005a; Collier 2010b; Messerschmidt 2010).
9 Globalisation theorists debate the origins, development, processes and merits of globalisation. Raewyn Connell (2007) suggests the three main strands of theorising regarding global and local processes include: modernity theorists (e.g., Beck 1999; Meyer 2000; Zhang 2001; Giddens 2002), postmodernity theorists (e.g., Featherstone 1995; Bauman 1998) and scholars who view global society as characterised by its constitutive capitalist dynamic (e.g., Hardt and Negri 2000; Ohmae 2005).
10 Connell (2009: 142) explains the patriarchal dividend as "the advantage to men as a group from maintaining an unequal gender order" (e.g., higher average incomes for men than women worldwide).

Chapter 1

Life in the City

Space, place and inequality

The City of London, also called the Square Mile, is an area in central London.[1] It is the financial hub not only of London and the UK but also of Europe.[2] The City of London's border runs along the River Thames to the south, the London Boroughs of Westminster and Camden to the west and north, and Tower Hamlets – one of London's poorest boroughs[3] – to the east. The London Stock Exchange and the Bank of England are located within the borders of the City, along with St Paul's Cathedral and the Tower of London.

According to the UK Government's City of London website:

> There's nowhere quite like the City. Not only is it the oldest, most historic part of London, it is the world's leading international financial and business centre with the unusual ratio of 33 times more workers than residents ... [it] is a small district at the heart of the capital...
>
> Established in around AD50 ... the City is the place from which modern-day London grew ... it's not just the Roman remains and medieval structures that make the City's buildings so unique; it is their juxtaposition with contemporary architecture designed to house the global business giants that have located here. This is where ancient and modern sit side by side.
>
> (City of London Corporation 2018)

The City, in its broader sense, also encompasses Canary Wharf and Mayfair's hedge fund industry, which are located in London's Docklands area and the West End, respectively. The City is home to over 500 banks, including 251 foreign banks, and is one of the world's leading fund management centres[4] (TheCityUK 2018). According to the TheCityUK[5] (2017, 2018), in 2017, the City was the world's second-largest hedge fund management centre after New York, managing more than 80% of Europe's hedge fund assets, 90% of European prime brokerage, and was the leading centre for management of European private equity funds. In March 2017, Reuters reported that London reached a $3 trillion daily foreign exchange turnover – a sum just over 50% of the global share. It is here in this thriving, historic business centre – the home of "business giants" and financial behemoths – where the men I interviewed worked.

In the official description of the City given above, the financial institutions and their elite workers are the visible and worthy actors shaping the identity and space of the City. They are positioned as the blood that pumps the "heart" of London and, as such, the lifeblood of the UK as a whole. It is hard to dispute the central role of finance in constituting London's identity as a global city, for, as Massey (2010) has argued, it is part of what differentiates London from other places and what provides it with its global standing as a hub of neoliberal capitalism. This powerful local and global positioning underpinned the UK government's bailout of the banking industry during the 2008 financial crisis. It has also featured heavily in political discourse around Brexit – the fear that key players in the finance industry may relocate some of their City workforce to places outside the UK, particularly if the country leaves the single market (Grafton-Green 2017; Treanor 2017).

The portrayal of the "giants" of business living side by side with other shorter- or longer-term inhabitants of the City is one that evokes a sense of harmony and peace. Indeed, what stands out in the description above is how London's prosperous development as a leading national and global financial centre is positioned not only as crucial but, more significantly, as inevitable and benevolent; through a supposedly natural development steeped in tradition and governed by history, powerful City institutions and their workers not only belong in and rightfully control the space of the City but do so for the greater benefit of all. This description helps lend the finance industry and its elite workers not just a legitimate dominance in the City, in London and in international finance more generally, but a moral one.

This moral dimension is highly significant. Suggesting that the business giants have simply and peacefully nestled in to the space of the City, not only preserving its integrity but adding to its character, disregards and renders unproblematic the socio-spatial and socio-economic divisions that powerful City institutions and their well-paid workers help shape and widen as well as benefit from (whether knowingly or not). The crucial contradiction, or what Sassen (2001: 323) has termed the "urban irony", inherent in this development of London as a global financial leader, is that the material and political power of wealthy City institutions and their highly paid workers is both dependent on and deepens forms of social, cultural and gendered inequalities. This results in a spatial organisation of London, whereby low-wage workers, who also play a crucial role in the day-to-day functioning of the City, its finance industry and related processes of globalisation, find it progressively more difficult to live there. Not only are low-wage workers increasingly priced out of the London housing market (rental as well as ownership), they also suffer from rising prices of goods, services and local amenities, including public transport.

Dimensions of socio-economic class and gender[6] intersect in these circuits of power resulting in men dominating the higher echelons of politics, corporate business and global finance. Reference to the masculinised nature of the finance industry portrayed through Tom Wolfe's (1987: 9) oft-cited nomenclature for the "master of the universe", his fictional Wall Street banker, was widely made in relation to City bankers in the wake of the 2008 crisis (see, for example, Hell 2010; HoC 2010; Rushe 2011; Stedman Jones 2012). The predominance of men working as highly paid bankers in the City has, however, often been merely assumed in studies of the finance industry in London, or at least not sufficiently interrogated through a focus on gender except when connected with very particular aspects of the workplace context such as "testosterone-fuelled" trading floors (see McDowell 2010). Collier (2010a, 2015) has noted how this reflects a broader tendency in academic discourse to either talk of corporate management in non-gendered language or discuss it in ways that can reflect stereotypical views of the kinds of men highly paid workers are and the masculine traits they apparently favour.

Meanwhile, global elites and the businesses they control in the City depend on a formal and informal low-wage workforce to support their needs, such as the mainly female migrant cleaners who clean City office spaces and who commonly occupy vulnerable positions within their host communities, working long hours, often in multiple jobs with poor contractual arrangements (Sassen 2002; Datta et al. 2007).

One can see, therefore, how processes of hegemony relating to space and gender overlap and intertwine, benefitting a few at the expense of the many, while maintaining an overarching common sense and positive doctrine. Prioritising the economic elite and their interests, praising their success and positioning it as de-gendered, natural and beneficial for all, masks and de-problematises both the processes and the consequences of unequal development; as a result, the needs and practices of many of those people who are particularly disadvantaged by the resulting inequalities are either seriously devalued or simply ignored.

What follows, then, is an exploration of how this process works – how it is constituted and perpetuated on a day-to-day basis. How do elite groups of men inhabit positions of power and wealth? How do they legitimate and reproduce social relationships that generate their dominance not only over women but also over other men? And what are the weak points in this process? Indeed, it is the successful *claim to authority* which is the mark of hegemony; as such, hegemony is never complete – it is always in contention and thus always contestable.

City streets: where the local meets the global

City streets

By 7am each weekday, a steady stream of commuters pours onto the streets from the mainline and London Underground stations servicing the City: Blackfriars, Bank, Cannon Street, Liverpool Street, London Bridge. By 8am, the road and pedestrian bridge spanning the River Thames from London Bridge station to Lower Thames Street throngs with sleek, suited men and women making their way to their gleaming, glossy offices in the City. Graham is one of them. He was 29 years old when I talked with him, and married with a young daughter, who was soon to start school. After living and studying overseas, Graham had returned to London with his young family and had taken a job working for a leading Asian bank. As a self-professed "poet and bit of a left-wing hippy", he viewed himself as a misfit in the City. He was eager to set himself apart from his fellow bankers, whom he referred to as "cocks in suits" who "barge people out of the way" as they march to work. He found the City "an ugly place to be" but worked in banking because it paid a "decent wage".

In the early morning, an hour or so earlier, the "cocks" in their smart black, blue or grey designer suits are not yet so visible. But the City is already hard at work.

Just before 6am, one bright but chilly spring morning in May, I caught a train to London Bridge station from my home in South East London. The train was busy with construction workers, wearing heavy-duty boots and functional clothing, who disembarked at the station and headed off to the various noisy, dusty building sites in the City. I too got off the train, and under clear blue skies, crossed the River Thames and walked up Bishopsgate and along London Wall. On my way, I passed a couple of window cleaners, their waists draped with bright green and yellow abseiling straps, dragging a red hose that splashed water over the limestone as it snaked along the pavement. I passed a woman wearing a vibrant pink tabard apron who was hard at work cleaning brass on the door of an old stone building until it gleamed in the early morning sunshine. I passed a man with dreadlocks and a powerful jet wash cleaning an open-air piazza encircled by glistening glass office buildings. And I passed site foremen in white hard hats and fluorescent yellow safety jackets directing large lorries reversing giant building equipment through temporary gateways and huge hoarding to the construction sites that lay beyond. The smell of bacon, freshly baked croissants and freshly brewed coffee wafted through open café doors and mingled with the smells and sounds of the streets outside. People laughed, chatted, shouted and whistled; heavy machinery whirred and thumped; and barrels of beer clattered noisily down a wooden ramp into the cellar of a City wine bar.

In the early morning sunshine, the space of the City is diverse, colourful, noisy and cheerful. Every weekday, during these early morning hours, the space of the City is groomed and primed so the "cocks in suits" can walk the litter-free streets to work, sit in their clean, shiny offices, "talk to people all over the world"[7] and get paid many multiples of what the early-morning workers receive. It is in this local space of the City where the global space of finance is controlled.

Creating, maintaining and reproducing the formidable positioning of global finance in the City is a collective process, one that occurs through a nexus of institutions, actors, social relations, practices and ideas. But while the process is collective, it is not egalitarian and is interwoven with potent forces of inclusion and exclusion,[8] of privilege and disadvantage, of opportunity and constraint – some more discernible than others.

By noon, the City's streets are ruled by gangs of suited workers who stride along the pavements talking on their phones while clutching take-away sandwich bags, coffees or bundles of dry-cleaning. They criss-cross in packs from one side of the street to the other in their shiny shoes and dull-coloured trousers. They are not the only people out on the streets – occasionally they are joined on the pavements by other pedestrians or a tourist with a backpack, or passed on the road by a cyclist. A few of the smartly dressed workers are women, but it is the gangs of striding men who visibly colonise the space. One gang wears blue suits, white shirts and blue ties; another gang wears black coats, black suits and black shoes. They have short hair and cleanly shaven faces. They are groomed and brushed, clean and polished. These shiny, glossy workers emerge from the shiny, glossy glass and chrome buildings through revolving doors that constantly spin. They walk, without a second glance, past the smart doormen who stand on duty outside. Collectively, these workers illustrate the wealth, authority and exclusive nature of the businesses they work for. Collectively, they exude an aura of confidence, busyness and collegiality. Collectively, their similarities mask their differences as well as their difference from the colourful yet now largely invisible workers of the early morning. Collectively, their humdrum presence masks the diversity of City space. Together, they create the public local and international face of the City: the "City built on business". They are the local face for a global space: the global face for a local space.

At 3pm, the gangs in suits are not so visible; most of their members have retreated back inside their glistening headquarters. On the corner of Fleet Street, close to the London Stock Exchange and St Paul's Cathedral, the finance industry seems more discreet than elsewhere in the City. In the warm afternoon sunshine, I watched as tourists climbed up and down the wide stone steps of St Paul's, and while buses, taxis, vans, cars, motorbikes and bicycles passed to and fro. While the gangs of workers may not "own" the streets so visibly at this time of day, the space is still shaped primarily for and by the needs and everyday social practices of these highly paid workers who occupy the office spaces in this part of London. There are sandwich shops, a champagne bar, an optician's, and a dry-cleaner's. There is a gentlemen's outfitter's, a barber's shop, a shoe shop and a shoe repair shop. There is a gym, a building society and an outdoor clothing and equipment shop. These amenities are not primarily geared towards meeting the needs of the tourists visiting St Paul's or, indeed, the needs of the colourful workers of the early morning. They are, however, important components of the social fabric that constitutes the dominant identity of the City space – components which, along with social institutions of the City (restaurants, bars, boutique hotels, private members clubs) as well as the low-paid workers who work in them, help knit the social and material local and international world of global finance together.[9]

The buildings of wealthy, prestigious banks still have a significant spatial presence in this part of the City, but this intermingles with an elite sense of identity – anonymity for the many, recognition for the few. As I stood across the road from one of the most wealthy and prestigious of all the City-based banks, I noted its lack of external signage (I myself walked passed it unwittingly on numerous occasions before I knew someone who worked there, despite its prominent location on one of London's principal thoroughfares). The sense of exclusivity this anonymity conveys was further reinforced by the doorman standing on guard outside the entrance; he resembled the doormen of expensive London hotels in his smart black suit, white shirt and black tie.

As I stood observing, a black cab stopped outside the bank and two men wearing suits and one woman wearing a skirt suit got out. They grabbed their bags, slung their jackets over their shoulders and walked confidently, one after the other, through the large heavy front door of the bank. The powerful presence of the buildings of finance, with their "juxtaposition of ancient and modern", extends to the power dressing of their well-paid workers: traditional suits in a fashionable cut; a mixture of old and new, stability and dynamism. These structural and material symbolic expressions of power, tradition and modernity work together to develop an image of up-to-the minute institutional, collective and individual dependability and rightful belonging.

Spending a day in the City enables one to see how the space of the City is temporal. The constant process of preservation and reinvention – of exclusion and belonging – signals the ever-shifting nature of the space, and this is important because it illustrates that the current process of spatial hegemony in the City that serves the finance industry and its well-paid workers is not fixed; rather it is fluid and transitory; and, as such, it is both contestable and changeable. The notion of space as perpetually shifting and integrally part of the everyday also brings into the frame the spatiality of politics and the spatiality of responsibility. In other words, it brings recognition that space is shaped through constant internal interactions and relations as well as relations and interactions with spaces and people elsewhere, and that these interactions and relations have a bearing on people's lives within and beyond the core, a process Massey (2005: 188) has termed "grounded connectedness".

Advertising a global industry

The appropriation of local space by wealthy financial institutions and their well-paid workers provides them with a physical dominance in the City. This physical power is combined with a metaphorical power to broaden banks' claims to authority, and further cement and legitimise their dominant position in the City. As Ho (2009: 304–310) has argued with respect to wealthy Wall Street banks and bankers – a global dimension is understood and used by banks and bankers as an indicator of institutional and individual authority and superiority, whether or not it accurately reflects the actual scope of business, or whether or not understandings of it are consistently applied. References to the "global" reinforce the relationship between strength, importance and size – the giants of the City, who were – who are (so we have been told – see UK Government 2017) – "too big to fail".

J.P. Morgan (2018a), for example, states that it is a "global leader in financial services, offering solutions to the world's most important corporations, governments and institutions in more than 100 countries"; Goldman Sachs (2018a) similarly explains that it is a "leading global investment banking, securities and investment management firm ... [with] a substantial and diversified client base that includes corporations, financial institutions, governments and individuals". It further details that it "prides itself on having pioneered many of the practices and techniques that have become standard in the industry" and describes how "our business is highly competitive, and we aggressively seek to expand our client relationships" (Goldman Sachs 2018b); Barclays (2018a), meanwhile, explains how its "global business model ... is focused on its strength as a transatlantic consumer, corporate and investment bank anchored in the two financial centres of the world, London and New York"; Deutsche Bank (2018a) explains that it is "a leading European bank with a global reach ... well positioned to pursue growth opportunities"; and Morgan Stanley (2018a) explains how it "lead[s] with exceptional ideas ... [to] build a better world", while staying at the "forefront of the financial services industry" (2018b).

The power associated with the apparent capacity to operate in this enormous spatial arena, while clearly an exaggeration of space, awards particular banks a dominant status in the financial and business world, increases their market appeal and success, and sets them apart – spatially, materially and metaphorically – from smaller, less-connected and less well-resourced firms. Crucially, like the official language of the description of the City seen above, the language of the global is juxtaposed with the language of the local, as seen particularly clearly in the following extract from Barclays (2018b): "Barclays was built over centuries" enjoying

> ... more than 325 years of history from our beginnings in Lombard Street[10] ... Our longevity is an extraordinary achievement, especially against the backdrop of multiple financial crises, international conflicts, and the agricultural, industrial and now technological revolutions.

Indeed, as Ho (2009: 310) remarks, in reference to Wall Street banks but equally applicably to City of London-based banks, "the global is not a totalising strategy ... [but represents] a situation of choice, flexibility and focused movement". And it is necessarily partnered with the local; it is part of, and feeds back into, the ability for these firms to occupy and direct their operations and market leadership from a spatial, local, position of authority – the City – and it helps justify the salaries they pay their elite City workers.

As well as using the language of geographic breadth, the official discourse of banking draws on the spatial language of innovation and expansion – the quest to "pioneer" and remain at the "forefront" of the industry, for example, or to "pursue growth". These expressions of exploration and discovery, with their echoes of colonial imperialism, along with terms that evoke a show of strength and the flexing of muscles, such as "leverage", or words which suggest the desire to dominate and control, such as "leader", present a particular value-laden message to the audience of this online material which helps depict, shape and legitimise forms of hegemony linked with City finance.

The specific language the banks use paints a portrait – real or imagined – of the ways they do/aim to do business, as well as the qualities they value and expect from their employees, whereby the language of domination, innovation and adaptability is juxtaposed with the language of strength, stability and endurance. The language helps masculinise the figurative space of elite banking and helps frame and define the environment in which elite City bankers work. What on the surface seems to be a rather uncomfortable mix of benevolent notions (freedom, opportunity, meritocracy) and more malevolent notions (aggression, pioneering) is significant for it exposes what Klein (2017: 48) has termed the "sales pitch of free market [neoliberal] theory" with its promotion and naturalisation of individualism, competition and greed, and its admiration of an insatiable desire to be the best. All of which are positioned (as well as veiled to a degree) on the one hand beneath an overarching banner of success, and, on the other, within a discourse of sustainability, both suggesting praiseworthy advancement and benevolent achievement. The sustainability discourse occupies a much more central positioning across banks' promotional literature in 2018 than ten years prior when I originally started researching banks' promotional literature. While this is not especially surprising, perhaps, given the ubiquitous focus on sustainability within contemporary national and international agendas, what is significant is that, despite this shift of overarching narrative, the minutiae of banks' language remains fundamentally unchanged.

It is perhaps also not surprising that the official language of banks is mirrored in the socio-spatial practices that elite City finance workers engage in on a daily basis, including the aggressive commuting practices Graham referred to, and the colonisation of urban space I witnessed in the middle of the day. This blend of metaphorical and physical aspects of banking illustrates the pervasive nature of hegemony, and helps consolidate and fuel existing gendered and spatial forms relating to global finance.

The relationship between language, hegemony, space and gender not only shapes institutional discursive constructions of banking, but also frames ways in which banks talk about their employees. Goldman Sachs (2018c), for example, describes how it "continues to search for talent in new places and in new ways ...". It further clarifies that:

> Although our activities are measured in billions of dollars, we select our people one by one...For us to be successful, our men and women must reflect the diversity of the communities and cultures in which we operate...we must attract, retain and motivate people from many backgrounds and perspectives. Being diverse is not optional, it is what we must be...We know the world of finance will not stand still and complacency can lead to extinction.
>
> (Goldman Sachs 2018d)

Deutsche Bank (2018b) similarly references the diversity and ever-evolving nature of its workforce, explaining: "We strive to create an environment which celebrates diversity. For us, diversity means an acceptance of the unfamiliar that brings strength through new perspectives".

It goes on to explain how it "... seeks to attract, develop and retain the best people, who reflect the communities in which we operate. Talent comes from all cultures, countries, races, genders, sexual orientations, abilities, beliefs, backgrounds, and experiences" (Deutsche Bank 2018c).

Morgan Stanley (2018c) meanwhile describes how its:

> ... skilled and creative workforce is comprised of [*sic.*] individuals drawn from a broad cross section of the global communities in which we operate and who reflect a variety of backgrounds, talents, perspectives and experiences ... Our strong commitment to a culture of inclusion is evident through our constant focus on recruiting, developing and advancing individuals based on their skills and talents.

Along with the many and explicit mentions of diversity, the sense of movement, evolution and constant development that permeates these descriptions of the global industry at both an institutional and individual level is celebrated, while contrasting notions of stability and uniformity are discredited and scorned – aligned with a sense of stagnation at best, "extinction" at worst. Through the use of such spatial metaphors, wealthy City-based banks portray themselves as progressive, innovative, dynamic, glamorous and benevolent – the latter lending an important moral edge that forecloses the space for criticism. Financial institutions are depicted as working in order to benefit the world with their "better ideas", their "balanced decisions" and their all-embracing diverse, representative and individually selected workforce – a local workforce comprising the global; a workforce selected, so we are told, from a talent pool of the most skilled and creative people in the world who collectively have the broadest knowledge of the global space the industry works in (see also Ho 2009).

This positioning of banks as uniquely skilled global benefactors is significant, for it helps legitimise their spatial claims to authority in the City and internationally, as well as claims to authority and entitlement by their elite workers. The narrative of a globally representative workforce, meanwhile, which while it rests on the centring of diversity and inclusivity, actually masks an exclusive homogeneity. Consequently, banks' global narratives legitimise their current unequal and patriarchal structures of recruitment and reward, which favour certain potential and actual employees at the expense of others (this is discussed in more detail in the following chapter). As such, the global discourse of banking must be recognised as constituting a crucial component of both spatial and gendered processes of hegemony linked to elite finance.

The physical and metaphorical spatial positioning of wealthy City-based banks is mutually reinforcing – the power of the global dimension supports their local positioning in the City, which lends wealthy banks and their elite workers a socio-spatial power that is not shared by all the constituent parts of the City and its workforce. In turn, this power is reflected in the dominant identity of the City as a global financial centre, which masks those very same numerous and vital but devalued elements that, along with global finance, necessarily constitute both the City's and London's economic and social fabric (Massey 2010: 41) and which help keep the wheels of global finance turning smoothly.

Narratives of a global industry

The five men I talked with who worked in the more prestigious jobs in City banking, and who received base salaries that alone placed them comfortably within the top 0.1% of "earners" in the UK[11] (Matt, Dan,

Paul, Dominic and James), drew on the institutional global discourse of banking when they explained their current roles and responsibilities. Each of these five men had entered investment banking straight from university. Matt was a 35-year-old banker who initially worked as a trader when he started in banking but had quickly risen through the ranks to senior management level. He told me that he was the "co-Global Head of ...", managing "a team of about 500 people globally". Dan was a 43-year-old banker, also in senior management. He described himself as, "Head of ...", and said that he worked with clients who "are worldwide based", and that he "cover[ed] European companies from London but talk[ed] to clients all over the world". Paul was 48 years old and was likewise in a senior role, describing himself as "Managing Director" who headed up a "global group". Dominic was 38 years old and worked in middle management. He referred to the "global operations" of the bank he worked for and described how he "personally [had] to deal with people globally". He also positioned himself as an integral part of the bank's operations by explaining that "we deal in every market virtually that we can deal in ... basically everywhere you want." James was 31 years old and was redundant at the time of interview.[12] Nevertheless, he explained that, for him, one of the appeals of working in banking was that it was a "global industry".

Like the banks' institutional use of the global discourse, these individual applications of it contribute to the global branding of the industry – a crucial projection of individual, institutional and industry-wide power, capability and connectivity which is both exclusive and normative at the same time. It sets particular firms and the individuals who work in them apart from other firms, but also positions the former as the benchmark by which the whole industry and the people who work in it are measured and valued.

Of further significance in the men's narratives is the emphasis placed on the centrality of London. London's dominant positioning as a global financial centre, for example, was reinforced by James, Dominic and Matt as they reflected on what were, at the time, some of the concerns facing the City's finance industry in the wake of the 2008 financial crisis. James, for example, suggested it was possible that some well-paid bankers may relocate overseas to work in a place with lower tax rates than London, should the UK government impose a higher rate of tax on top earners. I asked him if he thought firms might also start to relocate:

> That's a good question. The thing is, a lot of it comes down to time zones; London is significant because of the time zone. And because the States, they all speak English, so the next natural hub is London... You've got to be in London to do certain jobs, and you've got to meet clients face to face.

Dominic also emphasised the centrality and dominance of London as he talked about potential new regulations on the industry and how they may affect the appeal of the City as a prime location for the finance industry:

HL: Do you think London will keep its attractiveness for banking?

DOMINIC: Yep! Has always done, and will always do. It kind of lost that a bit to New York through the '90s, but it kind of got that back in the early 2000s – London became the kind of boom place. Umm, EU regulators are going to be pretty tough on banks but, you know, they're not going to move to Switzerland or France, or anywhere else. You're still gonna need a financial hub in Europe, and it's still gonna be the City. There's no point moving, you know. The good thing about London is it's very easy to attract people to come and live here: the lifestyle's pretty good, it's a major city, people can come and get their kids into good schools, buy nice houses, and do all the cultural stuff and all the stuff they want to do.

London's positioning as a global financial centre is reinforced in these extracts. And what is illuminating is that it is particular cultural features of the social relations of London – the language (James) and facilities for families (Dominic) – that constitute aspects of this. Dominic's comment, in particular, also begins to illustrate how lifestyle choice – both the act of making a choice and the choice itself – is intimately interrelated with the hegemonic processes of global finance, as is, of course, the very capability of people like Dominic to be freely able to make these choices in the first place. They are part of what Collier (2010a: 127) refers to as a "virtuous cycle of growth" whereby material rewards enable certain consumption and socio-spatial practices for elite workers, which, in turn, support notions of individual and institutional social status and who or what is able, capable, hard-working, successful, worthy and so forth. This cycle, itself, then fuels both geographic and social segregation and gendered forms of inequality. This segregation occurs through processes such as gentrification[13] of residential and business districts and the knock-on effect of this on the broader community spaces that service these areas. Increasing concentrations of high-income workers and residents produce patterns and practices of consumption and lifestyle that other people can also engage with wholly or partially depending on their material (and often social) resources, but which also help determine who is able to fully participate in society, as large swathes of the population are priced out of and thus excluded from participating in certain forms of social–cultural practice (see Sassen 2013: 24 for more discussion).

Elsewhere in their interviews, Dominic, James, Matt and Graham all referred to the same two or three cities that, together with London, comprised the global financial elite: New York, Hong Kong and Tokyo, although the latter city's status was disputed by Dominic:

> Tokyo's kind of died ... it was the Asian hub probably prior to the mid-2000s, early 2000s. Tokyo for 20 years before that was definitely the hub – all the banks' Asian headquarters were in Tokyo. Now it would mostly be Hong Kong.

Dominic's comment about Tokyo further acknowledges the centrality of space, power and flux to the functioning and hegemonies of global finance. It is significant for three main reasons. First, it appears to undermine the sense of permanence assigned to global financial locations, Tokyo or otherwise. It is a direct acknowledgement of the fragility of spatial dominance and, as such, it resonates with Dominic's previous comment about London's diminishing appeal during the 1990s, itself a tacit acknowledgement of London's concealed instability. Second, and in direct contrast, precisely because of Dominic's previous comment, it also serves to reinforce the superiority of London: London was able to weather the financial storm of the 1990s and re-establish itself thereafter, and was also expected to survive and perhaps even emerge stronger from the 2008 financial crisis. Third, regardless of whether London's dominant positioning is or is not durable, Dominic's comment illustrates one at the same time what is both the power and weakness of the hegemonic – its ability to adapt and reconfigure precisely because the assumptions underpinning it are not definitive. If London, like Tokyo, does at some point lose its current authority as a global financial city then either somewhere else, like Hong Kong, will seamlessly take its place and a similar hegemonic process will continue to the benefit of a few and the detriment of the many, *or* the assumptions underpinning this hegemonic process (and other hegemonic processes that interrelate with it) could be challenged and rejected.

Both the affirmation of the superiority of London and the instability of hegemonic assumptions, of course, take on new significance in light of recent and ongoing uncertainty surrounding Brexit (see Introduction). London managed to retain its dominant status as an international financial hub despite the 2008 financial crisis and the subsequent tightening of financial regulations. Following the Brexit vote, however, the sturdiness of London's dominant identity is once more being tested, and it is not yet clear to what extent London might need to or be able to renew and refashion itself in the wake of changes brought about by the UK leaving the European Union, if/when this eventually comes about.

While such a discussion is clearly beyond the scope of this book, what is important is recognising that different hierarchical and hegemonic processes intersect and strengthen each other. London's current spatial superiority as a global financial centre, whether or not it is natural, unquestionable, unshakeable and enduring, as suggested by official discourse as well as the men I interviewed, feeds into and benefits from other forms of supposedly cultural superiority (language, schools, housing and other symbolic confirmations of hegemony). And, as a result of this, helps constitute notions of individual worth and superiority on the part of employees, like Dominic, who are discerning enough to choose the City to work in. The hegemonic spatial positioning of the City is synonymous with the superiority of banks that are based there, as well as the bankers who work in them. As such, this spatiality feeds into infrastructural development, which feeds in again to this sense of institutional and individual worthiness while, at the same time, masking these same lines of privilege.

The same sense of self-worth and similar assertions of superiority based on spatial positioning were expressed by James, Paul, Dominic and Matt elsewhere in their interviews. For example, when discussing whether criticism over bankers' high salaries in London in the wake of the 2008 crisis was justified, Matt and Dominic made the following comments:

> People complain about what bankers get paid… I mean bankers are well paid, let's face it. But the reality is, do you do a job that can be done by a China man and expect to over time only get paid what the China man gets paid?
>
> (Matt)

> Banking's no different to any other industry … They go to China, they go to Thailand, they go to Indonesia and that's easy, India and that's cheaper. That's the exact reason [this bank] has got some operations in [India], 'cos it's cheaper. They don't have to pay someone to do the same job [there] as you do in London. They do … I wouldn't say basic operational stuff in [India] but fairly easy. You don't have to be very highly trained to do it, although it helps, it makes life easier. They're not really very highly trained and it shows: you know, you have to explain something to people in [India] five hundred times, whereas, you only have to explain it once or twice to the guy in New York. And, because of email, because of the Internet, because of the ability for people to fly out there if they need to quite easily, you don't need them sitting in an office in London, you stick 'em in, you know…
>
> (Dominic)

These comments about geographic location and superiority are significant because of the ways in which the spatial hierarchy distinguishing different places as well as the people who work in them is strengthened and normalised through associations (some rather contradictory to others) with better education, training and innate ability on the part of employees. These associations are used to justify the high salaries and bonuses paid to some people who work in global finance, and in turn, therefore, help legitimise the patriarchal structures of elite banking. The latter is also implied through both Matt's and Dominic's normalisation of *men* working in finance and the invisibility of women in their narratives and, in Dominic's case, men associated specifically with elite positions in banking – the "guy" in New York. Moreover, as James also remarked in his earlier comment above, it is apparently not just superior workers who are positioned in London but also desirable clients. What is also revealing is the way in which connectivity – actual (e.g., flying) and virtual (Internet) – rather than providing a means for transformation through developing a more egalitarian, horizontal workforce/firm, instead becomes a further tool for cementing existing inequalities and hierarchies.

It is perhaps not surprising that the men voicing these associations are the more highly paid bankers in this study's sample, precisely because of the interrelated strands and systems of privilege. The men's references to spatial positioning and the ways it is promoted as common sense – an understanding of the capabilities of people/workers from different countries these men assumed others share – underpin and help perpetuate existing hierarchical structures and practices of banking, which themselves shape, support and reinforce these same understandings of institutional and individual worth and value. Not only are high salaries and high bonuses apparently needed in a particular place (London or New York) to attract and retain the very best people, but spatial positioning also justifies paying these high salaries (the people working in banking in London, so we are told, are of better quality) and paying people working in banking elsewhere (in India, Indonesia and China) less money. The high salaries, in turn, feed into the cycles of growth that further fuel and cement socio-economic and spatial divisions.

This hierarchical spatial relationship is further complicated, however, by the fact that, as illustrated above, the global discourse of banking suggests employees who work in elite jobs have already been selected from communities all over the world. Thus, those who have been hand-picked to work in London (or New York) are, so the inferences are made, more intelligent, more skilful at and quick to learn how to do their jobs, harder-working, more discerning (according to Dominic, they recognise the benefits of good schools, housing and so forth) than other employees working elsewhere, and the other workers in the City who enable elite bankers to do the jobs they do. This blanks out the diverse lines and cycles of privilege – upbringing, schooling and so forth – that enable some people, including these men, to work in a particular place in the particular jobs they do, and renders unproblematic the discriminatory practices of recruitment, reward and remuneration in banking, not only in the City but in the global industry as a whole.

Comments made by James, when he talked about relocating to Sydney for work, further illustrate how this spatial hierarchy, which feeds into the hegemonic spatial arrangements of both the finance industry and people who work in it, as well as the process of hegemonic masculinity, is practised and reinforced:

HL: So did they fly you out [to Sydney] because of your expertise?

JAMES: Yeah, yeah. They wanted people who had a background, and who had first-hand experience of dealing with those types of clients ... The average Aussie is very laid back, so finding someone and training them up wasn't really an option. I think maybe they did look around at a few people in the market already in Australia but none of them really met the right criteria or the boss didn't really like them. So he spoke to a friend of his – the guy who got me out there, who really specialises in finding good people in London and sending them out to Hong Kong or Sydney. So that's how it was ...

Far from banks searching the world for the best people, what James infers in this explanation is that the best people are already located in very specific spaces – i.e., London – and are themselves flown around the world.

Collectively, these comments relating to spatiality made by the men jar powerfully with the apparent claims to diversity, inclusion and meritocracy put forward in the promotional material of banks, which suggest that all employees start off on an equal footing and are equally valued: employees hand-picked from all over the globe for their unique and precious qualities. They also begin to suggest some of the inconsistencies and ambiguities embedded in the structures and practices of banking that will be discussed in more detail in the following chapter (whether or not the boss "likes you", for example). Indeed, James' comment above is particularly interesting in light of the fact he was made redundant (and made so in a relatively short space of time) from the very position that he was apparently hand-selected for and flown halfway around the world to do (I discuss redundancy in more detail in Chapter 5). James is a particularly good example of the fact that the combination of the sense of exclusive entitlement to jobs and salaries and the supposed meritocratic nature of the financial workplace is a dangerous cocktail for employees – elite employees as well as others. As revealed later, when James talked about redundancy, he blamed his own shortcomings and not institutional flaws for the fact he did not succeed in this particular position.

A mobile identity in a dynamic space

A further element crucial to the process of spatial hegemony linked to global finance in the City is dynamism. Like the spatial hierarchy it combines with to feed into a double-layered process of mobility, the dynamic nature of elite City banking has both real and metaphorical elements. This mobility process comprises both opportunities for elite bankers working in certain places (e.g., London) to be mobile and the assumption they are and/or want to be mobile (these are, so we have been told, the people at the forefront of their field – the pioneers and adventurers). Although the boundary between these two elements is not always clear-cut, they combine to reinforce the superiority associated with bankers working in very particular locations (London and New York), which, in turn, reinforces the superior positioning of these places themselves. This relationship between space and mobility is complex, however. It can be understood, on the one hand, as contributing to institutional control: part of the seductive aspect of hegemony and the lure of the industry – the promise of overseas travel works in tandem with the enticing image of the dynamic, successful banker. On the other hand, and in practice, it is perhaps more full of contradiction than pleasure and excitement.

Mobility for those working in elite positions in finance appears primarily to consist of two forms. The first is a semi-permanent mobility, or the opportunity to work overseas for an extended period of time. The second is a much more fleeting short-term mobility – travelling overseas for work for anything between a day and a few weeks. The official mobility discourse of banks with regard to the former type – semi-permanent job prospects overseas – is linked with opportunity and a sense of freedom of choice, as the following extract from J.P. Morgan (2018b) illustrates:

> Thanks to our global reach, we can help you get where you want to go. Whether you sharpen your skills or gain something new, you'll have experience that will give you flexibility to move to another division or country if you choose to.

The emphasis on individual freedom and choice in deciding one's career trajectory is interesting in light of comments made by Matt, Dominic and James. I asked Matt if he had worked anywhere other than London:

MATT: No, no, I've always been based here.

HL: Is that your decision? Or would you … [*Matt interrupts*]

MATT: So given that I work for an American bank, there's always the slight assumption that if you want to progress you have to be in New York at some point. So I always used to say to my wife that someday they're going to say I've got to go to New York. And she was always, you know, fine with that. About three or four years ago, maybe longer, they asked me if I wanted to go to Singapore to run Asia. So I said I would think about do I want to go, if that's how it worked out, but it didn't happen. So it tends to work like that: they tend to tell you with not very much notice that, "we're going to do this".

Dominic made a similar comment when reflecting on the security of his role: "I guess, you know, all of a sudden they might decide to do the job out of Hong Kong, or something … I dunno, I obviously wouldn't want to move to Hong Kong particularly …"

And James told me how, after he was pipped to the post by a colleague and "good friend" to a job he had been promised in London (a job which, he explained, was created specifically for him (see the next chapter)), he was "pretty upset" and ultimately reassessed his future at the bank:

> So I'd interviewed for this job and everyone was, sort of, patting me on the back and winking and nodding. I then went on holiday and came back and everything was different. And I said, you know, "What's going on?" And my boss tried to gloss over it … So they said, "Look, how about you fly out to Hong Kong? There might be something happening with us there". And I spoke to a few people, but I knew it was going to take at least a year and a half to actually get a move out there. So I spoke to some other banks as well and I knew there was a job going at […] – not the job that I wanted to do, but I had interviewed there … In the end they offered me a job which was going to be Hong Kong, but at the last minute they said, "Well, what about Sydney?"

Not only is freedom of choice with regard to movement and opportunity missing from each of these personal narratives, despite banks' claims that it is available for all "deserving" employees, so also is the sense that employees' needs, commitment and career are of paramount concern. There is also clear indication of the banks' control over employees' private lives – both direct control and control channelled through the employees themselves: Matt, for example, explained how he told his wife they would have to move at some point, which does not suggest much room for negotiation. And yet, the invisibility of any concern for individual employees' needs (let alone the needs and desires of family members) appears to differ from the following definitive statement from one bank: "Here, you'll feel welcomed and valued … we work hard to create diverse, inclusive teams that support our business and each other" (J.P. Morgan 2018b).

Nevertheless, in large capital letters that shout out of J.P. Morgan's same website page is the word "TOGETHER". Along with the fact concern for the business is positioned before the individual in the above quote, this "togetherness" discourse is interesting. It is reflective, perhaps, of a concern for the well-being of the collective (i.e., the firm) that results in conveniently sidestepping – or indeed, as we shall see later on, overruling – concern for the well-being of the individual (Berman 2010), and yet at the same time paradoxically sitting uncomfortably with the ideology of competitive individualism (see Chapter 2). Regardless, Matt avoided answering my direct question about whether or not the fact he had only worked in London was a result of his own decision-making. Instead, his comment (along with those of the other men) implies that employees seem, in practice, to have quite limited control regarding their future in terms of where they do or do not want to work geographically, as well as the time they are given to make a decision. There are inferences in all of the comments above that decisions regarding mobility are made extraordinarily suddenly, and that job offers require immediate and rather astonishingly urgent responses. There appears to be little, if any, space for personal reflection or, in fact, much choice at all: no space to discuss such big decisions with partners/family when the so-called opportunities arise (the possibility that it might happen has to be raised beforehand); and no time to tender to one's personal needs (have a holiday) – indeed, as James found to his cost, to do so may result in the complete withdrawal of the job opportunity.

This kind of control exerted by banks has significant implications for all employees, but particularly for those who are not able to make that kind of decision immediately – those who have children in school, for example, or those who have different kinds of caring responsibilities – or those who simply do not want to be backed into a corner and forced to make such a decision on the spot. In some respects, however, this can be understood as a continuation of the aggressive undertones of the language of pioneering and colonisation discussed above, yet couched in the language of excitement, dynamism and opportunity. And, as such, it is both a product of and feeds back into the practices and identity formation of the elite institutions and workers of finance.

Of further significance relating to the semi-permanent mobility–opportunity discourse of banking is the fact that none of the men I interviewed had relocated to a different geographical location while working for the same bank, despite the fact most of them had been working in banking for some considerable time. In fact, the bankers in the most high-status and high-paying positions – Dan, Paul and Matt – had been working for their respective firm in the City for most, if not all, of their careers to date (Dan and Paul for over 20 years; Matt for about 14 years). Given these demonstrations of stability (and a concomitant loyalty), it may appear surprising that references to mobility are so pervasive in the banking literature. Yet regardless of whether or not this kind of mobility is real or metaphorical, it is clearly a crucial, central feature of the process of hegemony linked with global finance, and its presence in banking discourse remains powerful, alluring and unquestioned. As Matt's comment suggests, being asked to move to a specific geographic location (New York) can be an important sign of success and a signifier of status – a spatial confirmation that you have made it in the industry. As will be discussed in more detail later, the allure of potential rewards in banking, of which being asked to relocate to a prestigious location may be seen to be one, fuels existing processes of hegemony and the practices on which they depend, regardless of whether or not these rewards are ever realised.

The other form of mobility that feeds into a general dynamic sense of institutional and individual identity is a briefer form of mobility: short overseas business trips. This seems to be a form of mobility more of the men engaged in, although it was still, perhaps, not as pervasive as one might have expected. Like the semi-permanent form, it rests on contradiction and masks stability. While the idea of travel, as promoted by banks, may evoke a sense of glamour and adventure, in reality, business travel was referred to by the men as, at best, simply routine and somewhat tiresome, at worst, utterly exhausting, or as Paul described it: "brutal". Dan gave the following account, when I asked him if he had to travel much during the year:

DAN: A reasonable amount, yeah, absolutely. You have to go to Europe to see the companies, and then our clients are worldwide based, so we have to go and see those clients probably once or twice a year. But it does mean you have to travel quite a lot because there are quite a lot of different places to go because the client base is quite fragmented … beneath that, we do have less important clients who you can see when you go to that city, but you really go to see the top four to five clients … So it's a day-trip to Europe mainly once every two weeks, maybe an overnight, you know. It's not too bad … And then there's trips to the States twice a year, three times a year for like two days. I mean, not extended periods, maximum three or four days – yeah, I would say three times a year.
HL: You say your important clients … *[Dan interrupts again]*
DAN: Yeah, you know, the bigger clients – the bigger investors.

While there is a clear association of wealth with size and status in Dan's comments about clients, which mirrors the notion of the "business giants" in the official discourse of the City discussed above, what also begins to emerge from his description is the way in which London is positioned as the command point – the place from where the hand-selected elite workers travel to other places to establish and maintain business contacts and networks. Matt and Dominic made similar comments:

> We have branches all over South America, all over Africa and elsewhere. So there are obviously people there that I go and see. We also have clients who are based all over Europe, the Middle East and America, so yeah, yeah, I go to a lot of places. I'm not sure I've ever had an average year, but to give you a flavour: in March, I was in New York, Miami, Mexico City, São Paulo; in May, I was in Abu Dhabi and Beirut, Johannesburg, Cape Town, New York. At the moment, I'm kind of finding it quite irate, quite exhausting.
>
> (Matt)

> I try to limit [travelling] really. I have to go to the States at least once a year, probably twice, actually. We have a big conference in Europe once a year. I have to go to Hong Kong maybe twice, and Singapore – I went to Singapore earlier this year. I dunno, I guess I'm supposed to travel at the weekend – you're supposed to travel in your own time – but I do try and go Monday morning sometimes, if I can.
>
> (Dominic)

The mobility practices of these elite City workers help reinforce the spatial hierarchy of global banking, along with the hierarchies of the different employees working in different locations. Despite the fact that banks claim to employ people who reflect and represent the "diverse communities" they work in (banks who apparently have "offices around the world"), it is the elite bankers from the City – the men in high-status positions – who are sent to woo clients in other countries. Matt's listing of numerous locations especially, perhaps, reflects the voracious appetite of the finance industry for expansion as well as the colonising tendencies inferred in the official banking discourse.

In addition to the dependency on the stable, commanding position of the City, this form of mobility also quite clearly requires significant stability in the private lives of workers, like these men, who have caregiving responsibilities (it also requires accommodating partners who are willing to sustain an intimate relationship under these kinds of conditions). Overnight business trips and weekend travel require and assume there are family or caregiving arrangements in place that enable this kind of absence. It needs people, other than the men, to perform essential tasks and fulfil parenting and domestic responsibilities. This necessary dependency further strengthens the forms of gendered and spatial hegemony associated with global finance – the patriarchal nature of the elite financial workplace and the separation of work and home – as well as the combination of the two. And this combination, as I discuss in more detail in the following chapters, supports and perpetuates the authority of the masculine elite financial workplace over the feminised space of the home, and the authority of the public lives of the elite workers over their private lives.

Family relations are discussed in more detail in Chapters 3 and 4. But one interesting point to emerge from the ways in which the wives of these men talked about their respective husband's business trips that deserves a brief mention here is that overseas travel appeared to place little extra burden on the women over and above the everyday complexity of managing their husband's normal absence from the family home due to other day-to-day forms of work commitment (long hours, client entertainment and so forth). For example, Gwyneth, Paul's wife, lumped travel and other workplace demands together as she discussed Paul's routine – foreign travel, long hours, late dinners and functions – while Cath, Dan's wife, was quite matter-of-fact about her husband travelling for work:

> Because Dan's not around Monday to Friday, to be honest, it only bothers me if he has to go on Sunday night to America or something … but quite often I forget he's away, or whatever, because he normally isn't here anyway, so it doesn't make any difference to me [*Cath laughs as she says this*].

Meanwhile, Kara, Matt's wife, explained that despite the fact she hated Matt going away on all his business trips:

> Ironically, we have a sense of almost seeing more of him when he's travelling, 'cos we might get half of Monday and half of Friday. And he will always phone me from the airport lounge, you know, and we'll have long conversations for an hour or something.

The ways in which these women talked about their respective husband's absence from the home illustrate how the routine practices of the financial workplace impact on and structure family space. The fundamental interrelationship between the work and private lives of the men, particularly in terms of the need for the women's spatial and familial locatedness and stability, is thus a necessary and accepted counterpoint to the dynamics of the finance industry and its elite workers.

What the narratives of the men and women reveal is a link with hierarchy, space and a dual process of stability that necessarily accompanies the dual process of mobility. First, there is the stability of the City both as the command point for elite finance and as a source of elite workers who can be called on to travel anywhere in the world at short notice. Paul, for example, recounted to me how he might get home from a work trip to China on Saturday and then find out on Sunday night that he had to go to Chicago the next day. Second, there is the stability elite workers depend on in their private lives (and employers assume they have) to enable them to fulfil the mobility demands of their employers.

A contained space

As a stable command point of global finance from where the industry's mobility is directed, the City maintains its dominance through a complex web of processes, everyday practices and socio-spatial relations. As such, the space of the City is shaped primarily for and by the needs of wealthy City-based firms and their workers in ways that deliberately and by default further strengthen their advantage over other less well-resourced firms and less well-paid workers.

In the outside space of the City, as described earlier in this chapter, services cater for the needs of workers during the day – cafés and sandwich shops to buy coffee and lunch, dry cleaners to take work clothes to be cleaned – while others continue servicing them on into the evening – restaurants, bars and clubs – for work-related networking. These offsite services combine with onsite amenities offered by banks, which are promoted as demonstrations of employer care and concern about employee well-being and comprise part of the official institutional blurb to lure would-be recruits. J.P. Morgan (2018b) provides onsite "wellness programs" offering "health coaches, counselling and guidance services", and "employee programs" that include "back-up child care services, flexible work options [and] fitness programs ...". Morgan Stanley (2015) provides "a competitive and comprehensive benefits package" for employees and their families, which "aims to support [their] health and wellbeing" through a "range of lifestyle benefits to support [employees] at work and at home" – this includes an onsite fitness centre, physiotherapists and medical practitioners. Goldman Sachs (2018e, 2018f) provides "wellness offerings ... designed to enhance the health and wellbeing of our people", including "an on-site café, along with a fitness centre, medical centre and childcare facilities". It explains how it "... provides resources to help our people manage life outside the firm at every stage from parent resources to adult care as well as counselling services and medical advocacy programs".

These onsite services, as other studies of corporate employment in global cities have noted (see, for example, Ho 2009 and Collier 2012), together with the offsite amenities of the City, help blur the boundaries between work and home. They help develop an exclusive space by providing, in one place, all the material aspects employees need to stay fit, healthy, professionally connected and physically present at work. And they feed into the institutional image intended to coexist with, and be mirrored by, the characteristics banks want to foster and expect from their employees – characteristics that echo the global discourse of banking: outgoing, dynamic, fit and networked, and which help project a sense of success and affluence. Together, the different services – onsite and off – help constitute and sustain the dominance and stability of the City and the banks and bankers located there. They are crucial to the exclusive culture of banking in the City and the gendered hierarchical structures and practices of the financial workplace. They support and encourage, for example, certain forms of working, particularly long hours, which reinforce gendered divisions both in the workplace and in the home (I discuss this in more detail in the next chapter).

The provision of these kinds of onsite amenities, whether or not they are utilised by workers, helps banks exert considerable control over the space of the workplace as well as the private lives and family relations of elite workers. While the onsite services may be promoted as assisting work–life balance issues, they nevertheless promote a self-sufficient community based around work, which is quite different. Moreover, the existence of these facilities, and the ways they are promoted, forecloses the space to problematise current workplace practices and structures. The irony of this situation is of course, as Collier (2016) has noted, that these onsite amenities are, to some extent, only needed in the first place because of the existing workplace culture – the very same culture that produces the effects these facilities are trying to alleviate (long hours, hyper-competitiveness, etc.). So while such provision can, to some extent perhaps, be linked to a level of organisational commitment to employee well-being, institutions avoid engaging with the root causes of many of the problems, and instead continue to promote, expect and valorise them (Collier 2016). As Goldman Sachs (2018e) state: "From compensation and benefits to wellness and on-site childcare, we aim to support your commitment to your job …". So not only does the way in which these services are advertised create a metaphorical hierarchical divide between work demands and other non-work demands/desires, including family responsibilities, the physical spatial positioning of these facilities *in* the workplace also demonstrates this subordinate valuing of private, non-work space.

Banks promote onsite facilities, including emergency nursery and childcare provision, as if they are based on thoughtful benevolence. Yet those who, in theory, might benefit from this supposed thoughtfulness do not always view it in quite the same way. As this comment by Cath illustrates:

> We had just had Noah, and Dan came home one day and said "Oh, it's really good news, [the bank] have just launched a scheme for emergency childcare. They have 2 spaces reserved each day at a local nursery". And I was kind of thinking, "What? Who thought that would be", you know. Emergency childcare is either sending a nanny to my house, or letting you have the day off, or couriering you anything you need from the office. Not dropping your two small children at a nursery where they've never met anybody.

Of course, one can justifiably argue that such provisions are not designed to directly help non-bank employees like Cath, but to help bank employees like Dan (her husband). But this, in itself, simply further illustrates employers' separation of work and family concerns – the primary concern is to enable bankers like Dan to work in the workplace, despite the fact they may have young children who urgently need caring for. In reality, therefore, the primary beneficiary of these facilities is arguably the firm, not its individual workers.

Both the ways in which the onsite amenities are promoted and described and the kinds of provision on offer subordinate the people who may do these caregiving or other tasks outside the financial workplace, whether family members or not (and, as suggested by Cath, may also devalue the well-being concerns for children). The social value of these forms of work, and by default the people who do them, is positioned as secondary to the importance of high-status workers and the paid work they do. Indeed, what banks suggest in the ways in which they promote these provisions is that caregiving responsibilities and issues of well-being should not prevent an employee from being present at work; if an employee is organised enough, it is expected he or she can "fulfil" caregiving responsibilities in addition to and supplementary to engaging in high-status, intensive forms of working. This is not to deny the agency of individual workers who can and want to work in this way. Nevertheless, a further point of significance is that the suggestion that home and workplace responsibilities (in particular, those relating to demanding forms of employment) are easily compatible with one another sets the benchmark for expectations placed on *all* workers (elite or otherwise, bankers or otherwise) to combine and self-manage paid work and family responsibilities.

The banks' provision of such onsite facilities, combined with offsite facilities in the City, helps bolster the global standing of wealthy banks and, by default, the City. Because wealthy banks provide these support services, their employees are more able (as well as expected) to work hard. This reinforces the notion that these workers are more committed than workers elsewhere, that they work longer hours, are better at their jobs, and so on and so forth. This, in turn, contributes to the argument that these workers also deserve or "earn" their higher-than-average wages (some of which are, of course, considerably higher). While this masks lines of privilege that feed into the hierarchical reward system, it also legitimises and justifies notions of worthiness and the authoritative positioning of the men who continue to dominate the top echelons of power in global finance. This normalised structure of worthiness and reward has additional knock-on effects: higher wages mean elite workers can also, ironically, afford to organise additional support structures or extra help in their private lives (nannies, gardeners, cleaners etc.) over and above the institutional "work-life programs" they have access to, which in turn also enable the hard-working – long-hours – culture of elite banking (see Chapter 3).

Two employees who illustrate particularly starkly the gendered spatial divide between work and home, which is encouraged and supported by workplace expectations and facilities, are Matt and Dan. Since having children, both men had moved with their families out of London to locations that required between one-and-a-half and two hours' commute either way. Both men stayed overnight in London on average two or three nights each week. Dan stayed in an apartment relatively near his office, which he bought at the same time as buying the new family home. Matt, meanwhile, told me that he stayed at "the club". Both men explained the decision to move out of London in terms of the desire for a "better quality of life" for their families. And, although they both remarked that the biggest drawback was their now-lengthy commute, the ways in which they referred to the spatial divide between their work and home lives presented the decision as straightforward and unproblematic, thus foreclosing the space for questioning it:

> When we lived in London it was ten minutes in a taxi, or I could run it in 25 minutes. People ask me how I do the commute, but it's just what you want – it's what you want to make work.
>
> (Matt)

> Up until three years ago, we lived in [London] – literally 20 minutes away – and that was good because it was a much easier commute, and it meant you were home much quicker. But it's each to their own.
>
> (Dan)

Both of these men had wives who willingly (happily or not) acquiesced to this move, who assumed the day-to-day caregiving and domestic responsibilities of home and family, and who were thus complicit in hegemonic processes of elite finance. Processes which, along with each of their husband's lengthy commutes, encourage and dictate the ways in which the men were absent from the family home and the structures and practices in place to support their absences. To a significant degree, and perhaps rather ironically, the greater physical distance Dan and Matt had created between their family space and their working space offered them greater flexibility in the workplace. Because they both stayed overnight in London some evenings each week, they were able to work late – whether through choice or requirement – without the pressure or expectation of getting home.

Further comments made by Matt and Dan, along with the other two men who worked in the more prestigious jobs in elite banking (Paul and Dominic), offer insight into the ways in which the space of finance and the City, with its all-inclusive package of amenities and complex social fabric, actually serves as a space of ever-exclusive belonging. It is a place where bankers are expected to work and "socialise" with other people, people like themselves, and increasingly, it seems, marginalise their private lives. All four men explained how they were out, on average, at least two nights each week entertaining clients or attending work-related events. And Matt unequivocally explained that "bankers tend to hang out with other bankers". Further comments he made illustrate how the banking practice of evening work-related social commitments significantly impacts on bankers' private lives and consequently has implications for the ways in which their family relations and responsibilities are structured and divided:

HL: Do you commute up every day?

MATT: No, it depends on what I've got to do. If I'm going for a dinner – last night we had a dinner and presentations, so I went and had a dinner at 7 o'clock.

HL: And would you stay in a hotel in London?

MATT: Yeah, I would. I generally stay at the club, actually. If I'm in London, I'm probably staying up here on average two, maybe three, nights a week entertaining clients or going to a presentation or something.

Matt and Dan (along with their wives) had organised their lives so that work and family were quite significantly spatially separated. Paul, on the other hand, lived in London and explained that the important thing for him about living relatively near the City was that he could "always go home at the end of the day". However, he also had to stay out on work-related business until 11pm, or later, on average two evenings a week. Paul told me that he left the house each morning at 6am, and so it is clear that he did not really see his son during the week any more than Dan and Matt saw their children. What is also revealing in each of these men's accounts, other than the fact their schedules demonstrated certain limitations work requirements and expectations put on their family time,[14] is that there neither appeared to be little contestation made about these extracurricular work activities/duties nor much pleasure voiced about engaging in them. Ultimately, the men still did them – arguably to the primary benefit of the banks and to the detriment of other workers who cannot give this level of commitment. And perhaps also to the detriment (at least in terms of health) of those who can, as the following comment from Paul implies:

> I think it's all very tiring ... dinners and seminars. You're coming up and doing a day's work, and then you have to clock off to a hotel. And the other slight challenge is that when you stay in a hotel there are normally people from the overseas offices and they want to stay up 'cos they're awake. So you end up drinking till 2am, and then you're up again for normal day's work. All these things start adding up ... you can't do it like you could when you were in your twenties. You sort of know that, but still run your life as if you can.

To some extent, therefore, these evening work-related events might be understood as a third form of employee mobility, promoted, demanded and controlled by banks – a locally based mobility expected of elite workers in the City who want to maintain and enhance their career. It is a form of mobility that, like the other forms, blurs the boundaries between the personal and the professional. It can be seen as a form of mobility which feeds into the processes of spatial and gendered hegemony linked with global finance that help define and distinguish the employees who are supposedly more committed, hard-working, and therefore worthy than others, and by default help distinguish the institutions they work for. It is a further form of mobility that depends on, indeed demands, a significant level of stability in the family lives of elite workers and helps determine the gendered divisions of care and responsibility in the family. It is linked with the principles of self-management and responsibility for one's own well-being, and, like the other forms of mobility, with the dynamic, youthful image of global finance, the appeal of which, at some point or another for some, if not many, of these workers, starts to wear a little thin.

Conclusion

This exploration of some of the institutional and individual socio-spatial practices associated with global finance in the City illustrates how a process of spatial hegemony is at work, whereby the banking elite have established and are able to sustain their dominance and authority in and over the space of the City. The winning and holding of spatial power by the finance industry in the City has been achieved through a complex and ongoing historical process endorsed and facilitated by a number of different actors, including those in finance and politics. This dominance is positioned as natural, beneficial and common-sense. It also has seductive dimensions in the form of a discourse of dynamism and adventure, and moral dimensions in the form of sustainability and well-being. The spatial discourse of wealthy City-based banks interrelates with the physical space of the City and with spatial practices of banks and bankers (the latter at work and home) to develop the portrayal of an industry and its elite workers that is dynamic, committed, hard-working and rightfully powerful, valuable and valued. The next chapter looks behind this authoritative veneer to the exclusive gendered space of the financial workplace: the boys' club of global finance.

Notes

1 The City of London is a separate city and county located within London itself. It is one of the 33 local authority districts of Greater London – the other 32 districts are known as "boroughs".
2 At least, this is how it stands in 2018 prior to Brexit.
3 Tower Hamlets ranks among the bottom four of London's 32 boroughs for child poverty, unemployment, inequality in life expectancy, overcrowding, premature immortality and the number of people at 19 years old lacking qualifications.
4 See "London's Economic Plan" – part of the Lord Mayor's London Plan – online at: www.uncsbrp.org (accessed 27.10.18).
5 TheCityUK is the representative body for the UK-based financial and related services industry.
6 Along with other dimensions of difference that are not discussed here, including race, nationality and so forth.
7 This was a quote by Dan.
8 See Sassen (2014).
9 See also Massey (2010).
10 A key street in the City of London.
11 See Office for National Statistics.

12 I have included James here because, although he was not working when I interviewed him, he previously worked in investment banking in the City and was actively looking for similar work.
13 Gentrification was a term coined by Ruth Glass (1964) who first identified, in the mid-1960s, the way in which particular residential changes based on the upgrading of properties and a concomitant rise in the properties' purchase or rental values were fundamentally reconstituting the social fabric of districts in inner London through the displacement of working-class residents in favour of wealthier middle-class residents.
14 These are discussed in more detail in Chapter 3.

Chapter 2

Inside the boys' club of global finance

Behind the imposing stone and glass façades of the City of London's wealthy banks, the day-to-day peculiarities of hegemonic processes function and combine to shape gendered forms of hierarchy and authority which promote and sustain the dominance of the finance industry in the City and those who run it. Key components of these processes are the structures and practices of recruitment, retention and reward – aspects of which came under increased scrutiny from politicians and the media in the wake of the 2008 financial crisis. While much debate at the time focused on the disparity between the average UK wage and the high salaries and bonus payments awarded to City bankers, particularly those working at senior levels (see Toynbee and Walker 2008; Treanor 2010), some attention was also paid to gender inequalities and lack of diversity within the industry itself (see Hell 2010; McDowell 2010; Rushe 2011; Stedman Jones 2012). A 2010 UK government report on the City's finance industry, for example, showed that women were not always being paid as highly as men or receiving equivalent bonuses, with gender gaps as large as 55% for full-time salaries and 80% for bonuses (HoC 2010: 17). Figures compiled by the Cranfield School of Management (see Sealy et al. 2011), meanwhile, showed men still dominating top-management positions in financial services, comprising 84% of board members of FTSE 100[1] banks (see also Introduction).

Since the 2008 financial crisis, there has been increasing exposure of the economic benefits for firms of greater diversity and gender equality among their employee base and particularly at board level (Tucker 2010; Manfredi et al. 2016; Sealy et al. 2016) as well as a growing number of diversity, inclusion and well-being policies within the financial sector (Headworth et al. 2016). Yet men have continued to dominate senior levels in banking both in the UK and globally. In 2016 in UK financial services, women comprised just 23% board members (Chinwala 2016). Moreover, breaking this percentage down reveals even greater gender equality, with women comprising only 14% of executive committee members overall and just 12% at investment banks (ibid.).

The assumption that men predominate in the more prestigious positions in banking was reflected throughout the interviews I conducted with bankers.

Dominic, a 35-year-old banker working for an American investment bank, described how:

> There's a bit of a boys' club that happens in business. It's just how it works. The boys, you know, it's traditional for them to sit around in coffee shops around Fleet Street, from probably two, three hundred years ago, discussing and turning up and selling wares at a market place, which turns into a stock exchange, which turns into the markets, which turns into …

Dominic's matter-of-fact narrative resonates with the official description of the City given by the City of London Corporation as detailed in the previous chapter. By doing so, it reinforces the authority of this storyline and the conditions it underpins, not least the dominance of the finance industry in the City and in business more generally, as well as the dominance of men in positions of power. Dominic's comment evokes a sense of history, tradition, ownership, belonging and territoriality through the portrayal of the City finance industry as a "club", created by the "boys" for the "boys" – an inevitable consequence and colonisation of City space (which includes the spaces of socialisation (coffee shops) as well as business (stock exchange, markets)) that has evolved through "natural" historic development and progress. Dominic makes an allusion to class mobility, framed within a meritocracy discourse: rising up the social ladder from market trader to banker through hard work. Yet at the same time, this is an exclusionary narrative, like the official government description of the City, in the fact that it renders invisible and thus devalues women finance workers. This is particularly significant when considered alongside the sense of worthiness that successful City finance institutions and workers are imbued with (see the previous chapter), because it further suggests that particular banks and the (predominantly) men who work in the most prestigious and top-level positions in those banks rightfully dominate the industry – it is their club. Indeed, the power of this authoritative narrative, over and above its influence in shaping and assigning meaning to social practices relating to elite City finance, is that it compromises the capability of employees, like Dominic, either to consider the need for change or to willingly engage in processes that might bring change about.

In the elite financial workplace, such a narrative combines with other cultural ideas, and the social practices which support them, to feed into common-sense understandings of what constitutes and facilitates belonging, success and achievement. The ideology that underpins global finance promotes this workspace as not only competitive, but also meritocratic and collegiate – a space where one is personally in control of his or her destiny (Izurieta and Wade 2010; Connell 2012) yet institutionally supported and valued. For example, UBS (2018a) calls for potential recruits to come and "Grow with us"; it hails its "successful and long lasting partnerships with colleagues and clients", explaining that its ethos is: "We, not just me … Together. That's how we do things". J.P. Morgan (2018b), meanwhile, promotes itself as "A workplace for everyone", somewhere "you'll feel welcomed and valued" and where "doing first-class business in a first-class way" entails "respect, value and support [for] each individual employee". Goldman Sachs (2018e) explains how it "supports a culture of continuous learning, development and apprenticeship that helps our people achieve their full potential".

These narratives suggest that everyone starts out being equally valued and supported, whereby elite City banking is promoted as a space where those who "succeed" – those at the top – are the worthy winners and valued more than those who don't succeed – those at the bottom (Harvey 2011). It is a space, so we are thus told, where inequality is an inevitable and necessary consequence of meritocratic, "natural" market forces or the survival of the fittest. Yet, as other studies of elite financial workplace contexts have revealed, the apparent straightforwardness of this discourse is disrupted by the added insecurities embedded in the system. Substantial winners can very quickly become losers – their "growth" and "success" precariously gained – as the sudden collapse of Lehman Brothers in 2008 demonstrates. As Nomi Prins (2009: 166) has written, "a trader is only as good as his or her last trade … [a] firm is only as strong as its latest stock market position". Such disposability clouds the value-system banks promote.

The boys' club

The boys' club of elite City banking is characterised by opportunity and elitism, tradition and modernity, uniformity and inconsistency, individualism and conformity, teamwork and autonomy. It is both a local space and a global space. The challenge for those who gain access to this club, and who wish to survive and to thrive in it, is not merely to negotiate and manage these tensions, but also to navigate within a reward-based system that, despite its apparent "meritocratic" rulebook, seems neither straightforward nor consistent.

I interviewed four bankers – Matt, Dominic, Dan and Paul – in their workplace, which awarded me privileged, albeit still restricted, access to the highly closed and secretive indoor spaces of elite City finance. One of these interviews was scheduled for 11am on a damp and chilly autumn day.

A visit to the club

I arrived at the bank at 10.50am – ten minutes early – having nearly walked straight past the rather discreetly labelled building. The inside lobby of the bank was modestly sized with neutral décor and leafy pot plants positioned here and there. This inoffensive appearance was echoed by the quietness of the space, despite the presence of seven other people: three male security guards and four male visitors. A solid wooden reception desk faced the main door, and the two security guards who sat behind it looked up as I walked through the door and across the lobby towards them. Despite my smile and friendly greeting, the guard who talked to me was tersely polite. He put a tick beside my name on the list of the day's scheduled visitors and handed me a plastic security pass. He told me to walk through the bank of security barriers and take an elevator to the [fifth] floor, where someone would be waiting for me. The atmosphere was tense and serious. I may have been an invited visitor, but I was also an intruder, and I have no doubt CCTV cameras were capturing my every move.

The third guard stood on the far side of the security barriers. As I walked through the barriers, he beckoned me into an open elevator, which had no knobs on the inside, so he controlled where I went. When I emerged onto a quiet corridor, a woman – Jean – dressed in a smart dark blue fitted skirt and patterned crêpe blouse, stood waiting for me. Jean led me through a security-coded door into a large, busy, open-plan office with long rows of desks where people sat side-by-side and face-to-face working, their jackets hanging on the backs of their chairs. On one of the walls, a bank of large TV screens beamed out BBC World News, CNN News, Sky News and Bloomberg. Above the screens, a row of clocks showed the times of day in London, New York, Tokyo, Frankfurt and São Paulo.

Jean showed me into a smaller glass-fronted office, adjacent to the open-plan space. On the beige internal wall of the office, framed certificates of success and achievement hung alongside a large world map. On the desk stood four computer screens, with a further screen tuned into Bloomberg positioned on a separate table next to the desk. On a coat stand in the corner of the office, to the right of the door, hung a baseball cap, two ties and a college scarf. The room was neat, tidy and business-like but not unfriendly. Jean invited me to sit at a round meeting table in front of the desk. She apologised that the banker I had come to meet had been slightly delayed in a previous meeting but assured me that he wouldn't be long. I began to feel a little less like an intruder and more like an important client, and I couldn't decide if it made me feel more or less relaxed. In retrospect, I realise that neither identity was a reflection of my own positioning, but rather either a consequence of institutional power (the intruder identity) or a knock-on effect of this particular banker's individual status and power in this bank (the client identity).

The banker I was meeting was ten minutes later than we had agreed and was very apologetic at keeping me waiting. He looked athletic, suntanned and a little younger and shorter than I had expected. He wore a crisp, white shirt with red cufflinks, dark grey suit trousers and a large expensive-looking watch on his left hand. He had short, fair hair, a little longer on the top than it was on the sides. He was clean-shaven and had a big, broad smile and straight, white teeth. I stood up when he walked in and he shook my hand firmly before we both sat down. Like each of the men I interviewed at work, he began by warning me that he may not have a great deal of time and may have to leave at some point to go to another meeting. In the end, we talked for 1½ hours. As was the case with each of these other interviews, the potential interruption never materialised.

In theory, this banker was a "cock in a suit". In practice, in this particular context, I found him charming, affable, chatty and likeable.

The line of ascent

The conditions for hegemonic masculinity linked with global finance require not only the ideological prominence of particular values and norms, which serve the few but yet are seen to be in the best interests of all, but also the constant reproduction and thus legitimisation of these ideas and the social practices that support them. Certain similarities with regard to the men's lives and backgrounds indicate the social formation of the elite financial workplace in the City is, at least in part, defined by exclusive unity – or employee uniformity – rather than difference, despite increasing institutional claims to diversity (see, for example, Deutsche Bank 2018b; Goldman Sachs 2018c; Morgan Stanley 2018c). The men I interviewed were all white, from middle-class family backgrounds, and in heterosexual marriages, regardless of the fact these individual traits and social practice were not part of my criteria for participation. They also all, to one degree or another, enjoyed an elite British education. This latter similarity is interesting because it was not originally obvious – I searched out men who I thought had diverse educational experiences, and I only subsequently became aware of their broader similarity.

Matt, Dominic, James and David attended private schools at secondary level, and Dan, thanks to a scholarship, attended a private school at upper secondary level. All but one of these men – David, who was a 40-year-old corporate banker and a relatively recent recruit to banking having previously worked in a different corporate sector – went on to attend a high-status, Russell Group[2] university, from where they graduated with very-good-to-excellent degree qualifications. Such similarities are significant, because a number of UK studies of work and education have revealed a link between academic success, which in the UK is measured in terms of exam results and gaining entrance to high-status universities, and access to well-paid, high-status employment, particularly for children from wealthier family backgrounds and/or those who have been privately educated (Power et al. 2003; Jerrim 2013; de Vries 2014; Anders 2015). Furthermore, educational backgrounds have also been shown to have significance for employees already working in the banking industry, whereby being in what Prins

(2009: 151) has termed the "right line of ascent" (i.e., having the right education and/or knowing the right people and/or working for the right manager) can vastly increase an employee's chance of success (see also Ho 2009).

None of the men I interviewed made any link between their education background and working in the City's banking sector. Rather, those among them who received elite education were very matter-of-fact about it. Matt explained how he "went to [*X*] College" – an old and prestigious all-boys school – where he studied "maths, further maths, physics and economics for A levels" before going to [*X*] University to "read economics". Dominic similarly described how he "went to [*Y*] College" – also all-boys – "and did economics, double maths and biology", and then "went to [*Y*] University and did two degrees: political science and economics". Such a normalisation of elite education experiences both ignores and obscures this line of ascent into and within elite banking. Yet in the broader UK social context, this kind of education background is anything but normal, not least because such schools demand substantial annual fees, some of which (including those of the schools Matt and Dominic attended) are significantly higher than the average UK annual wage.[3]

Among the men who were privately educated, James was the only one who made any characterising remarks about his education. He gave the following account:

> OK, so I went to an all boys' public[4] [boarding] school. I studied technology, geography and art with art history. I enjoyed school and made some very good friends … Then, university, I studied architecture at [ ], which is the best place to do architecture in Europe.

Despite his more descriptive summary, James merely referenced his enjoyment of school, rather than providing any insight into the quality or value of the education he received. Comments he made about university appear to legitimise his unusual degree choice (at least for investment bankers) and thus render him worthy of being an investment banker despite his deviation from the norm.

While these matter-of-fact descriptions of elite education may not seem particularly noteworthy in themselves, they take on significance when considered alongside the somewhat value-laden remarks made by the men who were wholly or partly state educated. Dan, for example, explained his schooling in the following way:

> I went to a comprehensive school 'til I was 16, which I suppose was all right. I mean, yeah, it was all right, but it was a secondary modern turned comprehensive, it wasn't great. Then I went to a public school for two years, and then I went to [ ] University.

Paul similarly remarked:

> I just went to a, I guess a sort of comprehensive, secondary modern school. It was okay, I suppose. And, yeah, I did actuarial science at [ ], which is basically an economics degree with a couple of specialist modules.

Graham, meanwhile, insinuated that his school largely fell short except in one respect:

> I went to a comprehensive school. The only thing it had going for it really was it had GCSE and A level Japanese ... Then I went to [ ] University and graduated with a decent [language and literature] degree.

Although none of these men offered any more detail about their schooling or why they felt it was just "all right" or "okay", their comments evoke a general, shared sense of mediocrity linked to state schooling, even though a school with Japanese on its curriculum, for example, is very atypical among schools in the UK, state or otherwise. That the men felt it necessary to highlight a perceived mediocrity, along with the fact they had still made it into high-status banking positions despite the schools they attended, is more significant than whether or not they actually believed their education fell short because of the quality of the particular schools they went to. It illustrates the hegemonic nature of practices and ideas, which normalise processes of inclusion and exclusion that help characterise class dynamics, and the men's compliance with these. Regardless of whether the quality of education provided in the state schools these men attended was good or not, the absence of comments made by Dan and others with reference to the quality of education at various private schools serves to position private education as the norm – the benchmark by which all forms of schooling are measured. In contrast, the men's pejorative comments about state education help to distance them from it and from the majority of people who attend state schools. Of course, the combination of schooling discourses indicates that being privately educated is probably not nearly so uncommon among people working in elite City banking as it is among the UK population as a whole.[5] The general worthiness of the private schools is taken for granted in the men's narratives and needs no further qualification; it is the level by which the "Other" – the state schools – and the general population who are educated in them are perceived to fall short.

There had been no prior mention during any of the interviews of the merits of either private or state education in the UK, and so the men's comments required an assumption that I share their understanding – that I too buy into such normative definitions and ideas about UK schooling, and thus support the role these may have in the processes of hegemony relating to global finance in the City. This assumption is significant, not only because it suggests that such a perception of the differences in the worth of private and state education is widely held within elite City banking and the social circles associated with it, but also because it normalises this perception and renders it trouble-free. It is therefore important to consider ways in which this cultural stratification (both the actual and metaphorical dimensions of it), interconnected as it is to socio-economic privilege, is both perpetuated by and helps shape processes of recruitment and reward in this elite City workspace. Indeed, the combination of the men's normalisation of private education in terms of both their academic experiences and qualifications, as well as additional comments made by some of the men about recruitment processes in City banking, suggests that having a high-status academic history continues to be significant in terms of securing particular jobs in the City.

While these findings relating to elite education may not seem particularly revelatory, what is interesting is that reference to elite education as a "line of ascent" into elite banking did not figure in the men's narratives about their own positioning, wherein high-status academic backgrounds and qualifications were discussed in a relatively off-hand manner, rather than as an explicit indicator of belonging to the "club" of elite City banking. This contrasts with Ho's research on Wall Street, which details bankers' direct references to their alma mater (see Ho 2009: 60). But while this discrepancy may reflect a sociocultural difference between the two demographics based on their geographical location, it does not mean the equivalent line of ascent in the City is any less significant than on Wall Street in terms of either getting a job or a promotion. Nonetheless, the normalisation and the somewhat invisibility of the link between elite education experiences and working in elite banking in the City narrow the space for contesting it and contesting all the benefits and social practices associated with it.

In the men's narratives, privileged experiences of education become, instead, enmeshed within a complex discourse of worthiness based around assertions of innate intelligence and hard work. I asked the men what had led them to work in banking, and they all implied a relatively easy and inevitable transition into the industry based primarily on some sort of natural calling or ability. Matt, for example, said how he had "always known [he] wanted to trade; it's dynamic, well paid ...". And Paul, similarly, explained how he had "always wanted to work in investment". Dominic, meanwhile, described in more detail how it was essentially the combination of the fulfilment of a childhood dream and innate ability (or at least his own belief in his innate ability):

> I looked at the people my dad worked with and thought they had good cool jobs. They all sat there with big computer screens in front of them before anyone had computers. They sat there in these big trading floors,

> and that was just interesting, looking at the stock market. I used to look at the stock market when I was a kid, and I read about people who worked at [X bank] when I was a kid. I did economics at university, 'cos I knew what sort of job I wanted to do. I always knew I'd be good at it.

Dan used similar language to these other men as he described his own seamless passage into banking and was also very confident about his natural ability to do well in the industry:

> Well, it was obvious for me to work [in banking]. I always have been very maths oriented and, at the end of the day, I was always going to do something maths-based, it was just so obvious to do. It would have been ridiculous not to do it.

And while James also explained how banking suited his personality, he framed his decision to go into the industry as a process of gradual enlightenment (gained through his own pioneering initiative) rather than a calling he had apparently knowingly had throughout his lifetime:

> Midway through my degree, I thought working in investment banking seemed more appealing than architecture … I had a few interviews, made some progress [and] thought, "I've obviously got something going". Getting into banking was more dynamic, fitted better with my personality. It's just dealing with similar types of people – intelligent, switched-on guys – who work in a fast-paced environment.

The sense of innate ability to work in elite finance these men suggest they have, coupled with the ways in which they imply that working in banking was their destiny (something they had "always" wanted to do (Matt, Paul, Dan) or "always" knew they would "be good at" (Dominic) and/or a natural fit with their personality (James)), lends a strong vocational slant to their comments. While there are references to lines of privilege that brought some of these men to elite banking, particularly relating to socio-economic class (fellow students (James) or parental occupation and personal contacts (Dominic)) and to notions of gender (people who are like them – i.e., "intelligent, switched-on guys" (James)), they are overshadowed by the stronger inferences that these men were born to be bankers and have fulfilled their natural destiny.

The traits these men describe, such as dynamism, being "switched-on", intelligent, hard-working, good at mathematics, or even (by default) being "cool" and up-to-the-minute, may seem to contrast somewhat with those one might normally associate with a vocational calling (nursing, teaching and so forth), such as empathy, altruism or a desire to improve society for the benefit of others. To some extent, however, a similar sense of vocation, but one invoked on an institutional level, legitimised the government bailouts of the banking sector after the 2008 financial crisis, underpinned by the mantra that large banks in the City were too big and important to society to fail. Despite their financial and political clout, particular banks in particular locations are, as I have argued in the previous chapter, portrayed as existing due to a natural process of development and societal progress, and this imbues them with a natural sense of worthiness and rightful spatial belonging. This in turn fuels a sense of moral goodness, such that elite banks and bankers invoke, directly or indirectly, similar notions of self-worth. These ideas link with the global and local spatial positioning of leadership and pioneering to promote a sense that these institutions and workers, by doing the work they do, positively benefit the world they live in and the lives of those around them, particularly their families.

The notion that the elite financial workplace is somewhere one naturally either does or does not belong can also be seen to provide crucial support to banks' demands for dedication and commitment from their employees. Indeed, the sense that investment banking is a way of life that is instinctively understood by some is echoed in banks' promotional literature, which is widely peppered with references to some sort of shared culture or belief system. Morgan Stanley (2018d), for example, referencing a quote from its Chairman and CEO, speaks of: "Our DNA, our culture and our history"; J.P. Morgan (2018c) refers to its "great culture" and collective "passion"; and Goldman Sachs (2018b) to the "esprit de corps" of "our people" who share "a passion for excellence" (Goldman Sachs 2018g). There is at the same time both an inclusionary and exclusionary aspect to these narratives that project a self-protective image along with a sense of shared conformity as much as shared spirit or passion. Yet to a large extent, the negative aspects are masked by a sense of benevolence and solidarity which, when coupled with inferences by the men that they have always had an innate ability and/or calling to do well in elite finance, legitimates existing structures and practices of recruitment and reward.

Such narratives adhere to the neoliberal ideology that individuals deserve their fate, which is a corrosive notion that breeds a veneration of certain forms of employment (i.e., well-paid) and people who work in them and a concomitant disdain of certain others. Moreover, for the men I interviewed, and other bankers like them, these vocational inferences, along with the dedication and commitment to work they suggest and endorse, devalue other aspects of their lives, including family and domestic responsibilities relating to their roles as fathers and husbands. If banking is fundamentally what these men say they were born to do, then to what extent is this compatible with their other responsibilities, desires and/or dreams? It seems that such a discourse might, in fact, cause considerable tension for these men (and their families) as they try and live up to expectations they may have of themselves working as bankers, and/or as they try and negotiate changing desires and responsibilities over time that may or may not be compatible with the "culture" of elite banking.

Nevertheless, the sense of vocation is important for three additional and significant reasons. First, it helps legitimate a divide between work and private lives – it helps justify, for example, unequal and gendered divisions of family labour that employees may organise to help manage this divide (see Chapter 3). Second, with this sense of vocation comes also the implicit suggestion that elite bankers rule their own lives and are in charge of their own destiny. In other words, bankers, like the men in this study, have chosen this profession; they are naturally suited to it; and if they do not succeed in it, it is their fault. Finally, the emphasis on "natural" characteristics and ability masks important factors, such as an employee's education and family background and cultural ideas around gender, socio-economic class and/or other forms of social grouping, that could likely have important bearing on a person's ability to step into a well-paid, elite position in finance and progress upwards through management.

In one sense, then, "the boys' club" of City banking can be understood as a club for worthy, like-minded individuals – those with natural ability and a natural calling. In other words, a club, it seems, that people can belong to as long as they already – before they join – possess the right attributes, characteristics and attitudes. The powerful institutional and individual language of a shared, innate spirit or calling among would-be and actual recruits to banking masks the problematic of gender inequality within the industry by suggesting that people deserve their fate. While the implied gendered nature of the boys' club of banking suggests the normal rules are bent to let women ("girls") in, which in turn suggests that women are automatically placed at a collective disadvantage before they even set foot in the door, the vocational narrative implies (somewhat paradoxically perhaps) that those women who do get in should be equally able as men to rise to the top.

The best of the best

During their interviews, the men talked to me about their roles and responsibilities at work and, as they did so, referred to the process of recruitment. Their comments on this topic further point to an ambiguous financial workplace characterised by forms of contradiction but underpinned by a degree of consistency. Interestingly, while the significance of the academic line of ascent into and within elite banking may not have been outwardly acknowledged in the men's autobiographical accounts of their own transitions into City banking, it was explicit in their more general comments about recruitment. Dominic, for example, explained:

> We take basically the top ½% of, well, we don't take all of them, but we choose the best from the top ½% of the university graduates at Oxford,

> Cambridge, Bristol, Edinburgh, Durham – those sorts of places. It's the same in New York – Harvard, Princeton, you know …

Dominic did not refer to other attributes or any specific skills a person may need to get a job at the bank he worked for and did not qualify what he meant by "best". Rather, his comment suggests that possessing a certain kind of education background is the principal qualifying criteria required for simply being considered for a job let alone being successfully recruited for one. And regardless of whether or not this is, in reality, always the case, Dominic's comment illustrates the symbolic importance embedded in elite forms of education and in the association of elite education with elite banking (note that Dominic referred to very specific geographical locations – London and New York – even though the bank he worked for has offices in many other locations). And this association helps constitute and infer notions of individual and institutional worth and belonging.

There is an implicit sense in Dominic's comment that all those who are recruited into elite banking start off on an equal footing, with a shared and demonstrated natural ability to be "the best", which is made all the more powerful when considered alongside the vocational sentiments discussed above. Because Dominic suggested that the bank he worked for chooses recruits from all such available worthy graduates, men and women – and these are graduates that we should presume are all equally "naturally" motivated as well as academically gifted – the implication is that gender inequality among bankers at higher levels is a natural and an inevitable state. If the point of access to elite banking really is this egalitarian (in gendered terms), then all those who are recruited share the same ability and desire to be successful: those who succeed in this system deserve their success; those who fail warrant their fate.

Of course, Dominic's confirmation of the supposed quality of recruits to banking also made his own sense of entitlement to be a successful well-paid City banker explicit, rightful and unquestionable: not everyone can attend an elite university and not everyone who successfully graduates from one can go on to be an investment banker. Drawing on a broad social understanding of the merits of elite education, Dominic's comment is illustrative of a desire for consistency or conformity seen as necessary to maintain an image and understanding of the elite financial workplace in the City (as well as the well-paid bankers such as Dominic who are clever enough to get a job there) as rightfully powerful in the financial and business world. In turn, this awareness helps legitimise the high salaries and bonuses paid out to the elite employees who work in this particular geographical location. It also helps shape, justify and sustain specific socio-spatial practices these elite workers and their families are able to engage in because of and to further maintain these high remuneration levels.

Dominic's positioning of elite bankers working in the City as the "best of the best" was reinforced as he paraphrased a motivational talk he and his colleagues were given during a leadership training day. Dominic explained how the trainer had told them all that:

> [You] are the top ½% of people. As the top ½% you are used to being right, at the top and succeeding in everything. You are always used to being right – all through school and university you were always top of the class and the most successful.

Thus, one can see how what began as an implicit link with academic ability effortlessly broadens out into an all-embracing ability – an ability to turn one's hand to anything and be not just successful at it but the best – and a taken-for-granted, generic characteristic of investment bankers. Doing well at school becomes not only an indicator of academic worth, but also an indicator of general worthiness. While this severely narrows the notion of what constitutes worthiness and success, it also disregards the many factors that can help children to achieve academically (ranging from their socio-economic status, to levels of parental support, to the conditions in which they live, to the quality of schooling they receive, to who their friends are, and so on and so forth) (see, for example, Vincent and Ball 2006; Siraj-Blatchford et al. 2011). Not only does it infer value on people, like Dominic, who work in elite City banking, it positions this value as the general standard by which everyone else is also measured, including the wives of the men I interviewed.

Matt explained what he felt distinguished the best of the best and the best from the rest:

> There's a lot of perfect CVs – people with straight As and great degrees. You know, they went through the 20 criteria and ticked them all. But it's not that easy. I look for something exceptional. Essentially, a tiny proportion of people make a massive difference, so I look for someone who might have that unique quality, something which distinguishes them … I don't want a load of average people.

Like Dominic, Matt positioned high academic achievement not only as the norm among people he recruited (and, of course, by default worked with), but also as the "average" by which everyone is measured, whether they work in City banking or not. He also aligned individual success/uniqueness with institutional success, an alignment that helps obscure any tension between, on the one hand, the ideology of competitive individualism and, on the other, banks' emphasis on teamwork and collegiality. References to gender are also absent from Matt's account (as they were in Dominic's account above), which implies that those whom Matt said he recruits are the very best people selected from all capable applicants. But like Dominic's unqualified reference to the "best", it is not clear from Matt's comment what an "exceptional", "distinguishing" or "unique quality" might be that could set the chosen few apart from the discarded others. Yet his statement, again like Dominic's, reinforces his own sense of worth – not only is he someone who presumably possesses the extraordinary qualities he referred to, he is also someone who could spot uniqueness in others. As such, he positioned himself as rightfully successful and deserving of the rewards he had gained and, in the process, foreclosed the space to question any abnormalities or unfairness in the system.

Self-confidence and a lack of self-criticism on behalf of the financial elite – both individuals and institutions – are important components in constituting processes of hegemony in global finance. Both Matt's and Dominic's language strongly echoes the language used by banks in their promotional material. Leading banks in the City emphasise, exaggerate even, their "uniqueness" and their employees' sense of "uniqueness" and their "exceptional" attributes as a means to create and sustain the image of success and authority in order to attract clients and new recruits and thus preserve or strengthen their financial, political and spatial power and prestige. The following extract from Goldman Sachs' (2018b) "Business Principles" illustrates this institutional discourse:

> We make an unusual effort to identify and recruit the very best person for every job ... we select our people one by one. In a service business, we know that without the best people, we cannot be the best firm.

Although unique characteristics may be undefined once more, the naturalised sense of worthiness attributed to the exceptional, "best people" is apparent. Elite bankers are positioned as the benchmark by which other people are measured and to which these others – the mediocre "average" and sub-average – can only aspire. It is a polarising discourse of "them and us" that implies that people who do well in elite banking (including those who are paid extremely high salaries and bonuses) are entirely deserving of their professional and material success, which in turn does not problematise the unequal, discriminatory reward structures.

Despite the supposed search for unique, exceptional human beings at the point of entry to elite banking, Matt, like Dominic (with his comment about very particular feeder universities), also alluded to a concomitant need for consistency as well as a somewhat contradictory need for conformity among potential recruits:

> If [applicants] work for a charity at Christmas and they work for [this bank] in the summer [...] and they think that makes them look balanced, to me it looks, like, inconsistent, because no one is actually that perfect.

What appears to be Matt's rejection of the ideal of perfection seems contradictory to his desire for uniqueness. Nevertheless, his comment is, in some ways, further confirmation of his own sense of personal value (he was chosen) and discernment (he can spot fakes). But it is also illustrative of the ambiguous and inconsistent nature of the rules of elite finance and the blurring of the boundary between inclusion and exclusion. It also points to the masking of difference by similarity, which helps constitute the authority of hegemony. It suggests that employees may indeed experience significant tension as they try and negotiate between two conflicting requirements, conformity and individualism (the characterisation of which may or may not be fixed and is certainly not explicit), and justify their presence/worth in elite finance. Matt's comment also suggests recruitment and success may depend as much (or more) on chance as any other factor (e.g., the personal preference of who is conducting the interview), although it does reinforce the sense that the "boys' club" is for like-minded individuals. In light of this, Matt's reference to the need for "consistency" is interesting and is further emphasised in his subsequent remark: "A lot of people we recruit, we know who we're looking for".

Wealthy banks' consistent links with particular elite university graduates, as Ho (2009: 226) observed in her study of Wall Street, help maintain their and their employees' institutional elite image and thus position of authority in the financial and business world. Elite City banks, and the people who manage them, likewise benefit (or indeed need) a strong sense of coherence and constancy in order to maintain and legitimise current structures of recruitment and reward, including high salaries and large bonuses, which feed into existing processes of hegemony. The following extract from Goldman Sachs (2018b) articulates this cyclical process: "Profitability is critical to achieving superior returns, building our capital and attracting and keeping our best people".

In spite of institutional and individual claims to innovation and uniqueness, thinking outside the box by recruiting an "unknown" could be costly and damaging. The sense of coherence, coupled with the best-of-the-best notion, usefully masks irregularities and inequalities in the system. Nevertheless, through the notion of uniqueness (regardless of whether the uniqueness is real, manufactured or imagined), which corresponds with the neoliberal language of individualism and entrepreneurialism, banks are able to justify patriarchal processes, including the unequal division of profit and reward. In the level playing field of elite banking, all competitors are hailed as "uniquely" gifted and able to succeed as long as they apply themselves – failure is down to the individual and not the system. This ideology is promoted by banks: "Advancement depends on merit, and we have yet to find the limits to the responsibility our best people are able to assume" (Goldman Sachs 2018b), and bought into by employees: "We want people who are gonna commit themselves to doing this and you're going to pay them reasonably well, and really it's a case of do they want it or don't want it..." (Dan).

Yet the confident air the men exuded – including James who was not working when I interviewed him due to having been made redundant – disguised the contradictory fragility of their own positions and identities in the workplace. As discussed in more detail in Chapter 5, elite bankers' positioning is fundamentally precarious, with the threat of redundancy looming constantly over the workplace (see also Ho 2009).

Of course, Dan's comment above also alludes to an important motivational factor integral to the elite financial workplace: financial reward. At times, the men denied that making money was a major incentive, perhaps partly because of the damaged reputation of banks and bankers (particularly investment bankers) due to the 2008 financial crisis. Yet other comments made by the men single out the significance of financial rewards in banking, not only to employees but also to the functioning of the whole system:

> Shareholders want to have the best guys. They want their company to make as much money as possible. There are people here who work for me for whom their attendance record is not relevant to me. They're only here to make money. Some of them will be up all night working, right. And so whether they come into the office is just academic to me. Listen, if I make a lot of money for the bank, they're not going to question when I'm here.
>
> (Matt)

> The guys who are at the top, they generally come from a trading-type background where they've made a lot of money for the firm. So they might have done some exotic trading; they've always just looked after themselves; they've always just been your rugby-playing types, quite alpha male. And then they get the rewards and recognition for having made so much money for the firm everyone starts thinking, "I want to be like that guy". Banking is fundamentally about money, really. And people want to be successful, so they want to aspire to those rich, successful-type people.
>
> (James)

While this motivational factor may be somewhat at odds with the vocational sentiments of the men's narratives, it is a crucial element of the processes of hegemony, for it is further confirmation of innate worthiness and hard work, which shapes particular employees' position of authority at work and at home. Material rewards gained from elite jobs in the City provide not only status at work, but also allow bankers and their families to engage in particular consumption practices and lifestyle choices outside of work. These, in turn, reinforce bankers' commitment to their jobs and help legitimise workplace and family practices and structures that enable this commitment.

In both Matt's and James' comments, there is explicit reference to the "guys" at the top – the bankers who are "the best". This turn of phrase represents a simultaneous disregard of women among these so-called "best", most deserving and aspirational employees: while women are allowed into the exclusive City club, they have yet to prove they belong. While references to the men in power are, perhaps, a reflection of current reality, there is, nevertheless, a sense of inevitability about this gendered inequality, whereby women (all women) are by default, subconsciously or not, side-lined as naturally unsuited to fulfilling a successful, high-flying career in elite City banking. This gendered normalisation makes it difficult for employees to contest existing reward structures and practices, the value and worth imbued in them in and outside the workplace, and concerns over forms of inequality that may develop or be perpetuated because of them.

The members' room

Succeeding in an environment where everyone is seen as "naturally" brilliant requires not only some level of belief that you are better than the best (or rest), but the concurrent necessity to prove it. The consequence of the best-of-the-best notion, which works to favour banks in the City and those who own and run them, is a highly competitive workplace and the hard-working environment this produces. As Dominic explained:

> It's a competitive environment, it's meant to be a competitive environment, everyone's supposed to have the hunger to succeed and a drive to succeed, and if you succeed you go on.

The promise for individuals of promotion, high salaries, large bonuses, and the social and cultural forms and expressions of power these rewards provide access to, fuels the need and desire to prove one's value in this workplace. But couching access to this highly competitive field in naturalising language requires employees to prove they are capable of living up to the image of success and the right to membership of the elite club of City finance by effectively channelling their so-called superintelligence through an equally high level of "innate" competitiveness. Banks' official promotional material refers to this process. Goldman Sachs (2018b), for example, states:

> We have an uncompromising determination to achieve excellence in everything we undertake. Though we may be involved in a wide variety and heavy volume of activity, we would, if it came to a choice, rather be best than biggest.

UBS (2018b) similarly states that "we are continually looking for people who are able to do great things ... We aim for excellence in all we do ...". It further explains how it offers clients: "informed advice, tailored ideas and solutions and best-in-class execution" (UBS 2018c).

Intense competitiveness, like superintelligence, is naturalised to the extent that it becomes an all-embracing characteristic of those who work for wealthy, powerful banks, a characteristic applicable to all elite bankers in the City and one aligned with notions of success. J.P. Morgan (2018b) describes its "smart and motivated" employees. Under its Business Principles, it tells employees to, "Strive for excellence, don't settle for mediocrity" and "Compare yourself with the best", in order to help the firm "become the best and most respected bank in the world" (J.P. Morgan 2018d).

This contrived but naturalised image helps legitimise banks' claims to knowledge and leadership in the local and global financial sector; it attracts clients and legitimises high rewards paid to bankers. This ideology, as well as the language banks use, is mirrored in comments made by Matt, James and Dominic. James and Matt talked about elite bankers in general:

> Bankers tend to be quite driven, well-disciplined types of people ...
>
> (James)

> Now, if you have highly-paid, highly-motivated investment bankers, you don't normally have to spend a lot of time trying to get them out of bed, or trying to make a deal 'cos they know what the incentives are ... [These are] highly motivated individuals ... it's very different managing investment bankers to, say, managing a factory floor because I have got people who are really hungry for this job, they're really hungry to get ahead, rather than someone just turning up to get their pay cheque. It's just a different dynamic.
>
> (Matt)

Dominic, meanwhile, described what sets the very best of the best bankers apart from their colleagues:

> I just think drive. [They've] got more drive personally, more drive to get to the top. They will come in at 6 or 7 in the morning. They will stay there 'til 10 o'clock at night if they need to get the job done. They will work as a team but they all want to succeed themselves. No one's going to stop them from succeeding. They think about it all the time. Most people switch off from work; work's life for those kinds of people. They don't switch off at night when they go home or on weekends. They're always thinking, "Well, what can I do?"

The naturalisation or normalisation process that banks promote and employees engage with and express embraces and does not problematise current workplace structures and systems. Rather, it legitimises them by drawing on a broader neoliberal ideology, particularly the affirmation of competitive individualism and the supposed meritocratic nature of the workplace, whereby hard work inevitably leads to success and financial prosperity.

One consequence of understanding intense drive and competition as not just natural human traits but quintessential traits all elite bankers possess is that failure (lack of success) in elite banking becomes once more not simply the fault of the individual but a potential failing of the individual's innate being. That bankers, like James, Matt and Dominic, buy into this ideology is illustrative of important constituents of hegemonic processes: confirmation and compliance. This has ramifications for all those who work in finance as well as those who do not, but who are also judged by these same "ideals" and this same ideology. This includes the "factory workers" Matt referred to using an interesting metaphorical spatial segregation of elite, middle-class, worthy (i.e., hard-working and motivated) workers versus non-elite, working-class, less worthy (i.e., apparently less hard-working and poorly motivated) workers. In other words, Matt positioned both sets of workers – bankers and factory workers – as deserving of their current situation.

Institutional and individual use of the language of meritocracy combined with competitive individualism, like the language of natural ability, masks or ignores crucial factors that can help facilitate or limit a person's access to high-status employment in elite City banking, as well as a person's capability to succeed in it once employed, for reasons that may well be partially or totally out of her or his control. Such factors range from not living anywhere near London, to health and personal circumstance, to an individual's gender, to the bankruptcy of an important client, to fluctuations in global financial markets. It raises questions about how bankers like the men I interviewed may experience tension when confronting these ideals and other potentially conflicting ideals relating to notions of masculinity or fatherhood, as well as the kinds of traits they may value in others and encourage or support in their own children.

The naturalisation of both the gendered character of the financial workplace and its successful employees, and its association with a broader neoliberal ideology of competitive individualism, relieves banks from taking responsibility for the well-being of their employees by rendering individuals' wider needs, to some extent, a non-issue. Although banks are strong on their meritocracy rhetoric, there is a simultaneous and somewhat inconsistent undervaluing of the individual in the workplace, as the following extract from Goldman Sachs' (2018b) promotional literature demonstrates: "Our assets are our people, capital and reputation. If any of these is diminished, the last is the most difficult to restore".

This institutional devaluation of the individual in favour of the reputation of the bank is at odds with banks' claims that they search the world for the most skilled, creative and intelligent people they can find. It contradicts the best-of-the-best notion where employees are supposedly viewed and affirmed by banks as necessary assets to the firm – individuals, individually selected, cherished and nurtured – and it is illustrative of the contradictory nature of the elite financial workplace. However, the ambiguity banks demonstrate between the desire to recruit "the best" and the desire to retain the best creates an environment where employees need to constantly prove themselves worthy by working hard, securing new clients and generating more profit, which ultimately works in the banks' favour.

Being the best of the best supports processes of hegemony in elite banking – it is a mobilising force couched in normative language. Nevertheless, engaging in and supporting this ideology – for example, demonstrating worthiness by working very long hours and being highly competitive – may not sit comfortably with all employees. For such practices have inevitable, unavoidable implications for managing work and private lives and are potentially exclusionary for some employees who have obligations outside the workplace they cannot or do not want to offload onto a third party but who are otherwise arguably capable of success. Yet the process of hegemony works to confirm the current system and its regulation of who does and does not win. Employees who succeed have risen to the challenge: they have found a way to make it work; the "guys" who have "made it" to the top are rightfully there, and there is little space available to dispute this.

Projecting and sustaining the image of dedication, commitment and worthiness, however, is as important as the work practices promoted to prove one is worthy. It is a process of branding designed, as Klein (2017) has argued, not only to entice would-be employees and potential clients by projecting a very particular image linked with certain forms of working and the social values associated with them, but also to engender fear – fear of not being part of the club, or of losing one's place in it. And herein lie both the strength of this process and its weakness: on the one hand, it is a powerful, generative process; but on the other, because the process relies on maintaining a socially esteemed image, it is vulnerable to the whims of change. Nevertheless, although alternative forms of working, if they are equally valued, could lead to a new image/perception of what commitment and worth entail, this would require a change more fundamental than banks simply declaring a newfound allegiance to "sustainability" (see the previous chapter) or some other contemporary cause.

In living up to the current image and the practices which interrelate with it, employees are largely obliged to take responsibility for their own interests and welfare or at least conceal any difficulties they may experience when managing diverse and often conflicting demands or tasks they are not familiar with. This, of course, contradicts the institutional emphasis on welfare provision, whereby well-being, equality and inclusion policies and services at work are presented as valuable concerns of employers and promoted along with other onsite amenities (see the previous chapter). The provision of flexible working options or other support systems designed to help employees at work was mentioned by the men I interviewed, mainly during discussions about parenting and hence in relation to parental leave schemes. But the men also made other more general references about employee support structures, which further demonstrate how certain forms of working associated with notions of commitment, value and success undermine or are at odds with issues of well-being and employee choice. Matt, for example, referred to training programmes offered by the bank he worked for:

> We have on-going training and all sorts of mentoring ... It's a little bit about, there's an awful lot on offer, some of which is delivered at a mandatory level, some of which is there if people choose to take it. Because some people want it, some people don't; some people want to be spoon-fed and some people really don't want to be spoon-fed.

David and Paul, meanwhile, referred to official bank policies, with David's comment further reinforcing the naturalised masculine nature of senior management:

> There are procedures and policies but a lot of it's run by what your functional manager will kind of help you achieve, so if he's not helping you along with your next step in your career path because he doesn't think that's what you should be doing, then that's a concern ...
>
> (David)

> [This bank's] policies [on flexible working] are very good, but depending on the role you have, they're irrelevant. You can have stuff planned with your family for the weekend and on Friday night you'll be told that you'll be going to New York to do some deal over the weekend or something. So you are always disappearing ... if you're going to Asia, you tend to get a Sunday morning flight, get there and go straight to the office – you're away from home, you're away from family and stuff. It wrecks the weekend ...
>
> (Paul)

These extracts suggest that when initiatives designed to assist employees are offered, formal support systems may be tarnished through associations with immaturity (see Matt's comment), met with informal resistance (David), or be strangely incompatible with the very demands they are trying to alleviate (Paul). There is a sense that the people who truly belong in this workplace should be able to go it alone without assistance, regardless of whatever form it is available in. Thus, potentially detrimental and abnormal aspects of the financial workplace, such as working very long hours or high levels of stress, are accepted and normalised. It is perhaps no surprise, therefore, that when the men talked about problems in managing demands of the workplace, their comments were largely dismissive or distant; issues were either glossed over or discussed with respect to someone else:

> Trading is stressful, but you have to personally handle the stress; it's crucial. In order to make it as someone who manages risk, you've got to be able to handle how that risk influences you. I watch people – you can see whether or not they go grey, whether they eat healthily. I had a 26-year-old girl last year who got shingles mainly because she's extremely motivated and extremely driven, if you saw her you would never ... One of the problems is very ambitious young people can drive themselves into a kind of mess. If you're not very good at handling stress, you can kind of stress yourself even more, so you kind of abuse it.
>
> (Matt)

> Quite a few of the juniors do work quite hard – 70, 80 hours a week. I bet you at least half the department would sit there and tell you they have to work at weekends. But it's because they're slightly inefficient. I think stressfulness depends on ... I think it's demanding, I'm not entirely sure it's stressful, 'cos I think it depends what kind of person you are. Obviously I've worked in this industry for 20-odd years, and you can't afford for it to be too stressful; otherwise you're not going to survive. If you don't feel you're coping, and you're finding you're getting too stressed, then you know that probably that job's not for you.
>
> (Dan)

Matt's example of a young woman (a "girl") is particularly interesting for it lends further support to the argument that while some candidates (e.g., women) who make it in to the boys' club appear to have the right credentials on the whole, if they do fall short, it is not because of the faults in the system but because of their own innate weakness or immaturity and unsuitability – their inability to handle stress, for example.

Elsewhere in their interviews, Matt, Dan and Paul all admitted to working long hours. These long working hours clearly affected the time these men spent with their families, and they all admitted this when they talked about work in relation to their role as fathers (see Chapter 3). However, when their talk of work was centred on their role as bankers, potential systemic problems, such as long hours and abnormal levels of stress, were not questioned. In the context of work, it seems the onus of responsibility is placed on compliant individuals to manage and cope with any difficulties they may experience. Because of the naturalisation of this situation, an individual's failure to live up to this apparent innate ability – a failure to cope – is even, it seems, understood in terms of her or him self-harming, e.g., giving oneself shingles, turning one's own hair grey, stressing oneself out, or, as Graham confessed to, drinking too much:

> If I could find something to do that pays a decent wage and wasn't in finance and banking, I'd jump at the chance – I'd get out tomorrow if I could. The job I'm in, in theory, is the job that kind of reigns in the crazy people who are just lumps of greed basically. It's not good for you; it's an ugly place to be. When I get down, I hit the beer quite heavily …

Among the bankers I interviewed, Graham expressed the most dissatisfaction with his job but at the time was yet to break through into the more established and elite banking positions, which could have affected his mindset. Nevertheless, unlike the other men I talked with, he was critical about the competitive nature of banking. This is significant because it highlights a potential weakness in the system wherein it is possible to contest hegemony. It shows, for example, that not everyone who works in such an environment feels comfortable with it. Unlike Matt and Dan, Graham did not distance himself from a weakness to cope, and yet in some ways, he seemed equally compliant with the system. Despite his disaffection with banking, he still worked in the industry and elsewhere in his interview expressed desire for promotion. He was also acquiescent to the financial rewards of banking (i.e., his "decent wage") and, like the other men, adhered to the notion that high rewards are there for the taking (for anyone) as long as one has the right attitude and desire. As he argued: "It's there if you want it, if you're that way inclined, if you're that sort of person and you go for the jugular".

Whether an employee's ability to engage with competitive individualism is framed in terms of harming others or harming oneself, it is extremely significant that the responsibility and capability for succeeding or not succeeding in elite banking is placed in the hands of the individual not the system. That each of the men did this is important, for such compliance helps disguise ambiguities, unfairness and exclusionary aspects of the elite financial workplace, which in turn works to support the myth of meritocracy, both inside and outside banking.

The link between natural ability, hard work and success is complex and frequently contradictory. On the one hand, the men confirm the discourse of meritocracy, as well as imply jobs in elite banking are more accessible and inclusionary than they are with their suggestions that success and reward are there for the taking if you have the right attitude (whether or not you think this attitude is agreeable). The following comments from Dan and Dominic further illustrate this, as well as allude to a coercive element within hegemonic processes linked with global finance:

> The finance industry generally is quite demanding on your lifestyle but does actually kind of reward you for that.
>
> (Dan)

> No one should really sit there from 7.30 to 7.30, but unfortunately [bankers] do. Well they don't; they're forced to 'cos they'd prefer for you to work 7.30 to 7.30 than pay – hire – five more people ... But no complaints in our industry, 'cos you get paid reasonably well to do that.
>
> (Dominic)

While such compliance with the system supports the current patriarchal nature of elite banking, additional comments made by Dominic, Graham and Paul reveal the arbitrariness, unfairness and unpredictability of the rules of the game with regard to success, promotion and reward, even for those employees who have done very well in their careers. Importantly, comments made by these men hint at uncertainties that are largely masked in the dominant meritocracy-themed discourses of hegemonic processes in finance:

> It's a once in a right seat, right time. There's other people that work really hard, doing really well. They're number one sales guys with all their clients but because of the business that they do, a smaller-margin business, they might only book 10 million dollars' worth of revenue. But that 10 million they book is easily equivalent to the 100 million this guy does. Well, he just happens to be in a product that trades in the billions (Dominic).

There is a disconnect between the notion of meritocracy and discriminatory reward practices in elite banking, as a further comment made by Dominic also illustrates:

> I think if I could find the right hedge fund, I would consider moving. The good thing about hedge funds, or working for a private firm like that, is the pay-off's not asymmetric. [In banks], if they say "If we make 10 million this year, you'll get paid a million", then at the end of the year they say "well, we made 9 but we had these issues here and these issues, so the reality is, we can't really pay that in cash so we'll have to pay it to you in stock" – 70% stock or something. So you end up, your bonus is 500,000 but you get 350,000 in shares. So my biggest bonus is actually worth probably half of what I actually got paid because the stock price is less than half.

And Dominic hints again at the inconsistency in remuneration when he talks about his boss:

> You look at guys like my boss and you think, "Why are you still working here?" Honestly, he must have a fair amount of cash … he's probably – oh well, maybe he doesn't, maybe he doesn't; maybe I'm overestimating what he's been paid and stuff […].

Graham and Paul also suggest discrepancies in the supposedly meritocratic reward and retention structures:

> I'm close to 50 grand below the market rate. Just because I've moved internally, it's a bit difficult to secure a better wage.
>
> (Graham)

> They might consolidate some of the positions … they'll pool some of the roles into a Europe-wide role, and there'll be two of you going for one job and you know that if you're [X[6]] then you get the job and if you're not, you won't. If you're up against the [X] boss then you … you just have no control.
>
> (Paul)

Although these discrepancies seem to reflect the very antithesis of meritocracy, the uncertainty they create keeps employees constantly working hard as they try and prove their worth to themselves, their colleagues and their employers over and over on a daily basis. The meritocracy discourse provides the necessary legitimising force, for it supports the apparent worthiness of those who are recruited into the "club", those who survive and those who thrive. The instability of the system, meanwhile, provides the mobilising force. And threading the two together are the levels of reward that are possible (however likely or unlikely) – the million that might be paid (that is paid to some), the better wage that might be gained (that other employees already receive) – for this promise of reward both justifies and feeds back into the whole process.

Conclusion

This insight into the boys' club of elite City finance has further revealed how certain ideas and common-sense ways of thinking are simultaneously seductive and controlling. The exploration of the ways in which elite City bankers describe their jobs has helped to uncover hidden mechanisms of the reproduction of exclusivity and exclusions and expose many contradictions. Within these contradictions lie possibilities for contesting and changing processes of hegemony linked with global finance, as long as alternative choices are available and well-defined, which does not seem to be the case if one goes by the men's all-or-nothing narratives (i.e., that you either buy into the system or you don't). Paradoxically, however, the strength of the current system also exists not in spite of its ambiguities and inconsistencies but because of them. While it is not clear who will survive in elite banking let alone come out on top, to persevere in it, as the men's narratives illustrate, requires consent and compliance with its practices, which is fuelled by the seductive promise of reward and justified, in part, by the perpetuation of a collective sense of the intellectual superiority of those working in it.

The embedded nature and constant propagation of this system and its ideology has a bearing on the work lives of elite City bankers. It also has a bearing on bankers' private lives, as well as wider consequences particularly as it interrelates with broader cultural ideas and practices concerning success and failure, prosperity and deficiency, happiness and dissatisfaction. This relationship with banking practices to spaces beyond the elite financial workplace requires interrogation. This is because, while individual practices and actions on the part of elite bankers or banks may not seem, or even be, especially problematic in and of themselves, their cumulative effect can have often-unintended ripple effects that shape and compound inequalities and injustice and impact on the lives, opportunities and well-being of others (Young 2011) in and beyond the finance industry, including the families of elite City bankers. This is not to suggest that individual bankers or individual banks do not bear any responsibility for the effects of their actions but rather that it is necessary to uncover how practices and actions interrelate and what the consequences and impact of their cumulative effects are in order that they can be better understood and collectively changed. This recognition taps into the moral dimension of processes of hegemony that is so crucial to their legitimisation and which is discussed in more detail in the following three chapters with regard to the men's private lives and the 2008 financial crisis.

Notes

1 The FTSE 100 (Financial Times Stock Exchange 100 Index) is the share index of the top 100 companies listed on the London Stock Exchange.
2 The Russell Group comprise a group of leading public research universities in the UK.
3 According to the 2017 Annual Survey of Hours and Earnings compiled by the Office for National Statistics, the median gross annual earnings for full-time employees in the UK were £28,600. Meanwhile, the top ten most expensive schools in the UK all charge over £35,000 per annum.
4 In the UK, "public school" is a term used for an independent, fee-paying school.
5 According to the Independent School Council, in 2018 in the UK, 6.5% of the total number of schoolchildren under the age of 16 and 18% over the age of 16 were educated in the independent sector.
6 The nationality of the bank.

Chapter 3

Gender, space and family

Processes of spatial and gendered hegemony linked with global finance in the City of London bring together elites and systems of political, economic and sociocultural power. While these processes are characterised by the everyday practices and structures of global finance and the City, they are also unavoidably conditioned by and intertwined with wider social processes beyond the workplace within which banks and bankers are located. This broader positioning is crucial for shaping, solidifying and legitimising the authority of hegemony.

This chapter explores the ways in which well-paid City bankers negotiate and live their private lives and engage in socio-spatial practices that help bridge the divide between the terrains of work and family and in the process support or contest processes of hegemony linked with global finance. In particular, the chapter considers two interrelated concerns. The first concern is the family spatial arrangement, with respect, in particular, to the choice each couple had made about where to live. This choice is explored in terms of how it connects to ideas around freedom, work–life balance and fulfilment and interrelates with the different and potentially competing day-to-day responsibilities of the workplace and the family. The second concern is fatherhood and the ways in which the men and women talked about the responsibilities of parenthood, with a particular focus on the men's role as fathers and each couple's negotiation of gender relations and structures of care in the family.

In search of freedom

As discussed in Chapter 2, the strategic positioning of wealthy banks in key geographical locations such as the City of London or Wall Street is an important component of processes of hegemony that sustain the dominance and authority of global finance and elite bankers. Likewise, the geographical positioning of the family homes of City bankers has some bearing on these same processes of hegemony, not only in practical terms, such as determining the length of commute, for example (see Butler and Lees 2006), and other kinds of socio-spatial practices bankers engage in, but also in the ways in which notions of space shape narratives of family and parenting.

Of the bankers I spoke with, five lived with their respective families in London, while two (Matt and Dan) lived outside London in the Home Counties.[1]

A visit to the country

One unexpectedly beautiful summer's day, with the sun shining warmly and the sky a rich, vibrant blue, I drove out to the coast to meet Kara. As I neared my destination, I bypassed the local town, from where one can catch a train to London, and turned right, off the main road. The lane I found myself on meandered through flat green fields: flood plains bordered by low hedges and wide ditches. The scenery in this area is both rural and coastal, and the small towns and villages are picturesque and affluent. I followed Kara's instructions: I drove past a farm shop advertising organic meat, fruit and vegetables, free-range eggs, and homemade cakes and pies; a little further on, I passed a group of pretty cottages and a small stone church. A short distance past the old church, I took a right-hand turn down a secluded, narrow, private road (speed limit ten miles per hour) towards the sea.

A small number of large, detached houses, half hidden behind trees and shrubbery, loomed over generous plots of land between the road and the sea. Kara and her husband, Matt, were overseeing the building of their new six-bedroom house, complete with fitness studio and an adjoining two-bedroom self-contained annex. In the meantime, they were renting a sizeable house a few plots further down this same exclusive road. I drove slowly past the building site and shortly afterwards turned up the wide, sweeping driveway of the rental property. I parked next to Kara's small vintage car, in front of the house.

Kara opened the heavy wooden front door and greeted me warmly with a small kiss on either cheek. She was suntanned and wore a dark T-shirt, cropped lightweight trousers, sequined flip-flops, and a pair of large-rimmed sunglasses propped on top of her head. She was short, petite and friendly. Inside, the house was clean and ordered. There were adults' and children's coats, wetsuits and footwear neatly arranged in the entrance hall. Children's drawings decorated the large fridge in the kitchen. A piano sat in an adjacent, spacious living room, where large, sliding French windows opened out onto a neat patio. Beyond the patio, an expansive, well-manicured lawn bordered by pretty flowerbeds stretched down to the beach. It was a beautiful view – a view that Matt had told me previously was "worth the commute and £10 every morning just to get up and see" (a comment that signified both exclusiveness and personal worth). Kara saw me admiring the view and suggested we take a short walk on the beach after we finished talking. She offered me a glass of juice or water. I took water – it was a hot day and the drive had been long – and we sat down together on the patio in the warm sunshine.

Two hours later, after we finished talking, Kara insisted on buying me lunch at the nearby health and leisure club the family belonged to. When we arrived at the club, Max, her three-year-old son, ran up to greet her. He had spent the morning with the nanny taking his older brother and sister to school first thing and afterwards swimming in the pool at the club.

As I drove away from the club after lunch, leaving this affluent lifestyle behind me, and feeling slightly sunburnt and windswept from the sun and sea breeze, I realised with a tinge of disappointment that in our haste to get to the club, Kara and I had forgotten to walk on the beach.

Life in and around London

Desire for a better quality of life, along with a search for freedom and a sense of community, underpinned the lifestyle narratives of the two couples who had decided to move their family home outside London. Matt explained:

> We lived in Central London and I thought we needed more space. You know, money can't really buy space or enough space in London. So I said, "come on, let's find some space". And I convinced Kara to buy this house, on the coast. At the time, we weren't planning on leaving London, so it was just about weekend access. Kara said she didn't want to move out of London. Well, I thought she meant now, you know. And we spent probably two years going there at the weekends and holidays, and she loved it so much, she's like, "I want to live here". Well, I'd anticipated that she would say that; I thought that would happen. So then, I suppose once you tell everyone, you know, people say, "well, how do you do it?" Well! "How do you live in Central London?" You know! Sure, Central London – that's great for getting to work and getting home from work, but it's not great for children's activities or them running around in the garden or schools or expense – whatever – there's no benefit. Now we live there; they're extremely happy. So the only thing is, I commute to work. In an ideal world, it would not be two hours away [*he laughs*]. But if that were the case, then more people would live there; it would be too expensive; it wouldn't have the same feeling there.

Dan and Cath had two young children. They lived a similar distance outside London to Kara and Matt but on the opposite side of the Capital in a very different geographical location – inland and more semi-urban than rural. They lived in what Cath described as a "recently remodelled" six-bedroom house in an exclusive cul-de-sac of large, detached houses. Dan remarked how he and Cath:

> ... did the classic – we moved out of [London] for the usual combination of space, schools and community. And the last one, which I think is very important, I mean, there's just so many people in London, it takes ages to do anything, or get anywhere. And, you know, well again, it's each to their own, but bringing up children in the centre of London's not great. When you live out of London, sort of, the boys can be trusted a lot more by themselves. It's just that kind of a bit more freedom.

The references to and/or the search for community made by the men and women are explored in more depth in the next chapter. But what is interesting in both these quotes above is the way in which space, as the facilitator of freedom, happiness and personal growth – whether in terms of better activities for children (Matt) or a sense of community (Dan) – appears to be characterised through greater exclusivity rather than greater diversity, whereby the density of people in London is seen to curtail individual opportunity, rather than offer a richness of experience and community. There is a competitive defensiveness in the men's narratives, as they seek to justify their choices as better and more worthy than those of other people. But this is characterised, and in the process legitimised, by both men through the same moral dimension, which is concern for the well-being of their children. In Matt's case, this moral dimension extends to a concern for the well-being of his wife, Kara (which, incidentally, he implied he understood better than Kara herself). In both cases, this moral dimension is significant, for it helps support the men's identities as and embodiments of both successful fathers and successful bankers. It does not, therefore, problematise either existing workplace or family practices.

Matt talked in more detail about his and Kara's decision to move out of London, explaining the two-way relationship between work and home:

> It's just what you want to make work. To me, it's like Kara lives there, she makes her life as nice as it is now. I sort of plan it out and pull all the things together. It's about quality of life. You know, Kara will say that she doesn't work. She will say I work very hard and have to commute and whatever. Whereas, I would say, you know, I get to do this, and this. Fortunately, as I say, she thinks she gets a good side of the bargain, and I think I'm happy enough with my side of the bargain.

Dan invoked a similar sense of self-sacrifice to Matt with respect to comments he made about managing the distance between his home and work. He explained how:

> People do commute every day and it is possible. It's sort of the way you want to live your life, quite frankly [*Dan raised his voice here, perhaps*

> *to emphasise as well as defend his point*]. To be honest, it suits Cath and I 'cos we're not going to do anything on a Monday night, so it's much better to be [at work] till 9.30 on a Monday night, Tuesday night, and have the weekends a bit freer. But I do think, each to their own and what they want to do ... it does suit us.

The physical spatial distances between both Dan's and Matt's respective homes and workplaces resonate metaphorically in their narratives. Dan's comment indicates that in contrast to his wife, Cath, he was not at home very much during the week – a situation he explains "suited" them both. This echoes Matt's reference to the nice life that Kara was creating for herself in the family home (and presumably by default for their children). Both extracts indicate a gendered spatial positioning, whereby the men's positioning in the family space was secondary to their positioning in the workplace while the women were positioned primarily in the home. A more dominant, contrasting narrative of control and ownership linked with the men's City banking jobs, however, frames this narrative of belonging, and somewhat negates the sense that decision-making between the couples is mutually balanced. For example, Matt said he "convinced" Kara to buy the house and that he "plans it out and pulls it all together". Meanwhile, Dan explained that it suited him and Cath for him to work long hours during the week. This suggests unequal power relations based around the men's banking jobs may exist within the family space and between the spaces of family and work. This is important in understanding processes of hegemony in global finance, for it suggests a process of patriarchy linked with elite City jobs could function in the family – a key component of the process of constituting hegemonic masculinities (see Connell 2005a).

Both Matt's and Dan's private exercise of freedom to decide to live outside London and engage in particular socio-spatial practices linked with these decisions was to a large extent, of course, facilitated by the material resources each accrued through his job. For both men, high remuneration levels and savings enabled them to buy and maintain a large, expensive property and make particular lifestyle choices. Among other things, both men could afford a regular and pricey commute on the train to and from London. Both could also afford frequent overnight stays in London – Matt at "the club" and Dan in his apartment (see Chapter 1).

Despite the expense of such practices, however, both men received enough money through their jobs to cover a shortfall in family income due to their wives scaling back on paid work when they had children – at the time of interview, Kara had stopped paid work completely while Cath worked three days a week. Nevertheless, both couples also employed a nanny on a part-time basis to help with childcare. They were the only couples in the study to do so. Cath and Kara each explained how they employed an English nanny, even though they were more expensive. The young woman Kara and Matt employed used to work five days a week but had her days cut back to three when Max (Kara and Matt's youngest child) started preschool. Kara explained that:

> Having a nanny has sort of been necessary and helped us set up our life here so that it works with Matt being away. It all takes time, and I feel, if I don't have some time out, even just to do my admin and catch up with that, and prepare for the weekend when Matt's here, and rearrange the children's bedrooms – you know, anything to make their lives more interesting – there's always something that has to be organised over and above the day-to-day running of everything.

Kara linked the employment of the nanny with socio-spatial practices that support processes of hegemony linked with global finance in three significant respects: first, the spatial aspect of separation of their home from London/the City and thus the frequent absence of Matt from the family home due to work commitments; second, her capability to ensure a quality living/family space for her children; and third, her role in shaping the family space and the kinds of social practices Matt could engage in with his family at weekends, when he was around.

Cath talked similarly about her and Dan's decision to employ a part-time nanny:

> I've always made sure I've got some sort of help, you know, like my nanny. So I've never tried to work and [...]. I've always had a nanny to take [the boys] to school, so that it wasn't stressful for me, and so that my ability to go to work isn't compromised by [Dan] not being here. We could have a full time nanny, but I've got someone who does 2 or 3 days a week. I do think it's important for me to be around ... you can't pay for people to bring up your children for you. But sometimes that drives Dan bananas. I think part of him thinks, well, you know, lots of other guys in his position in the City, they've got full time nannies and the wife doesn't even work at all ... But that was my decision.

Despite the presence of nannies, in both Kara's and Cath's narratives, the physical presence of the mother in the family space is positioned as crucial to the well-being of children, in terms of providing either emotional support or physical/material happiness (rearranging bedrooms and so forth). There are also clear linkages in Cath's comment to the high City wages that Dan received, which serve to further signify his worth and justify the couple's lifestyle choices.

Dan's and Matt's accounts of employing a nanny are matter-of-fact:

> We employ someone 15 hours or so a week to help, 'cos Cath's at work ... Cath can't quite get in her mind what she wants to do and how many hours she wants to do and how many this person should do. I'm very

> clear in my mind in that we should employ this person who does the childcare kind of on the edge of more than is necessary, so that we can all achieve things, right.
>
> (Dan)

> Kara's a primary teacher so she wanted to spend time with the children. So in a way, having a nanny, you know, "what's she doing there?" But actually, it's about quality of life. It's an expense, but also we had three children under 3, so that was a lot of work. In a way, I think everyone gets to benefit from it. The nanny enjoys her job; my wife enjoys her job; the children enjoy what they do ... I think it works very efficiently for us. You know, I kind of talk to her, see what she wants, and kind of plan it out.
>
> (Matt)

The men's accounts similarly position the women as responsible (whether directly or indirectly) for ensuring the day-to-day hands-on caring of their children is fulfilled. This ties the women primarily to the family space. Yet the men position themselves as the parent who ultimately makes this arrangement materially possible, and this connects them primarily to the workplace. While the women are in direct, daily control of the family (and the nanny), the men are in overall control. The household arrangements are shaped primarily to accommodate the men's jobs and careers and not the women's, which are in contrast positioned as supplementary or superfluous to the well-being of the family as a whole. This gendered hierarchy, including the subordination of forms of work and care and the people who do them, is reinforced in the detached way in which Dan referred to the "person who does the childcare", the use of the impersonal term "nanny" by each of the other respondents and Matt's possessive expression "my wife". Incidentally, none of the women used the expression "my husband" at any point in their interviews, referring always to their husband by name. In contrast, all of the men, except David, at some point or another referred to "my wife" – Dan and Matt did it frequently.

In addition to a nanny, both Matt and Kara and Dan and Cath paid other people to help with household-related tasks. When I arrived at Cath and Dan's house, a man was fixing the light fitting in the downstairs toilet and shower room. Cath told me he was her regular "odd-jobs man". She also explained that two cleaners, busy at work in the deluxe family kitchen, came each week for a few hours, as did the two gardeners she also hired to help take care of the family's one-acre garden. Kara and Matt also paid a gardener and a cleaner for two to three hours each per week. Like the nannies, and like the workers who service the space of the City, these workers remained nameless and impersonal – their status and worth in and outside their workplace depreciated in the process.

Dan's and Matt's narratives about their spatial family arrangements, when combined with their ongoing ability to make these particular arrangements possible, support two significant identities linked with fatherhood. First, a super-breadwinner identity that positions the men as superior to their colleagues and other workers who do not make as much money as them or provide the same form of "quality" lifestyle for their families. And second, a super-caregiver identity, whereby the men's contributions to developing and sustaining a "quality" family life are positioned as superior to those of their wives. This latter positioning not only places considerable social value on material worth, but also connects money unproblematically to valued processes of care and responsibility (a point explored further in the following chapter with regard to school choice). As such, it both reflects and reinforces the cyclical relationship between forms of work and material and gendered social value fundamental to processes of hegemony in global finance. This dual fatherhood identity plays a significant role in contributing to both economic and moral dimensions of hegemony.

Each of the other five couples in the study lived in London: Paul and Gwyneth, Dominic and Jess, Graham and Ayami, and David and Emma lived in Inner London; James and Bibi lived in Outer London.[2] Paul and Gwyneth had one child and lived in an especially affluent area of London. Paul, like Matt and Dan, was paid an extremely high salary and generous bonuses. Although neither Paul nor Gwyneth told me exactly what Paul was paid, it was clear from where they lived in London, as well as remarks they made about their lifestyle, that Paul received a considerable income. Gwyneth mentioned remodelling the family home, as well as annual family skiing trips, for example, and their tendency to take two other family holidays each year to luxury destinations such as Dubai or North America. They also paid for their son, Zac, to attend an expensive local private school.

The area of London where Paul and Gwyneth lived is not a newly gentrified area but one that has long had wealthy residents and high house prices to match. It has wide, tree-lined streets, big detached Victorian houses and a large park. I wandered around the area for a while after meeting with Gwyneth. The "village" centre had chic clothing boutiques, a bookshop, a delicatessen and a florist's, as well as a few restaurants, cafés and old pubs. Gwyneth explained how she and Paul moved there shortly after they were married:

> We could afford to buy in a nice area. You know, it has the best of everything – the greenery and everything. We love it here, living so close to the centre of London. You've just got that idea that's where it all happens. And I suppose we had to be somewhere that was accessible to the City, 'cos Paul said he wouldn't commute 'cos he would never be home and would never see Zac. It's nice to have this compromise with being this close but being in a nice area. I suppose the downside is the money and the space – it's ridiculous, isn't it? You know, we could have acres if we lived somewhere ... But I wouldn't want to live right out in the country, 'cos I wouldn't like the isolation, and I'd hate it with the rubbish shops.

In Gwyneth's account, her and Paul's choice of lifestyle is once again positioned as superior – "the best of everything" – to all other available options, options which despite offering the possibility of more space were ultimately dismissed by Gwyneth as substandard with their "rubbish shops" and lack of community. One irony in Gwyneth's comment about the cost of space in London is, of course, the link between the high property prices in London and the Capital's affluent residents and workers – people just like her and Paul.

Paul, like Gwyneth, described the spatial location of their family home as ideal. He linked the appeal of living where they were to the relatively short and easy journey he had to and from the City:

> A lot of people move out to Sussex or somewhere, you know, and you can't get home very easily. I think from my perspective, and it's something we've discussed about how far you move out, is that neither of us wants to move out. It's a reliable [X] minutes commute.

Paul and Gwyneth, in a similar vein to Dan, both referred to the common social practice among high-status and well-paid workers of moving out of London, although they had to date rejected this choice. Indeed, Paul's comment suggests, like those of Matt and Dan, that he had made the more discerning choice among his peers – by remaining in London he had ensured a better quality of life for himself and his family. Gwyneth's account, likewise, not only positions this choice as one that signifies Paul's worth as a committed and present father (he could see more of Zac) but also signifies Paul's worth and status as a breadwinner (the cost of where they lived in London could have bought them "acres" of land in the country). Of course, that they had the choice to live in an expensive and well-located area of London in the first place was only possible because of Paul's well-paid job in City banking.

Each of the other couples lived in what might be termed relatively newly gentrified areas – neighbourhoods with attractive well-kept parks, tree-lined residential streets and a range of local amenities, including independent shops, cafés and restaurants. Dominic and Jess had three children. They lived in a semi-detached, four-bedroom house, with a good-sized garden and off-street parking. David and Emma had one very young child. They lived in a neighbouring borough, in a slightly smaller four-bedroom terraced house with a moderately sized garden. James and Bibi also had a very young child and were renting in a modern, luxury apartment complex that had various amenities for residents, including a swimming pool, gym and children's playground, and with other amenities at street level for the general public, including restaurants and shops. Graham and Ayami had one young daughter and were renting a garden flat in a converted Victorian property, situated opposite a leafy hilltop park.

Dominic and Jess both independently mentioned that they were considering moving out of London to the country at some point, although they had no immediate plans to do so. James, by contrast, remarked that he missed living more centrally and described living in the rental apartment as "a bit like living in a hotel" and that he and Bibi "plan[ned] to move back into town" when he got a new job back in the City. David, meanwhile, explained how he wanted to:

> Make sure that I provide for [my family]. So stay in a good, well-paid position to maintain a comfy lifestyle … we've been talking about where the next move for us would be, mainly because we've been thinking we need more space … And then, do you move out of London, because eventually we would do that? But the thing is, here's really convenient for everything at the moment. And really, I'm quite happy.

The men's and women's narratives of lifestyle linked with family space and private mobility and the promise of finding freedom and fulfilment, whether in London or the Home Counties, echo banks' institutional language of pioneering and discovery. Mobility – both private and public forms – is positioned as aspirational and somewhat glamorous, yet also readily available for those who want it, who work hard enough and who organise their lives to make it possible. It is a desirable, achievable state that simultaneously makes working in banking worthwhile and signifies one's worth as a successful banker. Not only that, but in much the same way that mobility in the public realm espoused by banks depends on forms of stability in the private realm, this mobility and quality of space in the private realm that the men describe (i.e., the freedom to move wherever one desires) depends on stability in the public realm (maintaining a well-paid City-based job). In these narratives, high remuneration levels enable private mobility (perceived or otherwise) and provide access to all the benefits and happiness (perceived or otherwise) that engaging in it yields. Money linked with global finance thus forms the infrastructure of both the private and public spaces of well-paid City bankers and the social practices that constitute these spaces. Yet the "freedom" and choices this money brings are positioned as though they are available to everyone, not only well-paid City bankers.

The two-way spatial relationship between the public and the private (regardless of the extent to which such lifestyle mobility in the form of moving to find more space is ever enacted), underpinned as it is by high City remuneration packages, is important for two reasons. First, because it helps bind City bankers like the men in this study to the elite financial workplace – either due to the immediate reality of sustaining a lifestyle choice or due to the aspiration of eventually being in the position to make such a choice or change one's mind about the choice one has already made. And second, because, as such, it helps legitimise the status quo, including notions and practices linked with status and worth, and further narrow the space for contestation. This private mobility discourse, therefore, should be recognised as a seductive and mobilising aspect of the processes of spatial and gendered hegemony linked with global finance: it is significant because the promise or dream of mobility and finding the ultimate quality of life helps form the basis of a powerful shared outlook.

Like Matt and Kara and Dan and Cath, each of the couples who lived in London, with the exception of Graham and Ayami, paid for additional help in the home. While each of them paid for cleaners, Gwyneth and Paul also paid for a weekly visit from a gardener who doubled up as an odd-jobs man when required. When viewing all the narratives together, it seems that the practice of buying in domestic and/or caregiving labour is closely linked with bankers' everyday routine work practices and norms, regardless of whether they live in or out of London. Indeed, despite Kara's and Cath's initial suggestions that they each employed a nanny to help with childcare because of living *outside* London and the impact this had on the time Matt and Dan each spent at home, elsewhere in their interviews they each mentioned that they had previously employed a nanny when they lived *in* London.

The practice of buying in domestic and/or caregiving labour, therefore, along with low-paid workers who do the labour, must be recognised as contributing to the day-to-day capability of global finance and its elite employees to operate and work in the ways they do (see also Massey 2010; Perrons 2010, 2015). This, of course, is not necessarily problematic if different tasks and people who fulfil them, whether inside or outside the financial workplace and the space of the City, are all valued. In the constitution and conferring of hegemony, however, the institutional and social structures and practices that evaluate, value and reward different jobs and the people who do them are beset with inequalities. The relinquishing of responsibility by the more privileged groups of society for certain vital everyday tasks, in order that the elite can work longer hours in highly paid jobs or engage in leisure activities of their choosing, devalues these everyday tasks and the people who do them (see also Donaldson and Poynting 2007). This continues to promote the idea that caregiving, domestic and household work are a cost and not a benefit for, or essential to, the productive economy (Perrons 2005: 397). This, in turn, helps perpetuate the unequal valuing – socially as well as materially – of different kinds of workers, including in relation to employment rights (see Sassen 2009b).

Similarly to Cath and Kara, four of the remaining five women I talked with had scaled back their work commitments after having children. Ayami worked in the fashion industry and had reduced her days from five to four per week. She spoke enthusiastically about her job and did not elaborate on her decision or mention any future possibility of either increasing or further scaling back on her hours. She and Graham each explained that they divided up household chores and caregiving responsibilities equally. Gwyneth and Jess, meanwhile, described their respective family arrangements:

> I always wanted to give up work and be a full time mum. And I guess we never really discussed it. I couldn't wait to give up work. And Paul earns much, much more than I ever did or ever could. I would never be able to support us all. And I did expect to have more children – I always wanted four or five, but that didn't happen – so I guess, I never really thought I would go back particularly. The little bit of work I do now is not much really. It gives me a little bit of pocket money.
>
> (Gwyneth)

> We didn't really discuss it because there's absolutely no point from our point of view. There's no way I could get a job that pays as much as Dominic gets paid. He earns ten times as much as I could, or more.
>
> (Jess)

While Gwyneth made no mention of any plans to modify her schedule in the future (she worked a few hours per week editing), Jess explained:

> If I wasn't looking after [the children], I'd be out working. It's the whole reason I'm at home. That's what I've chosen to do, and I know I'm really lucky to be able to do that. I do want to do something once all the children are at school. I don't really know what yet, but I don't want them growing up thinking women don't work.

Jess's comment is interesting for a few reasons. First, Jess devalued her role as a full-time parent – someone not "working". This supports the different, hierarchical valuations of forms of work, particularly paid versus unpaid work and the people who do them. As such, Jess positioned herself in the family space as somehow lesser than her husband, including in the eyes of her children. Second, through her reference to being "lucky", Jess implied she should feel a sense of gratitude towards her husband's job in facilitating her capability to be at home full time, which further subordinates her own positioning in the family in favour of her husband's positioning and justifies the rewards of City banking. Third, her comment serves to naturalise a more widespread gendered division of work through the use of the word "women" in the plural, as well as the fact she positioned the situation as her "choice". Moreover, the overriding sense that the current gendered divisions and valuations of work and family are fair and natural is further crystallised by the fact that at no point in her interview did Jess problematise the long hours Dominic, her husband, worked. Thus, the patriarchal nature of work and home is legitimised.

In contrast, Emma, a highly educated scientist, explained how she had felt compelled to leave a demanding academic career after falling pregnant with her daughter, Millie – a decision she partly attributed to discriminatory norms in her field that expect full-time commitment – and instead worked three days a week for a public research body. She discussed her and David's division of family responsibilities, suggesting they were based (in theory at least) along fairly egalitarian lines:

> Before we had children, it was pretty even-handed. Now it varies a little bit. Because I'm at home Thursday and Friday, I do tend to do the shopping. But we pretty much share putting Millie to bed and taking her to nursery. Well, David does two days a week if he can. But I think once you become a mum, you also, sort of become chief household manager; it's kind of expected of you.

Bibi, a highly trained medical practitioner, worked three days a week in private practice and two days a week for the NHS.[3] She confided:

BIBI: I think James is finding it quite difficult not working, you know – ups and downs.

HL: Yes, I'm sure it's very stressful for him trying to find work ... You mentioned that you find working five days quite exhausting, Bibi. If James gets a job, what would you plan to do, do you think?

BIBI: Ah [*she laughs*], my ideal situation would be to work three days a week and spend the other two with Oscar, absolutely. And probably try and get pregnant again. I ... when James starts working, Oscar will go to a childminder. He goes to one[4] at the moment if James has an interview to go to, and he just loves it. So I'm happy about that. For three days a week, that will be perfect.

What the extracts about divisions of labour in the family collectively reveal is that most of the women, therefore, in spite of their different circumstances, employment and education backgrounds, positioned childcare and hands-on parenting as their preferred priority. It was something they said they had willingly chosen to do, at least while their children were young, or in the case of Bibi, something she would "ideally" do once James was back working full time. A further significant similarity, which is explicit in Gwyneth's and Jess's comments and implicit in Bibi's, is the reference to high City salaries as a central component of this decision.

Paul and Dominic reinforced this association (as Matt and Dan did above):

> I've been trying to send [Gwyneth] back to work for years [*Paul chuckles*]. Umm ... no, it was really her decision. She gave up work when she was pregnant and we never really discussed it. I assumed she'd want to go back to work, but she never did. And I guess because I work in banking, it was never a financial imperative, so it just never came up.
>
> (Paul)

> It's Jess's decision, totally. You know, if she wants to work, fine; put the kids in nursery or whatever.
>
> (Dominic)

Graham, meanwhile, admitted that he had considered leaving banking, so that he could be "a bit happier":

> I'm not ruling it out. But Ayami can't see a position whereby she would get a job that would allow us to have the time we have together and pay the rent … I can deal with getting a bit pissed-off with my job every now and then so that she can do what she wants to do, and we have a fairly decent quality of life … If I can do one thing for my family, then this is what I'll do. I'll just bite my lip and get on with it.

Elsewhere, Graham, unlike Ayami who didn't mention her intentions to me, conformed to the same gendered narratives of choice and value as the other respondents:

> I'm actually hanging on a mini-promotion. I don't know if I'll get it, but if I do, I'll get a decent pay rise. And if I get that, I think Ayami will pack in her job. When she started work, basically, I just told her, you know, "as long as your wage covers nursery costs – 'cos it's not just about making money, it's about getting out of the house and getting your sanity back – and anything extra you make, just stick it in your pocket, and I'll sort out the rest …" (Graham).

There are four noteworthy points in the men and women's accounts of socio-spatial practices linked with family and parenthood. First, the suggestion that very little (if any) negotiation or discussion about the gendered separations of family and paid work occurred between each couple (with the exception of Graham and Ayami): the men worked long hours in the City and got paid well; the women had organised, or were planning to organise, their lives accordingly. Second, most of the hands-on daily care of young children – at least during the week – was the expected and/or naturalised responsibility of women, whether the mothers or paid-for childcare providers (note the nannies, childminder and nursery workers were all women). Third (leaving aside Bibi and Ayami), although the women may, whether through free choice or otherwise, on one level have been controlling the smooth daily functioning and practicalities of the family space, on another level, the men (positioned, it seems, as intellectually and materially superior) controlled the shaping of the family space and the practices which support it. And this was done in accordance with the structures, demands and rewards of the elite financial workplace and the men's well-paid jobs in City banking. Fourth, despite the men's and women's recognition of the benefits of high City salaries, the women's choices and the decision-making that underpinned them are largely separated in both the men's and the women's narratives from the attitudes, expectations and practices of elite City banking – in other words, the household space and the women's roles and identities within it are positioned as supplementary and not fundamental to the demands of the workplace.

Narratives of fatherhood

Like the narratives of space and mobility, those of fatherhood and family dynamics, as told by both the men and the women I talked with, further reveal the relational aspects of the private spaces of the family and the public spaces of elite City finance. Relational in terms of how these particular spaces are shaped by and through both relations with each other and their internal interactions (Massey 2005, 2010).

The ways in which the men and women I interviewed talked about the men's identities and roles as fathers offer insight into ways in which hegemony gains strength through the articulation and/or re-articulation of particular ideological elements in a process that may be seen to be both consensual and coercive (see Gramsci 1971). Two linguistic aspects of the men's and women's narratives, in particular, can be understood as both the product and partial producer of hegemonies linked with global finance, embedded as they are in a sociocultural process. The first is the use of finance and market-related language to describe family and emotional relationships – this is particularly evident in the men's accounts of fathering. The second concerns notions of worth, status and ease, which frame both the men's and the women's descriptions of the men's enactment of fatherhood and engagement in forms of care. Both these linguistic aspects illustrate how cultural ideas about gender connect with institutional authority in the process of constituting hegemonic masculinities (Connell 2005a).

Fatherhood and the language of the market economy

Financial lexicon infused the men's talk about fatherhood. It was especially evident in the ways in which the men assessed their family role and associated responsibilities within the constraints of the demands of their jobs, for example:

> You've got to be quite disciplined and I completely accept that I work quite hard, but actually, at the end of the day, to a degree that I'm quite happy with. I accept I won't spend as much time with my children as I would like to. Investment banking is quite demanding on your lifestyle, but does actually kind of reward you for that. And everyone has to make the choice of, is it rewarding you enough for the kind of detrimental effects on your life. And is it a detrimental effect on your life? You

> can have a big debate about that. Really it's a case of "Do you want it or don't want it?" It's each-to-their-own. And you do feel that of course you need to put in time with your children, and of course you'd like to see your children more, but the world doesn't quite work like that. But you do still see them quite a bit. But that's the trade-off, I think. Which must be everyone's trade-off.
>
> (Dan)

> I permanently agonise about it, re-evaluate it, probably more than anyone else. I spend a lot of time thinking about all the opportunities, all the tail risks – I think, am I getting it right? Am I getting the balance right? How can I change it? What do I need to prioritise? I look for people who I think have done it well, who've succeeded with that whole, sort of, balance… At the most extreme level [this] led to me taking six months off because I couldn't have a holiday. A lot of people said it's career suicide, etc., etc. But it was just a simple balance decision – this is where my family are, this is where I am personally…
>
> (Matt)

Market-related language can be identified in the men's references to discipline, hard work, reward, benefit, evaluation, prioritisation, opportunities and tail risks; meanwhile, Matt's use of the violent metaphor "career suicide" connects to the institutional language of aggression, immediacy, competitive individualism and self-responsibility discussed in the previous chapters. Similar language, including "benefit" (Dan) and "bargain" (Matt), can be seen above in the men's descriptions of their family spatial arrangements.

Use of market-related language illustrates how the City's elite financial workplace, and the ways it is positioned in and operates through the market economy, creates the terms within which the men (and by default their wives) negotiate their family responsibilities and desires. Such language is not only reflective of the discourses that confirm and normalise forms of hegemony related to global finance, but its use also supports and normalises the status quo and patriarchal conditions relating to reward and status within the industry. Such language infuses the men's narratives with a sense of rationality, and suggests the current demands of the elite financial workplace are fair and suitable not just for these men and for all workers in similar jobs, but also for the men's wives and children. Furthermore, the use of such language, as well as the ways in which it is used, supports the present situation more generally. It is illustrative of the ways in which hegemony "acts to saturate our very consciousness" (Apple 2004: 4), whereby common-sense interpretations of the everyday are seen instead as the only way and thus exclude or squeeze out other possible interpretations. In other words, market-related language supports the depiction of life in general as meritocratic (not only elite finance). When combined with matter-of-fact language, such as Dan's comment that "the world doesn't quite work like that", or Matt's reference to a "simple" balance decision, the men's market-infused narratives imply the status quo is fair for everyone, whether bankers or not, whether well paid or not.

Three interrelated discursive elements the men used stand out because they mirror prominent features and seductive forces of the hegemonies of global finance. The first is the link between hard work and material gain/success, which Dan's comment above suggests is quite straightforward. The following explanation by Dominic also makes this link, although his comment differs from Dan's by acknowledging (although notably not problematising) the unequal distribution of financial reward within the current capitalist-based labour market, despite neoliberal claims to meritocracy:

> I have to work quite late and stuff sometimes ... But, I dunno, there's nothing wrong with a bit of hard work. I don't really see the kids at all in the morning 'cos I leave pretty early ... But it's no different to factory workers, doctors, nurses, you know – they all work 12-hour shifts. No complaints in our industry, 'cos you get paid reasonably well to do that (Dominic).

Interestingly, hard work (or the demands thereof) is justified by material gain, which both recognises and reinforces the power and seductive dimension of material accumulation embedded within the hegemonic discourses of global finance, as well as the satisfaction this material gain supposedly brings. This justification links to the second element of market-centred discourse, which is the notion of the "trade-off", evident in all the men's accounts of fathering. This notion suggests that higher wages/material gains and the benefits money can buy make hard work and all the "detrimental" (or indeed as Dan suggested, "not detrimental") effects it may entail worth it in the end, effects that can include significant absence from the family home due to long working hours, business travel and so forth. Such a position supports the capitalist dream, which is an important, enticing and mobilising force in the processes of hegemony linked with global finance – the constant association and naturalisation of working hard with being suitably rewarded, which in turn leads to satisfaction at work along with happiness and greater well-being in the private realm, such as that supposedly gained through buying spatial freedom.

Of particular note in the ways this "dream" discourse was used by all the men, however, is the moral dimension they assigned to it: the fact that they justified working hard in City banking because the rewards they gained from it benefited their entire family – a point that echoes their spatial narratives. Paul explained how he felt "lucky to have got into banking" and that he believed his son and wife had "benefitted from it as well". Graham even more broadly claimed that by working in a bank he was "contributing to society" by, as he put it, "contributing to [my daughter's] life and making her a decent person in society so that she can be happy". This moral dimension, embedded here within the traditional breadwinner model of fatherhood, gives hegemony considerable power and endurance. It supports how hegemony preserves economic power in the hands of a few while positioning this preserve as a greater good (for family and/or society). In this case, the wealth and profits of global finance are positioned as though they eventually benefit everyone in a trickle-down process from top to bottom. This helps justify the ways in which the men and their wives had organised their private lives and responsibilities, such as their choices about where to live (see above) and where to send their children to school (see the next chapter). It is also a cyclical process, for in turn, these choices help justify the high salaries of elite City bankers, and this helps keep these men, and other workers like them, working in the jobs they do in the ways they do even if, like Graham, they express dissatisfaction (see the previous chapter).

The third related element is the suggestion that achieving an ideal work–life balance is actually possible, even though the men's comments suggest in practice it had to date proved elusive. None of the men categorically admitted to achieving perfect work–life balance, but the potential for them to do so, like the lure of the high City salaries that apparently could or do make it possible, is clear in their narratives. The appeal of perfect balance – whereby through working hard (in a particular way) one can reap rewards and bring happiness to oneself and the whole family – and the desire such an ideal invokes contribute to the men's compliance with current workplace practices and structures. As such, it is an important driver in processes of hegemony linked with global finance.

Yet in the men's search for perfect balance, it was, somewhat surprisingly perhaps, not always the demands of the workplace that were seen as needing to be reassessed, as the following comment by Dan illustrates:

> I think work impacts me, every father, hundreds of different ways. On the one hand, you can't necessarily pursue the career you want to. I don't know how many people would say this, but it is career-limiting to have children, which sounds a completely bad thing to say but it's true.

This is an interesting comment, of course, considering the number of high-profile men who are fathers (including bankers, businessmen, entrepreneurs and political leaders). To that end, it could reflect the uncertainty of success in global finance and the lack of consistency regarding who wins and who does not, as discussed in the previous chapter, and thus provide a convenient excuse for Dan not yet having reached the highest rungs of the career ladder. When Dan made this comment, however, I asked him whether he felt it had been the case for him, to which he replied, somewhat contradictorily, "No, I don't necessarily feel that that's the case".

Regardless, Dan's comment is also interesting specifically in relation to his family arrangements at that time. Cath (Dan's wife) was working part time in order to look after the daily needs of their children. During her interview, she framed this decision as her choice despite linking it explicitly with the demands of Dan's job:

> I did want to go back to my job when I'd had Cal … but, you know, like a lot of people, when you have, you can't imagine what it's like until you've had the baby, and I realised that I did only really want to work three days. And I realised that, however much Dan was gonna be involved as a dad, he was never going to compromise his work … If you're going to be married to someone who works in the City, you have to accept the advantages and disadvantages; and that's the way it is.

Cath's decision, and the way she explained it, suggests she felt a sense of desire, duty and necessity not to work because of concern for the well-being of her children, which, when compared with Dan's narrative, helps reinforce the notion that childcare is primarily and naturally the responsibility of the mother. Cath's comment also suggests a sense of obligation to comply with the expectations of elite City banking, justified through her explanation of how she married Dan already knowing the deal. In addition to reducing her paid work when she had children, Cath and Dan both independently mentioned that the nanny was employed so that Cath could undertake her paid work two to three days a week. In other words, Dan's work commitments were positioned as superfluous to both Cath's decision to work part time and her and Dan's decision to employ a nanny, in that it was assumed Dan would work full time regardless of how the care of his children was fulfilled (this is discussed further below). When viewed together, these decisions and narratives around childcare mean that it is not entirely clear in what way having children might in any way have disadvantaged Dan's career.

Nevertheless, it is very interesting that Dan saw the fact of having children as potentially detrimental to one's career and not vice versa. Even if in reality this is not true, or at least not true for everyone, cultural ideals and representations are powerful components of processes of hegemony. Dan's representation of reality is, on the one hand, a direct challenge to the suggestion that the ideals of present, hands-on fatherhood and egalitarian forms of parenting might inevitably and readily upset existing processes of hegemony linked with global finance, for his comment prioritises and values the space of work over the space of the family. It implies that while the space of the family can be reconfigured to accommodate work needs, the space of work (or at least, the space of elite City banking) cannot successfully be reconfigured to accommodate family needs. And this helps legitimise Dan's decision to spatially separate his work and home life.

Given the sociocultural context in which Dan's comment was made, it can be understood as a strong legitimisation of existing patriarchal systems and gender inequalities in both public and private realms linked with global finance and more broadly. In respect to the workplace, it implies that anyone who has children, whether a man or a woman, is penalised (equally), and as such, it endorses the gendered exclusivity of the elite financial workplace where some people (women, so we have heard) simply do not belong and where those at the top deserve their success. In respect to the relationship between work and home spaces, it must be considered in the context of the fact that current structures and divisions of parental leave, not only in finance but also in the UK in general, combine with gendered sociocultural norms relating to parenthood and parenting which still position women as the primary carers, especially of very young children (see, for example, Olchawski 2016). As such, it helps perpetuate the sense that women are naturally less committed to their careers than men, effectively reinforcing Dan's worth as a banker.

On the other hand, however, Dan's comment is interesting because being a father in reality seems anything but a hindrance to a career in elite City banking. On the contrary, the narratives of the men and women I interviewed help to illustrate how fatherhood provides a moral justification both for the men working according to the existing demands of the elite financial workplace and for the high salaries and bonuses that elite City bankers get paid. This, in turn, is useful for banks and their shareholders because it helps keep men, like Dan, committed to their jobs.

Later in his interview, however, Dan explained how he found having young children particularly time-intensive:

> You must realise this, but for the last 5 years it's been a bit more stressful because you have to be with them all day. I don't really mind all of that 'cos I'm quite fit and energetic, but the kind of thing that really annoys, not annoys, that's wrong, but, you know, you can get a bit of cabin fever if you spend all weekend together.

And Matt made a similar comment:

> I'm not sure I've got the perfect balance. Actually, sometimes I get too affected by what the children want. They can be real sponges on your time. You can spend all this time with them, and still they don't think that you're spending time with them.

These are the same men who commented on the trade-off between their work in the City (which resulted in frequent absence from the home) and their ability to make their family happy or to provide for their family in ways that satisfied everyone. Yet Matt's and Dan's comments about time spent with their children to some extent imply that they assumed their wives, who at the time both spent considerably more hands-on time with their children regardless of help received from part-time nannies, did not feel the same way – or at least did not have the same manoeuvrability or autonomy within the family space to consider their children to be, as Matt rather interestingly put it, "sponges" on their time, and choose when and how to engage with them. In fact, quite the opposite given that both women had given up full-time paid work when they had children.

While the men's comments may indicate some resistance to the hands-on fatherhood ideal, they do not suggest the men reject it. But nor do they suggest the men either resist or reject existing hegemonic processes linked with their City banking jobs. On the contrary, neither Dan nor Matt (nor in fact any other of the five more highly paid bankers in the study) made equivalent explicit comments about how the demands of their jobs consumed time in ways that were detrimental to their family time. In fact, elsewhere in his interview, Matt again referred to the benefits (for him at least) of the more-work-less-family model of work–family balance:

> I suppose I'd like to be [at home] a bit more but being away from your children a little bit more than you want means they really like it when you are there. My wife who's there all the time, the children aren't going to get excited seeing her 'cos she's there all the time.

Such a sentiment does not appear to be one that fully supports a change in the status quo.

James' situation, as a father and caregiver, was in some ways very different to the other men because he was not working in paid employment when I interviewed him but was caring full time for his young son. During his interview, he reflected on his recent redundancy:

> I don't really get out that much… It's been quite difficult coming off a trading floor, dealing with some pretty difficult people, being very mentally active, to suddenly sitting at home with a baby who can't talk. It's quite a big change. Realistically, if it had to be one parent at home and the other working, it would be the other way round and Bibi would be at home. Coming home and seeing your wife and baby would be a lot better.

James' gendered narrative contrasts with the following reflection based on field notes I made after visiting him in his home:

> When I arrive, James is in the process of changing Oscar's nappy on a mat on the living room floor. James tickles Oscar's tummy while fastening the poppers on his son's stripy bodysuit – Oscar smiles and giggles. I comment on how happy Oscar is. James agrees, but also tells me he thinks Oscar is teething at the moment so his gums are hurting him a little. Later, as we sit on the sofa, Oscar climbs up next to James and gives him a kiss on the cheek.
>
> (27.01.10)

Despite his obvious caregiving capability, James concurred with Matt and Dan that spending too much time with young children is not just a drain on one's physical resources but also on one's mental/intellectual capacity and sense of well-being, especially if you are a man. James' circumstances at the time were, of course, shaped by the added strains and stresses of not only coping with a relatively young baby, being made redundant, moving from Australia back to the UK and trying to find work – all of which would likely be stressful enough on their own. Nevertheless, he explained:

> I used to be a lot more driven but sitting at home you just do slow down a bit. But I suppose a lot of this is out of my hands, there's nothing I can ... You know, it's a bit of a reality check, and I think the last 6 months is probably the hardest thing I've had to deal with ...

James' example is interesting because the expressions of care he demonstrated conflicted with what he said. This illustrates the need to look beyond the rhetoric of the new hands-on, caregiving father *and* the practices which support contemporary ideals of fatherhood in conditions of change. The potential for these ideals to upset existing forms of hegemony is brought into question by each of these men. For what is reinforced through their narratives is the power of current processes of hegemony in global finance: the separation of work and home and the gendered socio-spatial practices that support this separation, the primary importance placed on paid work (for men) and the concomitant devaluing of caregiving (for men) and interrelated notions of masculinity and fatherhood which legitimise patriarchal structures at work and home. When viewed together, the men's narratives and actions afford glimpses of the power of hegemony in terms of the relational gendered power dynamics embedded within it and perpetuated by it, as well as the power hegemony has to endure, not by rejecting change but rather by absorbing it and remoulding as a result.

James also, in comments he made about the contrasting work ethics of Sydney and London, strongly inferred that elite bankers in the City work harder and are more able and expected to focus on their jobs, a focus justified by providing for one's family:

> In Australia, the work ethic is a bit more laid back, you know. It's more of a family-type environment because, you know, you've got more space, less population, so family is perhaps a little bit more important to people. They're very understanding of having a family, whereas London doesn't have that dynamic – basically, you're there to work and you've got to let your family take it easy out in the sticks.

While James' comment metaphorically separates the spaces of work and home, it also draws a link between more space and a better quality of family life, which is a further endorsement of the dream discourse discussed above. But also what this comment does is to reinforce both the superiority of London as a hub of global finance and the people who work in banking there who are, so it is implied, harder working and more focused than workers elsewhere (i.e., Sydney) – as evidenced in part by their well-organised and detached family arrangements that ensure their family lives do not impair their commitment to work.

Fathering: an individual approach

The notion of perfect balance, and the suggestion it is possible to "make it work" (if not perfectly then acceptably) if you try hard enough, is an important element of ways in which the men positioned themselves as fathers. It may also be seen to contribute to levels of value bestowed on the men by themselves and others, including their wives, as not only fathers but also elite City finance workers. Issues of balance entail not only combining demands and desires of work and private lives, including facilitating and engaging in particular spatial living and working arrangements, but also combining traditional and new forms of fatherhood – both breadwinning and hands-on caregiving. Both forms of balance, spatial and gendered, feed particularly into ways in which the more highly paid bankers in this study were positioned – in their own narratives and/or in the narratives of their wives – as uniquely superior: the optimum father to other fathers; the optimum parent to other parents, including their wives. This positioning is significant for it reinforces the suggestion that City finance workers excel at everything they do. They are, so we have heard, the best of the best.

As Dan explained:

> You've got to balance up working and socialising and seeing your children. But I think everyone's got a bit of a different view of how you split those compartments in your life … you can't really be critical of other people to say, "Well no, you should do it another way". I suppose this is maybe me being different to everyone else, but you do try to balance family life, work life…

And Matt:

> I have an individual approach to parenting. I think about things a lot. I do think that if I spend a lot of time thinking about it, I'll probably, you know, have a more considered opinion than other people by the end. From about 10 years ago, I realised that if I thought about things more than other people, I would probably get it right more often than them. This is a kind of work philosophy of mine, and I apply it in private as well.

And Paul:

> I have a different perception from most parents of what parenting is about. I'm pretty relaxed. Gwyneth is much more old-school-type stuff; there's a little bit of "Wait till your father gets home".

Despite differences between them, these accounts all reveal a competitive edge to the men's approaches to parenting, which resonates with the neoliberal discourse of individualism and entrepreneurialism. This is not to suggest these men did not think carefully about their role as fathers and the level and type of care and lifestyle they wanted to provide for their families, nor that this was not commendable – indeed, the men's comments illustrate a positive sense of responsibility and desire to care (see Elliott 2016). Yet they also demonstrate, albeit in individual ways, a shared underlying sense of intellectual superiority and personal worthiness: thinking about things more than other people (Matt), having a better perception of parenting than others (Paul) or trying harder than other parents to find a good work–life balance (Dan). All of these are interesting claims considering the gendered family structures and social practices the men and women had organised and engaged in in order to facilitate such "exceptional" parenting. They are also interesting in that they additionally imply the men's superiority over their respective wife – Paul's comment does this explicitly while both Dan's and Matt's do it implicitly – and, in so doing, patriarchal relations within the family are legitimised.

Nonetheless, the men's self-professed claims of superiority were echoed and validated in the women's accounts. For example, Cath explained how:

> When Dan's around, he's absolutely great – much, much better than my friends' husbands. I could say that one of Dan's strengths, many strengths, is that he sort of does 120% wherever he is. When he's with the children, he's with them 120%; when he's at work, he gives 120%; when he's here at the weekend, he's playing football – he takes the boys to football practice and he helps coach football on a Saturday morning. He's really involved in their lives. Whereas some dads would go off and play rugby or whatever, he gives them his whole weekend.

Gwyneth made a similar comment about her husband, Paul:

> As a dad, Paul has always been absolutely, totally hands-on, probably more than any other parent I see at school ... more than any other parent I know. He's always done everything. He and Zac were close the minute Zac was born. I think they did the initial bonding thing. They've always been incredibly, incredibly close.

And Kara explained how:

> [Matt] is constantly revising how we can make the most of our lives. He's always writing these little lists and things, and I think, "gosh", you know, "you're off doing this massive trip, with basically 10 hours of meetings every day", you know – every day, "and you have time to think about us". It's amazing!

These accounts are significant in that they support relational, caring forms of masculinities and thus present a positive view of men's abilities and capacities to care, and I do not wish to undermine the value of care and the critical role it can play in men's engagement in gender equality (see further Elliott 2016). But these accounts also illustrate the limitation of change because they additionally help strengthen existing processes of hegemony in global finance in terms of both spatial arrangements and gendered power relations. Through their narratives, the women reinforce the worthiness of their husbands to work in elite finance in spite of their hands-on caregiving abilities and activities, which, in turn, helps legitimise current practices and structures of reward in elite City finance. The men are depicted as dedicated, hard-working and brilliant at being hands-on fathers despite the limited time they spend with their children. Kara's comment, meanwhile, further devalues her own position in the family by suggesting that Matt would inevitably be justified in viewing her needs and those of her children as secondary to his work demands.

Cath, however, went on to explain how:

> It does slightly drive me bananas when I have to go and drop the children at an activity in the evening and go back and pick them up when that would really be dads collecting them. But I would never change anything.

The gendered narrative Cath uses about "dads collecting their children" is interesting because it supports a gendered division between different kinds of caregiving tasks that appear to link with men working longer hours than women outside the home. But while Cath did question the unequal division of family tasks between her and Dan, she ultimately dismissed it as unproblematic.

Thus in general, therefore, these women acquiesced to the level and type of engagement in the family that their "hard-working" husbands performed. This acquiescence (whether willing or not) forecloses the space for challenging the level of achieved balance between work and home, both for the women and their husbands, as well as the distribution of family-related tasks and activities. The following two comments further illustrate this point:

> I do think we wouldn't be here if it wasn't for Matt working so hard. We're so lucky to live here and be able to do what we do. I try and do all

> the meal planning and the shopping for it, and all the planning of activities for the weekend – I try and get it all done in advance so it doesn't interfere with any family time with Matt.
>
> (Kara)

> I really don't mind doing everything with the children; I don't mind because I'm not working and I see that as my job really – my job's being at home. And, I don't know, I mean, Dominic would never, would never, ever complain if he came home and I asked him to cook dinner. He'd never say anything, it wouldn't annoy him, I don't think. But maybe he would be thinking, you know, "it's only fair", when he's been at work all day, and working really hard. And I would rather he got that time to spend with the children.
>
> (Jess)

The women, particularly Kara, tended to draw on quite emotive language when talking about family relations and dynamics, in contrast to the men's accounts which were much more matter-of-fact. This helps reframe and de-problematise unequal gendered power dynamics and relations in the home (see Jamieson 2011). For example, Kara described how she gave up her teaching job when she had her first child, Esmé. Although she did a little bit of tutoring in-between the births of Esmé and her second child, Leo, she told me that she had chosen to stop that also when her third child, Max, was born:

> I really felt that, actually, they were so tiny, and my passion is, you know, the young age and it'll all be over so quickly. And, umm, Matt was very supportive in that, and we could afford to do that, so it was lovely.

She continued:

KARA: I found tutoring really rewarding. I always came back feeling, sort of, a lot taller and almost a better mother and wife for it. Because, you know, it gave me confidence outside of this, of what's going on, the big change at home with two little ones. But it was wonderful.

HL: Do you plan to do it again?

KARA: No, I, umm, the thing that concerns me about going back to teaching, I don't want to put myself in a position where I'd end up, you know. If I've only got my children, at the end of the day when they're tired and hungry and need to do their homework, and I've got to prepare lessons and I'm tired as well, I think that could be tricky. I don't want to compromise them.

Kara's narrative flips her husband Matt's narrative on its head: rather than view parental caregiving as a strain on her work commitments, Kara positioned it the opposite way round. This provides further important support for existing processes of gendered hegemony linked with global finance through endorsing, on the one hand, sociocultural norms and expectations around motherhood (i.e., that women both naturally desire to and should put the needs of their children first) and on the other norms and values relating to paid work (that it is more stimulating and high status than childcare).

In both the men's and women's accounts of fatherhood, the men are positioned as hard-working, deserving, devoted and committed to both breadwinning and hands-on caregiving. The women and children, meanwhile, are predominantly positioned as the lucky beneficiaries of the hard work the men do (interestingly none of the men talked about the work their wife did in the home in any depth or with a similar sense of gratitude). This positioning serves to elevate the importance of the men within the family space, while concomitantly subordinating the women and obscuring the obligatory work the women do to cover the absence of the men from the family home *and* make possible the kinds of intensive father involvement that might occur in the evenings or at weekends (see further Dermott 2008).

Bearing these aspects in mind, this particular interdependency of private and public realms, in spite of different forms and degrees of spatial separation, may thus be understood as constituting a circuit of patriarchal power. This is not to suggest the men were not committed to meeting the daily needs of their families. But it is to suggest the competing pull between the need for the men to combine work and family responsibilities, underpinned by gendered assumptions and practices linked to the professional culture of City banking, strongly shaped how the men and women organised their work and private lives, and the ways the men enacted fatherhood and engaged in caregiving.

Conclusion

The narratives and observations of socio-spatial practices and family arrangements explored in this chapter help illustrate the cyclical relationship between the work and home lives of elite City bankers – a relational dynamic that empowers City bankers as both workers and fathers. Despite a lack of homogeneity between the men and their lifestyle choices, their narratives and those of their wives collectively reveal elements of a powerful, shared outlook that resonates with the ideology that legitimises processes of spatial and gendered hegemony linked with global finance. This outlook has a bearing on everyday practices and relations within the family, including the gendered divisions of care and labour. It combines elements of aspiration and pragmatism with notions of worth and value that unequally position and reward different people and the kinds of work they do. It is also underpinned by the high remuneration levels of elite City banking, which both facilitate and justify certain choices and practices.

This shared outlook has both gendered and socio-economic dimensions. There are important elements of some kind of shared identity relating to fatherhood. But this is an identity that rather than disrupt existing processes of hegemony linked with global finance seems instead to reinforce them by effortlessly combining not only newer ideals of hands-on fathering with older, more traditional ideals of breadwinning, but also with competitive individualism, which limits the relational scope of care (Held 2006). The very identity of the men as fathers is not only strengthened through this process of individualism, but also presents a moral legitimisation for it. It seems to be, paradoxically therefore, a shared identity built on both a desire and justification for distinction rather than solidarity and empathy. As such, it might be seen to extend what Savage (2000: 115) has described as the individualised process of class identity, which "rather than evoking a sense of belonging to a collective group, invokes a sense of differentiation from others", by including those with whom you might be expected to feel some sense of connection. In other words, it narrows the basis for building a more comprehensive, collective and reciprocal sense of well-being, care and responsibility for others. Because not only does it obscure significant and interconnected lines of privilege linked with gender, socio-economic status and other dimensions of difference, it also obscures the ways in which our lives and how we embody, experience and enact them are inextricably intertwined with the lives of others (see Young 2011).

Notes

1 The Home Counties are the counties of South East and East England which surround London but do not include London itself.
2 London, or Greater London, comprises a group of 12 London boroughs and the City of London which together form Inner London with Central London at its core, and a further 20 surrounding boroughs that form Outer London.
3 UK National Health Service.
4 James mentioned that the childminder was a woman in her 50s.

Chapter 4

Exclusive communities

A sense of community can be understood to hinge on a common human need or desire to belong and feel connected to the world we live in (Klein 2017). One way in which this might be achieved would be through embracing difference and diversity, which would entail a broad and eclectic sense of community. But another way in which this might be achieved is through selection and differentiation – by erecting boundaries around who or what we feel we are or want to be connected to – which would entail a narrow, more homogenous sense of community.

The notion of community was a common thread running through the family and lifestyle narratives of the men and women I spoke with. To some extent, it was closely linked with ideas around freedom and discovery, and a widening of experiences and outlook, which appears to connect with a broad sense of community. The concept was also, however, entwined with narratives about schooling and education in ways that connect with the narrower, more exclusionary and selective sense of community. As illustrated in Chapter 2 and explored further in this chapter, education experiences and the perceptions of worth they invoke can feed into processes of hegemony linked with global finance in ways that reinforce inequalities and forms of spatial polarisation in London and beyond.

Within a market-based system of education, such as in the UK, choices about and experiences of education are both imbued with notions of worth and worthiness (status signifiers) *and* feed into a cyclical perpetuation of privilege (status producers) (Cox 2011: 2664), whereby education is a tangible asset through which parents can pass on their own advantage to their children (McNamee and Miller 2009: 65; see also Ball 2003). In this sense, as Connell (2013a) has argued, it is privilege rather than education that is the commodity, while good parenting can easily be equated with buying the best services for one's own children (Connell 2011: 56). While this can cause significant parental anxiety, it also raises important concerns about social justice and equality, the relationship of money to notions of and practices supporting different forms of identity, care and responsibility, and ideas and judgements about people's intelligence, worth and entitlement (Swift 2003; see also Sandel 2010; Wilkinson and Pickett 2010, 2019).

Recognition that some parents are advantaged in navigating a marketised education system feeds into the fierce debate about school choice and whether the merits of a market-based education system are fair or not. Advocates of school choice argue that competitive market pressures drive up individual performances of schools, which concomitantly leads to a rise in quality of education provision across the board (HoC 2006; Rouse and Barrow 2009). Critics, however, argue that it leads to greater stratification in education and hence society because some parents are unfairly favoured and able to make different choices from parents with less material and sociocultural resources (see, for example, Swift 2003; Francis and Hutchings 2013). Advantages may include moving into catchment areas with "better", more desirable schools (Power et al. 2003; Cox 2011). Other critics argue that good quality education should be an intrinsic human right and should not be treated as a commodity and that the practice of selling education and increasing competition between schools imbues education with market values, including performance targets and incentive programmes (Sandel 2012: 53; Collini 2013). Meanwhile, an associated, lingering debate in the UK, revitalised in 2016 under the Conservative Government of Teresa May, is whether or not to expand selective state schooling[1] (Asthana and Campbell 2017). This debate has resurfaced despite evidence that selective schooling increases rather than decreases various forms of inequality, including educational outcomes, future earnings and so forth (see, for example, Burgess et al. 2017). Importantly, however, what the existence of these debates illustrate is that a market-driven education system, which results in competitive schooling provision and the positioning of knowledge as capital (Olssen and Peters 2005: 330), continues to be given virtue in the UK and appears unlikely to change.

Elite City bankers are highly likely to have first-hand knowledge and/or experience of the social and economic advantages that privileged forms of education can bring because of working where they do (see Chapter 3; see also Ho 2009, with respect to Wall Street bankers). They are also advantaged in the process of school choice because they are already proficient at engaging in market processes at work, including investment. As such, they are likely to positively value market processes (Connell 2011) and may already be familiar with spending money on forms of care in the private realm (see the previous chapter). This intertwining of work and family experiences and practices suggests school choice may be an important domain wherein processes of hegemony linked with global finance may be contested or reinforced. Bearing this in mind, this chapter explores the ways in which the men and women talked about the process of choosing schools for their children, as well as the kinds of education and educational experiences they wanted their children to have. It also looks more closely at the different choices themselves.

A trip to market: tales of school choice

The bankers' tale

The highest earning men in the study – Matt, Dan and Paul – had already, along with their wives, made the decision to send their children to private schools at the time I talked with them. James and Dominic, the next highest earners, were also considering private education for their children. James' son, Oscar, was still very young and had not yet started school, but James told me that he and Bibi planned to educate Oscar solely in the private sector. Dominic's son, Ted, was, at the time, attending a state primary school – this seemed to be (as I discuss in more detail below) due to the preference of Dominic's wife, Jess, rather than Dominic. However, Dominic and Jess each told me that they intended to transfer Ted to a private school, at least in time for his secondary level education. Of the remaining two men in the study (David and Graham), David remarked: "If my salary improves, my view is that, having been educated in [the private sector], it seems a lot more... Certainly, the facilities and activities were much, much better".

All the couples I talked with, therefore, except Graham and Ayami (neither of whom made any mention of private education as a choice they were considering for their daughter) were engaged with the question of choosing private education for their children in some form.

The ways in which the men who had chosen private education talked about their engagement with, and negotiation of, a hugely competitive education market are interesting, not least because the men appeared to downplay its competitiveness and any potential concerns they had about this. This renders the competitiveness somewhat invisible or at least normal and insignificant. It also renders unimportant, the inequalities that are integral to this competitive market. Dan explained his choice with regard to his children's schooling in the following way:

HL: Did you look at schools before you moved [out of London]?

DAN: You know what, I can't remember precisely. Umm, we did a quick look; we didn't really look very, very hard. I mean, it's not like we did day tours of the [private schools], or scrutinised them, you know. I think we probably knew there were two or three fee-paying schools, but we didn't really sit there and say, "that's definitely the school for them, we must move there". We certainly looked at the schools to check they were OK, you know. And we knew there were enough that we were bound to find one that suited them.

Paul similarly described:

HL: So in terms of your schooling choices for Zac, was that something you both... [*Paul interrupts*]

PAUL: Umm, the only decision we had was between which private school. I mean, the choice [in our borough] between private and state is not really a choice you make if you can afford it... That decision was a very straightforward one. The discussion about which private school in particular, as it turns out to be, is completely random, and you don't know in reality. So much depends on the individual teachers, I think.

Somewhat in contrast, Matt explained how, once he and Kara had made the decision to move permanently from London to the coast:

> The question then was really about schools. So, we wouldn't have moved there full time if there wasn't a school there that was fantastic. So once we saw that, it made it very easy 'cos it was like, there's a brilliant school... I was really impressed with it, and the facilities that were there. And the headmaster was really nice. It was, you know, we couldn't fault it at any level. So... and it was close, so it was sort of a done deal really.

The lack of references to competitive market pressures by the men is interesting because one assumes they chose to send their children to particular schools precisely because not only were they desirable schools, as defined specifically by this competitive market, but also, as the men have indicated elsewhere in their interviews, desirable schools in the eyes of the sector of the labour market in which the men worked (i.e., elite City banking). School choice, within this marketised system, where such desirable forms of education are both for sale and valued in relation to this, along with high social status and advantages associated with them, is aligned with notions of good quality parental care and concern. The men's comments about the ease of choosing schools feed into the general inference from their talk about fatherhood in the previous chapter that not only caring for children but caring for children well is a rather effortless process. This, in turn, supports the general presumption in hegemonic financial discourse that elite financial workers are good at everything they do. It also feeds into the related inference that fathers who are not able to buy this same level of care, or who make a different choice, have somehow fallen short of their caregiving responsibilities.

There are, however, differences as well as similarities in the ways in which these three men who had already chosen private education for their children talked about their choices. Dan and Paul downplayed any difficulties they may have experienced – Dan gave very little weight to the initial choosing process, suggesting he felt little anxiety about it (whether or not this is true); meanwhile, Paul depreciated the actual choice by suggesting the quality of schooling is ultimately not controllable, even though he was paying considerable money for school fees, and one would assume he would not pay for something he did not think was good quality. Both Dan and Paul, therefore, renounced the onus of responsibility for their choice, which depersonalises it. Matt was rather more explicit than Dan and Paul about his and Kara's desire to find some sort of high-quality school for their children. Nevertheless, he also implied that the choosing process was relatively easy, and similarly suggested, through the phrase "done deal", that the choice he had made was unquestionable and thus uncriticisable.

On one level, it seems the men's narratives reflect a general lack of room for self-reflection and thus self-criticism: the men either do not want to take responsibility for their choices (Dan and Paul) or they foreclose the space to question them – as Paul said, it was "the only decision", and Matt explained how "they couldn't fault it" and "it was a done deal". On another level, however, and in light of the men's comments about their own education backgrounds and those of their colleagues, it is quite possible that they considered that by limiting their options to a certain kind of school (i.e., private school) that any choice would be "adequate" and lead to good quality education for their children and, subsequently, to high-status employment. Indeed, recognition of the significance of school choice as an important form of parental investment encompasses both the immediate investment in the success, well-being and happiness of one's children while at school, and an investment in the future success and well-being of one's children into adulthood.

Of course, underpinning the men's matter-of-fact narratives about choosing private education is the neoliberal market logic that the more you pay for something, the better quality it will/should be. In accordance with this logic, therefore, the private school is the site of quality care, and sending one's children to a private school is the epitome of good parenting. This is the same market logic that legitimises the men's high salaries and thus the men's worth as bankers and fathers. Indeed, the high salaries of elite City banking are justified both by the desirable forms of education the men themselves received and because they provide the means by which the men were able to purchase the same kinds of desirable education for their children. It is the cyclical process of this same market logic that feeds back into broader naturalised notions of individual sociocultural value and worthiness. Incidentally, each of the schools these three men had chosen is among the more expensive private school options in the UK, which suggests the process of choice was more carefully engaged with than the men made out.

The presumed link between quality and private education or selective education (whereby pupils are selected on the basis of exam results) seems to be supported in the comments the same men made about potential secondary school options:

> I think Gwyneth is quite agitated about it, but I'm not. I know [Zac's] going to a school where there's a focus on teaching, on good manners,

> and churning out reasonable human beings. And I'm not convinced I can control much more than that.
>
> (Paul)

> We're happy sending them away to school for weekly boarding. What we basically said was that we need [the schools] to be kind of within an hour and a quarter from where we live. So let's pick the best schools... But it's not necessarily about the perfect school, because if the perfect school is in Scotland, you know, well, that's a whole day away, so then that's not the perfect school. Do I think that will ruin my children's childhood or education or what have you? No!
>
> (Matt)

And Dan:

> I suppose we're not totally wedded to going fee-paying because there's a grammar school[2] here, which is obviously good. We haven't made any real decision, so we'll see, although we're not kind of 'see what happens' people.

The men's accounts of the process of choosing primary and secondary schools for their children as "easy" (Matt), "straightforward" (Paul) or relatively "unforgettable" (Dan suggested that he couldn't really recollect the process and that he and Cath "probably" did certain things) display a lack of concern regarding the inequality underpinning the freedom that economic advantage (high income) can offer and thus the ethics of buying and transferring privilege in a socially segregated education system. It is not that this inequality is ignored but rather that it is used as justification for choosing particularly selective forms of education. There is the same inference in the accounts of secondary school choice as those of primary school that private or selective schooling is the only worthy choice, that it offers the best kind of education – one where children are educated properly and shaped into worthy ("reasonable") human beings, which implies, of course, a danger they would not be in other kinds of schools.

Moreover, within the men's comments there is no discernable anxiety about or reference made to any difficulty regarding their child's/children's opportunity or capability to get into the schools they had chosen for them or were thinking of choosing for them, or in terms of the actual quality and value of the education their children would receive, or whether their children would enjoy going to the school and/or do well there. With regard to primary school choices, Matt explained the decision was simply a "done deal"; Paul said "the only decision [he and Gwyneth] had was between which private schools"; while Dan described how he and Cath had briefly considered which school but "didn't look very hard" or "scrutinise" the different options (even though he later claimed, somewhat contradictorily in his comment about secondary school choice, that he and Cath "are not see what happens people"). The ways in which these men talked about school choice, therefore, suggest an unbounded freedom to choose to send their children to whichever school they wanted to, as well as an unbridled confidence in their choice.

In the men's descriptions, however, there is a clear juxtaposition between the importance of education, the complexities of the education market and the sense of randomness (in Dan's case, this extends to nonchalance) about the ways in which they described the process of choosing schools for their children, regardless of whether or not this was actually the case. This downplaying of such an important investment decision seems at odds with the attention to detail the men were likely to put in to their day-to-day decision-making with regard to financial markets and client investments. Dan, for example, worked as a financial analyst, while Paul was an investment consultant; thus, one assumes both men would scrutinise potential individual or institutional clients to determine if their investments were worthy or not. One suspects more thought went into the process of choosing schools than the men let on, but it could also be that their apparent attitudes are reflective of their knowledge and experience of market ideology and the fluctuating and temporary nature of market fortunes. As Paul remarked, for example, making the right choice "is completely random" and the result relatively "uncontrollable", depending on "individual teachers" who come and go.

Nonetheless, the fact all of these men had chosen costly private schools signifies that perhaps they considered that this limited the potential for their choice to turn sour and their investment to flounder. It is also possible that their demonstrations of confidence and/or insouciance were grounded also in some measure of self-assurance, whether conscious or subconscious, that their investments need not be permanent or total. Despite the high fees they were already paying, the men enjoyed sufficient economic and social resources to change, modify or supplement their choices through, for example, changing schools, supporting children with homework, paying for extracurricular activities and/or paying for tutoring. And while the men did not mention such practices, references to additional support did figure in the women's accounts.

The wives' tale

The ways in which the men talked about school choice were echoed in the accounts of their wives, particularly in terms of the lack of direct references to the quality of education provision. Matt, for example, described his and Kara's choice of school as "fantastic" and "brilliant", even perfect: "fault free". But from his description, it was not clear what it was about the school that made it ideal, other than the "impressive facilities", the "nice" headmaster and its geographical location. Kara similarly explained:

> We looked at two schools [*both private schools*]. We looked at one in [the nearby city] but it was such a town school, with small classrooms, that we felt it was no different to what they'd have gone to if we'd been in London. At [X], you drive in this drive, and it's got cricket fields, you know, pitches and big open spaces, and beautiful mature trees, and just so much space. And the teachers are really lovely. And it was almost a sort of foregone conclusion, you know. And they had places for them... We liked it so much, we didn't waste any time looking anywhere else.

Kara's description of the school is more visual than Matt's, but like her husband, she made no reference to the standard of teaching and learning. This is quite surprising considering she was a trained primary school teacher. Instead, the picture of the school Kara painted, through her references to the quality and ambience of the space as well as the "lovely" staff, appeared to be enough to justify her and Matt's decision. Through her description, Kara embellished her and Matt's acclamations of the perfectness of the school, which in turn justifies and romanticises not only their choice of school but also their decision to move out of London. The link Kara and Matt each made between the quality of the school and its spatial features – its geographical location, its grounds with its "beautiful" trees and its large classrooms – mirrors the ways they talked about their home and the space in which they had chosen to live. Both these spatial choices (living and schooling) are mutually supportive of one another – as Matt explained, "We wouldn't have moved there if there wasn't a school there that was fantastic", and the school "was close so it was a done deal". Because Matt and Kara's choice of school lends support to the spatial separation of Matt's work and home life, it also helps legitimise the high City wages he received and the patriarchal structures at work and home that enabled this spatial separation.

In a similar vein to Kara, although not quite as romantically evocative, Cath and Gwyneth referred to the ease of choosing a school based on non-academic considerations, such as facilities and the diversity and quality of the school space:

> It wasn't really that ... it was pretty easy. There's two schools in [X] – private schools – and I think the problem is, once you've seen what you can get in the private school, it's very difficult to not do it, because there is just so much. They've got a swimming pool, squash courts, tennis courts, cricket nets, cricket pitches, and badminton courts. And they have a music teacher, a French teacher. You have it all. What they can get is amazing – not just education but the whole education experience. And because we can afford to, you should do the very best.
>
> (Cath)

> I think we always thought that's the way we were going. One of the good things about the private school is all the wonderful facilities and all the things they get to do, like playing tennis and things. If you can afford it, then do it.
>
> (Gwyneth)

The men and women's narratives, therefore, present what appears to be a process of co-construction by husband and wife of the ease and straightforwardness of school choice. This includes the image of a certain lack of effort expended with regard to either making the choice or the working demands of elite finance which support their ability to make this choice (e.g., long hours), an unquestioned acceptance of the lifestyle it depends on i.e., the men's frequent absence from the family home and the patriarchal division of work and responsibility in the family that was facilitating this absence, and the loveliness and quality of the school, particularly in terms of space, that each couple had chosen to enrich their children's lives.

In the women's comments, like those of the men, there is a similar unquestioned acceptance and normalisation of having this choice in the first place, in relation to both the market-based system of education and the current structures of the capitalist job market, which justifies the men's high incomes. In both Cath's and Gwyneth's comments, at least, the moral element of the choice appears to be neither the dilemma of having this choice nor of choosing private education but rather the justification for doing so based on the grounds of doing the best for your child/children. This positions the choice, as both women explicitly stated, as the right and only one that any parent in a similar position should make, as well as the standard by which any other choice is measured, in terms of the quality of education being chosen as well as the worthiness of the parents who make the choice. This is echoed to a certain degree in Paul's remark about choosing a school that can "churn out reasonable human beings". Such a normalisation of private education as well as the decision to send children to private schools resonates with findings from Maxwell and Aggleton's (2010) study on privileged forms of education in the UK, which reveal how private education experiences are frequently positioned as "ordinary" by those who enjoy them, which, in turn, implies that any other form of education is seen by such people as inferior.

What we see in the men's and women's comments, however, is the buying not so much of good quality academic education but of an all-round lifestyle for one's children – a non-contestable package of privilege in a site of high-class quality care. This compliments the lifestyles the men were said to have been providing for their families in the home. Nevertheless, despite all the "amazing" and "wonderful" facilities at these schools, all of the children of these men and women were enrolled in additional paid-for activities outside school, including Cub Scouts (Dan's and Paul's children), football (all the boys of school age), cricket (Matt's, Paul's, Dan's and Dominic's sons), ballet

(Matt's and Dominic's daughters) and sailing (Matt's and Paul's children). In addition, all of the women whose children went to private schools mentioned the likelihood of paying for some kind of extra tutoring in the future. For example, Gwyneth explained:

> I haven't met a mother yet who hasn't tutored them before their Common Entrance Exam[3]... Well, not necessarily tutoring them, 'cos, you know, they're clever, you know, in a clever way, but tutoring them in an actual practical way to get through the exam, because they all [*i.e. the schools*] have their little ways.

What these references to additional activities indicate is that school choice needs to be viewed in the broader context of social and cultural systems within which individual achievement and advantage can be maintained, strengthened or perhaps diminished through a range of educational experiences (Ball 2003: 58; Vincent and Ball 2006).

The joint constructions of the process of school choice by the men and women demonstrate an absolute acceptance of the current market-based UK education system: the inequalities it both fuels and depends on, including the specific discourse of worthiness it promotes, and that higher cost equals more value and thus higher worth. The men's and women's narratives also show a dual commitment to the monetisation of care and the role of the men in materially providing this care for their children – a role which gave the men a position of importance in the family their wives did not share. The narratives of school choice help shape and justify particular notions of fatherhood exalted in the elite financial workplace based on the breadwinner model that facilitate the social practices which enable this expression of care and division of caregiving responsibilities and the patriarchal structures at work and home on which these particular social practices depend. One can also begin to see, in some of these comments, how the discourse of worthiness extends to refer to the type of education that is bought, the type of people who send their children to these schools and the children themselves – the children who are, as Gwyneth explained, already "clever, in a clever way", irrespective of the schools they attend.

A place of community: narratives of exclusive diversity

None of the men in the study whose children were attending private schools (Matt, Dan and Paul), or the men who were considering private education as a future option for their children (James, Dominic and David), expressed concern over the ethics of having or making the choice to educate their children privately. Other anxieties relating to the stratified nature of the UK education market were, however, referred to. These concerns track to the men's narratives of personal advantage with respect to their own education backgrounds and work trajectories discussed previously in Chapter 3. In all of the men's narratives of their own education experience, including Graham's, private education is positioned as the norm and aligned with social worthiness, while state education is positioned as substandard. Those men who were educated wholly or partially in the state sector (Dan, Paul and Graham) had, it seems, been able to rise above this handicap, which, in the narratives of both Dan's and Paul's wives at least, apparently demonstrates an even greater level of individual worthiness.

References to state education were made by some of the men and women with respect to the process of choosing suitable schools for their children. For example, Paul spoke about the local state school options his son could have gone to:

> At the time, the [council] was talking about mixing up the [local state] school with nearby areas, you know, bussing some of the children from [one area] where there's big problems up here. Basically, in [this borough], you go all the way down to [the neighbouring borough], umm, which has got a massive immigrant, non-English speaking population, and you've got obviously [X and Y] [*two other neighbouring boroughs*], and there's obviously big social issues there. So it was really a very straightforward choice.

Paul, in order to justify sending his son Zac to a private school, draws on assumptions about worthiness and quality based on markers of social and economic distinction and not the quality of education provision. Moreover, Paul's use of the word "obviously" indicates his belief that these assumptions are widely held. The children that Paul suggests would be attending state schools in neighbouring boroughs are positioned as not only problematic but potentially damaging to his son's entire schooling experience. By directing his prejudice to people living in three neighbouring London boroughs, Paul established clear boundaries around the community space in which he and his family lived. In the process, he reaffirmed the quality and exclusiveness of the space, as well as his own worth in choosing to live there. This, in turn, helps justify the high City salaries that enabled this choice in the first place, and the processes of hegemony in global finance that continue to facilitate and legitimise it.

Dan also commented on the available local state school choices, explaining, "They weren't really an option, right. We sort of knew that before we moved there".

Dan, like Paul, transfigured the inequalities that underpin the British education system in ways which reconstituted these differences as a reason to choose privileged forms of education not reject or problematise them. This mirrors Stephen Ball's (2003: 55) recognition that some parents opt for private schools simply because they are not state schools and because they are seen to offer a certain kind of education (see also Swift 2003). Yet while supporting the social exclusiveness of private education is in itself problematic in social justice terms, Dan's and Paul's comments are also problematic because the implied "quality" of private schools remains undefined. Instead of qualifying their choices through direct comments about the quality of education provision they were buying, they measured it through negative comments about the local state school alternatives they had rejected and by extension the people who go to these schools (this extension is explicit in Paul's comments and implicit in Dan's).

Dan's dismissal of local state schools is ironic, given that elsewhere in his interview he stated specifically that one of the "biggest positives" about moving out of London was the "community schools". In Paul's case, his sweeping and seemingly derisive remarks about the children who attend the local state schools and the impact the perceived social mix of pupils in state schools might have had on his son, Zac, are ironic for two reasons. First, because Paul was himself educated solely in the state sector – a fact his wife, Gwyneth, singled out as an unusual (at least for men who work in elite City banking) yet extremely beneficial experience. She explained how Paul's state schooling background enhanced his "excellent" managerial skills because it enabled him to relate "to all the different kinds of people he works with because he's just a normal bloke". Second, it is significant because of Paul's subsequent comment about the mix of children his son went to school with:

> Despite the fact it's a private school, it is ethnically very, very diverse. I think, certainly, you know, when we've been on these skiing holidays when you get all these kids that live in London, they just don't bat an eyelid when there's kids who are Chinese, Asian, Black, whatever; it's just not an issue at all. It's just they've been brought up like that, that's just what human beings are like; that's just what the UK is like. Whereas, if you go out to [the Home Counties], you barely see, you know, a couple of Chinese people who run the Chinese takeaway and that's it!

In Paul's comments about school choice, there appears to be a suspicion of difference based on socio-economic class as well as of racial or ethnic difference when combined with lower socio-economic class – i.e., the "non-English speaking immigrants" in the neighbouring boroughs. Yet there is an acclamation of difference based on race or ethnicity when this difference is combined with higher socio-economic class. This is evident in Paul's reference to "skiing" (an expensive choice of holiday), because this implies the parents of the diverse group of children Paul referred to were of similar socio-economic background to him.

These findings reflect those from Reay et al.'s (2007) research on schooling choices among the white middle classes in London. Reay's research (p. 1048) found the same inconsistencies in parents' deliberations about and actions resulting from exposure to difference, arguing that they were used to mask prejudice about forms of socio-economic inequality as well as prejudice based on racial difference (i.e., that children with different ethnic/racial backgrounds who do well at school are the exception and must come from caring families). Similarly, Paul's acclamation of diversity in the form of ethnicity relating to the children who go skiing blanks out consideration of social difference based on socio-economic inequality and forms of discrimination that occur due to sociocultural difference (Giroux 2011).

A further crucial point of interest relating to Paul's acclamation of difference is his oblique inference to a sense of moral superiority, which he suggested his son was developing as a consequence of living in London and mixing with a diverse range of people, in contrast to children who live in the home counties – i.e., the fact his son "doesn't bat an eyelid" when faced with "difference". A sense of moral superiority or leadership is a key component of processes of hegemony, and, as such, Paul's inference is hugely significant for it helps to illustrate the cyclical nature of processes of hegemony linked with global finance.

Graham and Emma (David's wife) each made similar remarks to Paul about London's ethnic diversity in relation to the benefits their respective children were gaining from living among people from different country backgrounds. Interestingly, like Paul, neither Graham nor Emma, however, referred to comparable benefits of socio-economic difference. Emma, for example, remarked:

> I think it's good for Millie to grow up in a diverse community, and I don't think you really get that in many other places… To me, it's quite important that she's very tolerant and accepting of people of all nations.

While Graham explained:

> Thinking in terms of quality of life and a place to bring up a mixed-race child, you know, London's probably the best place in the world, I would imagine. People from all over the world live here.

As well as offering vital support to the residential spatial decisions each of these respondents had made, these comments about London and community support the references the men made about the superiority of both London as a city and the people who work in elite finance in the City (see Chapter 1). In the remarks of Graham and Emma, like those of Paul above, a similar link between space and notions of worthiness occurs in the suggestion that children who grow up in London are more accepting of difference than children who grow up elsewhere.

Paul's comments about diversity also legitimise his economic advantage – as he explicitly remarked, "despite the fact it's a private school…". In other words, Paul's reference to the diverse cohort of students in his son's school helps to justify the fact he was paying for this schooling experience. As such, this supports the association between monetary value and valuations of individual worthiness in the financial workplace. It thus also supports the association of desirable forms of fatherhood in the finance sector linked with the monetisation of care, including buying extra forms of educational "experiences" for one's children in the evenings and/or at weekends. In Paul's case, this also extended to paying for his son to attend the homework club at school so that he and Gwyneth didn't "...have to have all the battles about homework". Paul did not suggest he engaged in a deliberate consumption of ethnic difference unlike his deliberate consumption of socio-economic similarity – i.e., he did not suggest he chose the school his son went to because of its ethnic mix. Nevertheless, it does seem as if he, and Graham and Emma, positioned ethnic diversity as beneficial for the development of their children into well-rounded, non-judgemental people – morally superior, therefore, to people who do not grow up exposed to such difference.

Comments about school choice made by Dan's wife, Cath, and Paul's wife, Gwyneth, support the ways the men talked about forms of difference. They similarly demonstrate a discursive link between school choice and residential choice: each of these men and women justified their choice of school through references to the local area. For example, Cath elaborated on the reasons she and Dan chose to send their two sons to a particular school:

> For the last ten years, nobody in this road, in this area, has sent their kids to the state school. It's diabolical. Obviously, I teach in the state sector, and I know what the state sector is like. When you don't have good quality... We knew from the beginning that this area... We kind of knew we'd have to stay in the private sector. And I sort of think, well, it's our decision. And when we lived in London, it was a disaster: the catchment area [we lived in], in a million years you wouldn't want to send your kids to this school. It was used as a dumping ground for temporary housing, and it was just awful; it was an awful school.

Cath, like Dan and Paul, appeared to limit her bias about state schooling to the local context. Nevertheless, she used the same argument about the poor quality of local state schools in two completely different geographical locations – the "diabolical" school in the area where they currently lived, and the "awful" school where they used to live. Furthermore, Cath's remark about her inside knowledge (as a practising state school teacher) of the supposedly questionable quality of state school education means that her bias needs to be considered as more than just a locally confined prejudice. Rather, when viewed as a whole, Cath's comments once more position private schooling as the benchmark for good quality schooling and all state schooling as substandard. Nonetheless, Cath's remarks about the local area and the local schools are significant because both she and Dan specifically talked about wanting their children to be part of the local community. Yet, despite this desire, her comments dismiss the majority of the local population – both the London community they escaped from and the desirable Home County community they sought out – who have little choice about where they send their children to school. This points to an extremely narrow sense of community: a community developed around forms of similarity rather than difference, and a community that centres on an ideal of exclusivity built through high levels of disposable income.

Gwyneth also made references to community space while explaining her and Paul's choice of school for their son, Zac. She, like Paul, made reference to a recent council initiative:

> They had this funny thing in [our borough] mixing up the schools. And we thought, "No! Our child isn't having that", you know. And Paul often says to Zac, "Look, if you're not going to work at school, then we'll take you out and send you where other people go. You're very lucky to go there"... And we always say, "Look, we never had those opportunities, and we're paying for you, and you have to make the most of them". 'Cos I think what Paul did was fantastic considering he went to a comprehensive [school] as well. He must have shown great dedication and focus to do as well as he did. Even if Zac could do as well as Paul, we don't want him to have that struggle.

A number of issues emerge from this extract. First, Gwyneth, like Cath, positioned private education as the benchmark by which to measure the quality of all forms of schooling. And although Gwyneth similarly attempted to limit her dismissal of state education to the local context, through her comment about Paul's remarkable ability to excel at school both despite and because of attending a comprehensive school, she made a sweeping judgement about the general substandard quality of all state school provision. Needless to say, her judgement also extends to the people who attend state schools – the "other people" (which includes her and Paul). These are, of course, the kind of people from whom Paul managed to escape through (according to Gwyneth) his sheer hard work and "dedication". Incidentally and perhaps rather poignantly, Gwyneth's statement subordinates her own achievements and ignores differences in family background and personal experience that feed into children's educational achievements and of course differences in the capabilities of teachers to teach effectively (if we agree with Paul's earlier comment about teachers above). The process of privileging certain forms of education, therefore, not only supports notions about good parenting, but feeds into broader forms of prejudicial thought and social judgements about people's intelligence, worthiness and so forth, based on aspects of people's background over which they may have little or no control (see also Wilkinson and Pickett 2010, 2019; Kenway and Kohl 2013; Friedman and Laurison 2019).

Both of Gwyneth's positionings – her positioning of state vis-à-vis private education and her positioning of Paul as an exceptional pupil – justify both her and Paul's decision to choose private education for their son and also Paul's high earnings. Paul deserved his high City salary because he showed exceptional "dedication and focus" in rising above the burden of state education; plus the money was also being put to good use (which, in turn, justifies his high salary level even further): first, by paying for "opportunities" for Zac that she and Paul were not so "lucky" to have been given and, second, so that Zac does not have to "struggle". Gwyneth's narrative also, of course, assumes two further points that link with the capitalist dream discourse and the myth of meritocracy: first, that by working hard (like Paul) you will succeed (likewise, as long as Zac works hard he will inevitably succeed), and, second, following on from this, that those who do "make it" (like Paul) thus deserve their success.

Gwyneth made additional comments about schooling and community, which add to the contrast in levels of worthiness she bestowed on the majority of people who go to different kinds of schools and seem to justify spatial segregation:

> Maybe if we lived in the country and had fantastic state schools, we might have thought differently, but not living here. What I worry about now is when Zac gets older, because I think well, you know, I worry a lot about that, because I just think people – there's such a mix of society, that people are gonna pick on him for going to a private school and having a posh accent, or whatever, and there's gonna be all that, you know. People get mugged on the bus here and all sorts of stuff!

In this comment by Gwyneth, the privileged elite – the privately educated – are positioned as optimal, worthy human beings who benefit the broader community they live in (regardless of whether or not they work hard at school), unlike the "other people" – the less-civilised delinquents – who pollute the space and are a danger to the people around them. If one views Gwyneth's comments alongside those of her husband, Paul, what is especially illuminating is that while living in a diverse London community is said to help develop children like Zac into better, more accepting human beings – those who "don't bat an eyelid" at people's differences – the same diverse community makes the "other people" more judgemental, more unworthy and more dangerous (these are the people who "mug" the worthy few because of their different accents). Furthermore, there is the implication in Gwyneth's comment that everyone shares these same valuations of social worth: that those people who do not go to private schools are inevitably going to be envious of the people who do. And it is this implication of shared ideas about worthiness combined with the link between private education and higher morals that is particularly troublesome.

Alternative communities

Neither Matt nor Kara, in contrast to Dan and Cath and Paul and Gwyneth, made any reference to alternative state school options when they talked about the school they had chosen to send their children to. State school options did not appear to have figured at all in their decision-making. Given they were both privately educated, perhaps they did not see their choice as unusual and/or in need of explanation or justification. Nonetheless, Kara did talk about her desire to be part of the local community:

> Sometimes I have a cup of coffee after my exercise class, and that's really nice. And you get invited to things in the village – it's lovely. Because our children are not at school in the village, I've always felt it's very important to be part of the village. There are some lovely people here, and the pace of life is very different. It's not, sort of, influenced by London… Elsie does her ballet in the village, and sometimes [the children] play tennis just up the road, and we go to BBQs at the sailing club, windsurfing club…

Unlike previous comments about community discussed above, which are disparaging of local state schools and mistrusting of people who attend them, Kara's narrative does not evoke a similar sense of danger about the broader local community. On the contrary, Kara expressed a desire for her and her children to be active members of the local community – a community that Kara directly aligned with the local school; a community that she and Matt had not only partially bought into by living where they were, but also one they had (rather ironically) partially excluded themselves from precisely because they had chosen not to send their children to the local school. Nevertheless, the local benefits Kara highlighted – the spatial distance of the village from London, the ballet lessons, the nearby tennis and sailing clubs – paint a more homogenous and exclusive social picture of the local space than the areas depicted in the other respondents' accounts. In other words, Kara's notion of desirable community was thus perhaps not so different after all.

The sought-after communities in each of the above narratives seem more like elite enclaves based around divisions of class, for they are enclaves that require significant economic resources to join. The unknown and unfamiliar: the excluded "others" of the community, such as the Londoners (Kara), the immigrants in the neighbouring boroughs (Paul) or the strangers prowling the streets or riding the bus (Gwyneth), are greeted with suspicion or as potentially dangerous and criminal, or at the very least are positioned as further justification for making certain privileged spatial/lifestyle choices with regard to deciding where to live, where to send children to school and/or where to go to enrich children's lives with extracurricular activities.

Jess, like Kara, expressed a desire to be part of a local state school community. Furthermore, she was the only respondent among any of the men and women in the study who explicitly referred to the benefits to her own children of mixing with other children from different socio-economic backgrounds; not only that, she also referred to the risk of *only* mixing with people from the same socio-economic class – considerations that contributed to her decision to send her son, Ted, to the local state school:

> We wanted a Catholic school. And I really wanted Ted to go to the local one so we could walk to school. So we didn't really look at any other options. But I did speak to a couple of parents who sent their children there, and because they were happy, I was happy. Also, I knew there would be a mix of backgrounds, which I thought was particularly important if he goes to a private secondary school, as I don't want him growing up thinking he's better than anyone else.

Dominic was far more concise than Jess, and reasonably non-committal, in the way in which he expressed his feelings about the school his son was going to:

> Ted goes to the Catholic school at the moment, which is pretty good. Jess was quite keen for him to go somewhere local. I mean, yeah, it's fine.

Dominic did not, either in his own account or the way in which his preference of school was described by Jess, suggest that he shared his wife's understanding of the benefits for his son of mixing with a broader socio-economic group of children through attending the local school. Rather, he placed the responsibility for the decision on Jess. By doing so, Dominic, like Dan and Paul, renounced personal responsibility for the choice of school as well as the consequences of this choice (whatever they may be). By contrast, Jess's comment seems mildly ambiguous. On the one hand, she expressed desire for her son to benefit from a similarly diverse community experience the other respondents also claimed to want for their children but ultimately rejected. On the other hand, however, she also obliquely referred to inequalities in the education market and justified her choice of school based on informal market research (garnering the opinions of friends), which to some extent formed a safety net around her choice: it was not just any old school. That the school is a Catholic school also implies a mild form of segregation with regard to the intake, which also, perhaps, suggests a minor level of appeal about the perceived kinds of families that send their children there.

It is difficult to know, therefore, the extent to which Jess embraced or would embrace difference and whether she would still have sent her son to a local state school without similar assurances from friends, especially given the preference of her husband – for, of course, such a lack of assurance may have led to stronger opposition to the decision from Dominic. Moreover, Jess's choice is also partial because she said she planned to conform to Dominic's preference for private education at secondary school level (both with regard to their son and later their two daughters). Jess's desire for social mix was also framed more in terms of its benefits for her son and his all-round development, rather than in terms of social equality, although, arguably, it could loosely support the latter in terms of breaking down the myths of worthiness relating to different social classes (i.e., both readings are illustrated in Jess's comment that she didn't want her son "growing up thinking he's better than anyone else").

Nevertheless, the fact Jess explicitly stated this aspiration for her son's social awareness is significant, for it is a clear rejection of the discourse of individual worthiness based around forms of education that shapes the other respondents' comments discussed above. This includes comments made by her husband, Dominic, who elsewhere in his interview (as discussed in Chapter 3) made explicit references to being the "best of the best", where best is specifically linked with academic achievement gained through privileged forms of education. Jess's rejection of this "best-of-the-best" discourse will not necessarily, of course, prevent her son from thinking he is "better than other people" if this continues to be the discourse promoted elsewhere. Nor had it stopped Jess engaging in social practices which support the patriarchal structures that result from it, particularly giving up paid work to care for children, which she attributed not only to her choice to be at home with the children but also to the "much" higher salary Dominic received (see Chapter 4).

Future communities

The overriding sense emerging from most of these accounts of school choice is that the process is influenced by a desire to ensure one's own children attend schools with similar sorts of children, as well as a belief that schools influence the kind of person a child develops into. James suggested his motivations were similar. His son, Oscar, was still very young at the time I talked with him, but in the context of reflecting on his own and his wife, Bibi's, schooling, James explained the kinds of schools they were considering:

> I think, yeah, we probably, definitely, want to send him to a private school, but not a boarding school. I really enjoyed my time at school, which I think has made me a certain type of person. Bibi, umm... In [X] [*country, where Bibi grew up*] there are only two private schools in the

> whole country. And I think the standard of teaching there is probably much better than it is here. Her education is probably every bit as good as mine, maybe even better. Like the curriculum is quite different. So I think she's had a better all-round education, and probably socially she's better educated as well.

In this extract, there is some acknowledgement of the benefits that people may gain from certain state school options. But James' comments about social mix are somewhat ambiguous, for there is the suggestion that the social exclusivity of private schools is one at the same time both beneficial and detrimental. James' comments, however, like those of Dan and Paul, could be taken to mean that in different circumstances (i.e., in this case, living in a particular country), state school education could be an option for his son. In other words, James, like the other men, has placed a cordon around the area in which he affirms the better quality of private schooling vis-à-vis state schooling (and vice versa). In James' case, of course, the cordon embraces the whole of the UK, but it still has the same effect of localising the problem of poor quality schooling in order to justify the final choice. Similarly, it is impossible to know, of course, whether or not James would freely choose a state school for his son if there were a local option he deemed suitable (however he measured this). Meanwhile, Bibi seemed to be of a similar opinion:

> If there is a state school [option] that is good, then maybe, but if I am a bit unsure and we can afford private, then I would definitely go private. If it's a state school, it will be with probably extra private tuition, 'cos I do believe in that.

The partial, localised dismissal of state schooling by the men and women may have been a way of legitimising their preference for private schooling in the eyes of others (including me) who might question their choice; it certainly narrows the space to contest it.

Of the other two couples in the study, David and Emma also conformed to elements of the hegemonic discourse in elite finance regarding the link between types of schooling (private versus state) and notions of worthiness, as well as social practices relating to different forms of schooling. They each explained that if David's salary were to rise then they would consider privately educating their daughter because of the better facilities in private schools. If David's salary stayed the same, however, then they were planning to send Millie to a local state Catholic school. Emma, like Jess, qualified her and David's choice of school through referring to peer recommendations: "We would have a look around at different schools, but [X] Catholic School would be my preference. And from what I've heard so far, it is quite a good school".

David, on the other hand, like Dominic, renounced personal responsibility for the choice:

> Emma's Catholic and she is keen to bring Millie up in the Catholic faith and wants her to go to a Catholic school. So I think if we managed to get Millie into one of the local Catholic schools, we'd be happy. I would prefer private education because of the facilities, unless you could find an area that offers a diverse… all the activities that you would do.

Neither David nor Emma, therefore, explicitly mentioned the community benefit of going to a local school; the potential community benefit appeared to predominantly derive from the Catholic element, with the nearness of the school a supplementary but not vital benefit.

Graham and Ayami were very matter-of-fact in their accounts of school choice and were the only couple who placed the decision as one of "the system": a consequence of the official process of state school allocations in London, rather than negotiations within the family. They did not go into much detail about the process of school choice or the actual choice itself. In the case of Graham, this could reflect his self-professed left-wing political leanings (i.e., that he rejects the principle of private education, although he did not state this). With respect to Ayami, this could reflect the fact that she grew up overseas and may have had differing understanding of and opinion about the UK education system to the other respondents. Nevertheless, both Graham and Ayami commented briefly on the issue, explaining and approving of the fact that the school their four-year-old daughter, Mimi, was going to go to was in close geographic proximity to their apartment.

> Mimi is going to the school on [X] Road, which is really handy. Yeah, so that's good.
>
> (Ayami)

> Once Mimi's school had been decided, that was good. She's going to the school just round the corner, so that makes it a bit easier.
>
> (Graham)

As a final point of interest in thinking about the "future communities" of schooling, Dan, Paul and Matt commented on future aspirations they had for their children:

> I don't know if other parents say this, but as long as they're stretched academically as far as they should be stretched, that's kind of fine. You know, I'd feel very disappointed if I felt they hadn't stretched themselves as far as they could stretch.
>
> (Dan)

> I want Zac to be self-motivated, and I want him to be confident, and I want him to… not be gullible. 'Cos he's frighteningly honest, and it could be a problem, because people can take advantage of him. I mean, in any competitive situation, you know, there are an awful lot of people who take advantage of, you know, gullible people in the world.
>
> (Paul)

> I don't have massive aspirations but, you know, I want them to be happy. And you realise, you know, you think, "Well, oh god, maybe it doesn't matter if they don't go to the prize-winning school or this, that and the other …".
>
> (Matt)

It is important to reflect on these extracts for two reasons. First, because they align with the men's narratives on school choice and confirm the merits of each of the men's choices. Second, they reaffirm the indicators of the men's own material and social worth highlighted in their earlier narratives about banking and fatherhood, including intelligence, hard work, competitiveness, and ideas around winning and being successful. These final extracts are thus significant because they confirm, support and further illustrate the cyclical nature of existing processes of hegemony in global finance. In other words, they illustrate how social practices in the family, including school choice, along with the ideology that underpins these practices, in turn support social practices in the elite financial workplace along with the ideology that underpins them, and vice versa, in an ongoing loop of privilege transference and embodiment.

Conclusion

Education is a crucial site of and for social justice (Unterhalter 2007; David 2014). It is a contested terrain where different social, cultural and institutional complexities limit the possibilities for empowering all individuals because certain gendered ideologies, organisational structures and processes and individual and collective identities are valued over others. Decisions relating to school choice discussed in this chapter, along with the ways in which these choices are explained by the men and women, reveal how a cyclical process of privilege, operating within the families of elite City bankers, supports and strengthens processes of hegemony linked with global finance. It is not just that children with affluent parents already have one step on the social ladder, although this is incredibly significant in and of itself. It is also that, in both the men's and the women's narratives of school choice, socio-economic/class-based divisions are reinforced in ways which assert and justify the economic authority of the men and their families. Moreover, this combines with acclamations of intellectual and moral superiority associated with privileged forms of private schooling and the people who attend private schools and the concomitant disparagement of other social groups. This, in turn, combines with ideas around desirable forms of community linked with notions of space, freedom and belonging.

What is gained through exploring these narratives of school choice, therefore, is valuable insight into hegemony's organisation of "experience through an esprit de corps" and its ability to sustain an "uninterrupted historical continuity" (Gramsci 1971: 7) across generations. In the search for particular forms of community – including communities for their children to live, be educated and socialise in – the affluent workers of City finance, with their selective and expensive residential, lifestyle and schooling choices, help widen the ever-increasing spatial polarisation between rich and poor not only in the global city of London but beyond. While the notion of community is often framed in the men's and women's narratives as though it is a coming together of people, on closer inspection, it is a coming together of particular kinds of people embodying particular kinds of diversity and difference. It is not, therefore, a broad, all-embracing notion of community. Instead, it is a narrow notion of community that works to preserve its own interests and cordon itself off; and much like the elite City workplace community it is connected to, it is a community that requires significant resources to join. So while developing, enacting and conferring a sense of community and shared identity can signal a desire for and process of cohesiveness that brings people from different walks of life together, it can also, as explained above, involve an inward-turning process of introspection, discrimination and exclusivity.

Notes

1 State schools that select their intake based on some form of entrance exam.
2 A form of selective state schooling.
3 Common Entrance Exams are set by the UK Independent Schools Examinations Board and are taken by children as part of the admissions process to senior-level independent (private) schools in the UK (see www.iseb.co.uk/Parents/What-is-Common-Entrance).

Chapter 5

A community in crisis

This book has explored the reciprocal relationship between the work and family lives of elite City bankers. In order to complete this self-perpetuating loop of privilege and the book's momentary insight into it, this chapter returns to the City to consider what City bankers' narratives of redundancy reveal about processes of spatial and gendered hegemony relating to global finance.

The collapse of the US housing market in 2007 marked the beginning of a widespread period of economic decline that the International Monetary Fund has termed "the Global Recession" (Cerra and Saxena 2017). It was not until September 2008 and the shock bankruptcy of Lehman Brothers, a 158-year-old Wall Street Bank, however, that the community of banking was really thrown into turmoil. When I started my fieldwork a few months after the collapse of Lehman Brothers, there was a great deal of adverse publicity about banking fuelled by this latest financial crisis. This hostility intensified as severe government austerity measures were announced in the UK at the same time as substantial government bailout payments were made to wealthy City-based banks, including Royal Bank of Scotland and Lloyds (Wintour and Elliot 2010; Treanor 2012) (see Introduction).

The 2008 financial crisis was not, of course, brought about exclusively by the actions of profit-hungry banks or bankers (Ho 2009: 298); many people working in the industry lost their jobs during swathes of redundancies, including within prestigious banks based in the City of London and on Wall Street, with the fallout deep and long-lasting. For example, in 2015, Reuters reported that British banks had cut 186,111 jobs since the crisis, with thousands more losses still planned (Edwards 2015). Nevertheless, the structures, practices and cultures of financial institutions did play a significant part in the crisis and have since faced considerable scrutiny from politicians, media, academics and financial regulators. Concerns raised include: lack of diversity (both gender and racial) in parts of the finance industry – particularly at elite levels – and how this might lead to "group think" or complacent "herd behaviour" (Tucker 2010: 11; see also HoC 2010; Sands 2013; Sealy and Vinnicombe 2013); and lack of regulation in the industry, particularly in the context of the "free market" discourse, with prominent issues including bankers' remuneration levels, and whether or not all practices bankers engage in and all products banks promote and sell are ethical (see, for example, HoC 2009; Deloitte 2013).

Banks responded to the criticism of the finance industry by articulating a discourse of morality and trustworthiness, which since the crisis has featured evermore prominently in their promotional online material. Deutsche Bank (2018d) and Goldman Sachs (2018h) have each drawn up a "Code of Business Conduct and Ethics". Deutsche Bank (2018d) has additionally appointed an "Integrity Committee" that reviews the bank's Code "with a view to [foster] ethical and moral conduct within and outside the bank". Goldman Sachs (2018b), meanwhile, declares, "integrity and honesty are at the heart of our business". In Barclays' Code of Conduct – "The Barclays Way" – the bank outlines, "...the Values and Behaviours which govern our Barclays way of working across our business globally ...[including] act[ing] fairly, ethically and openly in all we do" (Barclays 2015).

Credit Suisse (2018), meanwhile, states that "long-term success depends on our ability to inspire trust and achieve client satisfaction". The bank also has a "Code of Conduct" within which it explains its "vision to become the world's most admired bank" and presents a "framework" to "maintain and strengthen our reputation for integrity, fair dealing and measured risk-taking" (Credit Suisse 2010). J.P. Morgan (2018e), similarly, aspires to foster "a culture that stresses the highest ethical standards" in its "aim to be the world's most trusted and respected financial institution".

This industry-wide morality discourse of trust, integrity and ethical responsibility embraces formal institutional systems and practices as well as informal organisational cultures – all of which feed into processes of hegemony relating to global finance. As such, it implies there exists a widely shared sense of what acting fairly, ethically and openly means, in practice not just in rhetoric (Klein 2007; see also Harvey 2010; Ventura 2012), and could signal a significant change in the zeitgeist. It is not clear, however, whether or how such principles can truly coexist with other values that continue to be promoted by global finance (see previous chapters) and whether this presents, therefore, any kind of substantial opportunity to disrupt and change existing hegemonic processes. For example, Caterino and Hansen (2009: 88) have argued that competitive individualism, with its focus on bettering the self above all else, undermines democratic values and opportunities (see also Ventura 2012; Wilkinson and Pickett 2019). The irony here, of course, is that many of the above extracts from the banking literature unproblematically combine an ethical responsibility discourse with that of competitive individualism (e.g., J.P. Morgan's aim to be "the world's most trusted institution") and a sense of superiority (e.g., Goldman Sachs' suggestion that it is the agent of morality). Yet, as Connell (2010) has noted, the neoliberal discourse of market rationality, evidenced through desensitising language of opportunity, innovation, efficiency, rationality, progress and market leadership, helps strip emotion and compassion from the workplace and justify certain practices, such as downsizing.

As discussed elsewhere in this book, however, inconsistencies and irregularities are already commonplace in the systems of elite finance, not only sustaining but also strengthening existing processes of hegemony. The inherent incompleteness of hegemony, meanwhile, allows it to absorb new components and refashion itself accordingly, all the while rearticulating and promoting a common-sense narrative. This is not to undermine the response of financial institutions to calls for greater responsibility and accountability in the industry, but it is to suggest that such change may not actually destabilise existing processes of hegemony relating to global finance. On the contrary, it could be that this new moral dimension simply provides existing processes of hegemony with increased legitimacy in much the same way that new ideals of hands-on fatherhood have been absorbed (see Chapter 3).

What has not been particularly clear, however, either during the immediate furore surrounding the 2008 financial crisis or subsequently, is how elite City bankers have positioned the banks they work for and themselves as bankers in all of the debates about the morality of the industry and its practices. This positioning is important to consider because elite City bankers are central actors in maintaining the processes that support the domination and authority of global finance in the City, in the UK and elsewhere. With this in mind, this chapter focuses particularly on the ways in which the bankers discussed redundancy, because while conditions within elite finance have seductive dimensions, they are also shot through with instability, and the process of redundancy is a key component in what Ho (2009: 274) has described as the "risk-reward bargain" nature of elite finance. Elite City bankers, as Sassen (2009b) has observed, may be paid very well, but they have no claim over the capitalist system in which they work and are seen as a disposable resource by banks even in prosperous times, let alone in bad – a situation that in itself problematises the self-proclaimed ethical and responsible nature of global banking. Nevertheless, findings discussed in other chapters of this book reveal the close intertwining of the work and family lives of the bankers in this study and suggest the everyday practices of bankers and their families are heavily enmeshed in the current system and existing hegemonic processes of global finance and predominantly favour maintaining the status quo. Bankers' narratives about redundancy at a time when the prospect of losing one's job was heightened and the industry faced intense criticism offer a valuable window into issues linked to both the social responsibility and the competitive individualism discourses of global banking, as well as any contestations that may exist between the two that could represent the unsettling of processes of hegemony.

Redundancy and the game of elite finance

The decision

Redundancy was a common theme in the discussions I had with the men, even though I did not include a specific question about it. While in general, it was referred to in the context of the financial crisis, what was said offers interesting insight into the more general process of and practices relating to redundancy.

The two most senior bankers I interviewed – Paul and Matt – talked about the process of redundancy in terms of making colleagues redundant:

HL: So you mentioned the job losses in the City – has [this bank] had many redundancies because of the cri ... [*Matt interrupts*]?

MATT: Yeah, yeah. In 2008 we did but not massively.

Matt spoke in a very off-hand way, as if not wanting to go into any more detail and finished his comment abruptly. Perhaps this was not particularly surprising given the criticism of the industry at the time, as well as the unpleasantness of the task at hand. Nonetheless, Matt had been very forthcoming and chatty throughout his interview, and so I probed a little more:

HL: Are you responsible for doing some of that?

MATT: I have been, yeah.

HL: And do you find that a bit stressful?

MATT: Umm, err, it varies – it can be. I'm not a particular fan of it. But I think that some ... I think you can kind of work on open communication with people. So people should understand what the parameters are. We have evaluation committees; people get feedback. But not everybody gets it. The first person I ever made redundant said to me, "Matt, if I were in your position, I would do exactly the same thing" [*he laughs*]. It was quite extraordinary. But I've let other people go who just don't get it at all. And you can get lawsuits. I was quite taken aback by it when it first happened – they didn't have legal grounds at all; the legal case got dropped in a heartbeat.

Despite Matt's reluctance to divulge much detail about redundancy, his comments raise some interesting points. First, the words he used adhere closely to rational market language and reveal little in the way of emotion. This supports the discourse of meritocracy in elite banking and the apparently rational process that leads to either success or failure in the industry. This is interesting because findings discussed in previous chapters of this book suggest quite strongly that the routes to success in banking are not necessarily always clearly defined, logical or consistent.

Second, and seemingly contrary to Matt's reference to a straightforward rational process of "quality control" or performance management, is the way in which he expressed surprise that someone who had been identified as not meeting the latest grade shared this knowledge and agreed that he or she should be dismissed. It could be, of course, that Matt's surprise related to his own inability, as an extremely and rapidly successful banker, to understand why, if someone was seemingly clued-up enough to get into banking in the first place and understand the "parameters" therein, they would not succeed, or not want to succeed.

And the final point of interest is Matt's reference to the lawsuit filed by the ex-employee he mentioned, which underscores the dispassionate and contradictory character of the financial workplace. Contradictory because the lawsuit implies, from the point of view of the ex-employee, that the rules of elite finance are not necessarily clear or rational, yet from the point of view of banks and those in charge of them, that if an employee does not understand the rules of the game then he/she does not deserve to be playing it anyway. In Matt's anecdote, the rules of elite finance are portrayed as steadfast, including in the eyes of the law, and are therefore the only viable rules – redundancy, however unpleasant, is a rational, inevitable end for those who do not, for whatever reason, follow the rules.

Paul made a similar reference to rationality and some kind of universal assessment criteria when he talked about making colleagues redundant during the financial crisis:

> There are people in there who, you know, there's half of them you should have got rid of anyway, 'cos they're basically underperformers. OK, there's a bit of soul searching about a couple of names, but it's normally generally quite straightforward, you know – the underperformers. I mean, some people have been taking the piss for years and stuff, and you can finally deal with them … It's a bit harder at the moment … you try and make rational decisions, but you have to start cutting into people you like, people who work hard and are good at their job, and you try not to let that influence you. But you know it's right because the firm won't survive otherwise …

The detached nature of the language Paul used to describe the normal process of redundancy (i.e., "straightforward", "underperformers") is quite explicit. And, despite glimmers of contestation seen in Paul's references to "soul-searching" and "cutting into people" he likes, it is significant that the demands of the rational market, rather than compassion for individuals, appear to ultimately dictate and justify the process of redundancy as it normally occurs in good times as well as bad. As Connell (2010: 784–5) has written, downsizing is positioned as good for everyone, even though it means inevitably some people lose their jobs (and potentially much more because of it);

while redundancies of colleagues may occasionally be considered unfortunate or even sad by managers like Paul, the market-rationality discourse positions redundancies as inevitable and how it has to be – necessary for a firm to "survive", stay efficient and maintain competitiveness in an ever-changing "free" market (see also Giroux 2007, 2011). This rationale reinforces the separation between the workplace and people's private lives, and the prioritisation of the former. It also problematises banks' supposed concern for employee well-being by promoting a pragmatic engagement with what are essentially very personal processes, as well as disembodiment from the social consequences of these processes (see Hearn and Parkin 2001; Connell and Wood 2005). It is a method of developing detachment and dispassion that Richard Sennett (1998) has termed the "corrosion of character", which culminates in humane qualities such as empathy, loyalty and caring for others being considered signs of weakness and set in contrast to other, exalted traits, such as dynamism, competiveness and individualism. It also seems at odds with banks' self-professed focus on developing a culture of ethical responsibility.

The continued dominance of rational market ideology underpins the patriarchal nature of the elite financial workplace – both Matt's and Paul's comments reflect the meritocracy discourse of elite banking and imply the people who do not succeed in banking, in "normal" times at least, are essentially not cut out for it anyway: not smart enough, competitive enough or sufficiently hard-working. This legitimises the structures and practices of reward in elite finance, which continue overall to favour men over women in remuneration and promotion practices. It also further implies that the particular group of men who dominate the higher echelons of City banking (men like Matt and Paul) rightfully do so. Paul's reference to "underperformers" is especially significant, for it appears to place the long hours culture as not only central to individual success in the elite financial workplace but also the benchmark by which everyone's institutional and individual worth is measured: those who do not work as hard as others do not deserve to be there; they are the people who "take the piss". This, of course, renders invisible or unimportant the kinds of private family support structures in place that enable many high-status bankers (Paul and Matt included) to work the long hours they do.

The process

Dominic and Graham also talked about redundancy in the context of the 2008 financial crisis. Neither had been involved in redundancy first hand, but both provided illuminating insight as observers of the process.

DOMINIC: There are plenty of people that have lost their jobs and plenty of people that, you know … Err, one guy I work with is going to lose his job.

HL: Really? Does …

DOMINIC: It's pretty hard, you know. I know this guy and can't really say anything to him. Well, obviously, I can't say anything to him; I can't say *anything* to him. But you know that within a week's time he's not going to be – he's going to be packing up.

HL: Do you know why? Is it because …

DOMINIC: Well, he's in a group where there's like seven of them, they're probably massively, I think most people would think that group is over-resourced given the amount of revenue they've generated, or whatever else. Umm, yeah [*he sighs*], and he's one of the newer guys in there, one of the more junior-ish guys … To be honest, I think he's actually pretty good, there's two or three others I would get rid of before I got rid of him, personally. But it's all about who his manager, you know, who the manager of that group wants to get rid of.

Much of Dominic's story resonates with the comments of Matt and Paul above: the focus on market demands and performance – in this case a clear focus on performance and returns. There is also a direct reference to Nomi Prins' (2009: 151) line of ascent argument that advancement can depend as much on whom you work for as how well/hard you work (or seem to be working) or, indeed, your future potential. This also links, to some extent, with Paul's account of having to personally decide whom to "get rid of" despite the supposed rational rules of the game that should, so we are told, naturally weed out the wheat from the chaff. The disciplining control such practices of downsizing have over workplace regimes is significant: they coercively make people work hard as well as curb people's emotional attachment to colleagues. Although this is in keeping with competitive individualism, it seems quite removed from the all-embracing, nurturing and collegiate workplace banks depict in their promotional literature as well as the discourse of ethical responsibility they have increasingly endorsed.

Graham also described the process of redundancy at the bank he worked for in the context of recent waves that had occurred due to the 2008 financial crisis:

> There were big rounds last February. We lost a quarter of our partners. My boss is, umm, I wouldn't say he's a 'yes man' but he's quite keen to show he's very proactive. So, you know, some fought really hard, whereas my boss sort of turned round and said, "Right, the first cut's the deepest". But it's quite scary seeing the brunt of it. We knew the date was coming as well. So you sat at your desk – you had to be at your desk at 2pm. In another department, if your phone rang, it was you that was … you know. They didn't do that to us, but I don't know how they did it really. As far as I was aware, everyone was at their desk at 2, which is what you were told to do. I get a feeling they told everyone and then

grabbed the people who were getting it before 2 o'clock because it came to sort of 3 and I hadn't heard anything and then I realised the girl who sat across the office hadn't come back from lunch yet, and I thought "Oh … oh!" … She sat right there and I didn't even notice. It's not nice, not nice at all.

Graham offered quite a stark account of the process of culling unwanted employees, as well as the ways in which colleagues (soon-to-be-ex or otherwise) are positioned in such a process as faceless and anonymous beings, like "the girl" he sat opposite to. Although Graham was highly critical of the process, his use of the diminutive term "girl" served to position his ex-colleague as a vulnerable victim within a heartless power struggle. In other words, this dispassionate process designed to engender fear and compliance as well as the way in which it was described conforms to the narrative of "survival of the fittest", or the "survival of the most powerful" (Graham's boss) and the concomitant discarding of the weakest (i.e., "the girl" in Graham's office, or the "newest guy" in Dominic's). The hierarchical structure of worthiness in banking is, both in Dominic's and in Graham's account, infused with a corresponding hierarchical structure of power and authority, which governs the elite financial workplace through fear and compliance. The fear element is important for it can spur on the competitors who survive by providing a further source of adrenalin along with the rush one might experience from closing a deal, winning a new client or earning a large bonus.

The experience

James was the only banker in the study to have to date been made redundant during his banking career (or at least, he was the only one who openly admitted to it). I interviewed him six months after he was made redundant from his job in Sydney. He explained:

JAMES: So, I was made redundant when Oscar was three months old. You know, Bibi wasn't that well when she had Oscar – she had to go back into hospital. So I guess they were quite good about it in a way 'cos I just said, "Look, I've got to take the time off", and [I] took a few days straight away, you know, paternity and some holiday as well. When they did make me redundant, they said, "it's been on the cards for a while". So I don't know if they'd actually delayed it a bit because my wife was pregnant, so they just wanted to wait until we'd had the baby. And maybe they waited a couple of months to make sure we weren't going to go nuts and then, you know, dropped us in it then.

HL: Did you think about staying in Sydney?

JAMES: Yeah, yeah, but … you know, I had wanted to work there for at least four years, and choose when to stop, not be pushed out. And I thought

> my job was secure: they got rid of all the people who weren't very good at their job in the first wave and then some more people in the second, and I was in the third wave. And the other thing is, you only have 30 days to stay on on your visa once you are made redundant, so we didn't really have a choice to stay. And Bibi couldn't work because her qualifications are valid in Europe but not in Australia. But, you know, in Sydney I was doing some pretty interesting stuff. And I wouldn't change anything. I think it's, you know, I learnt a lot by going out there; it was a really good opportunity.

James did not go into detail about the actual dismissal itself, although his wife, Bibi, referred to it briefly:

HL: So did [James], do you think he suspected he would be made redundant?

BIBI: No, umm, no, not at all. Umm, the way it worked – they were told one day and they had to clear their desk and leave immediately.

James' account of the broader aspects of the process of redundancy, including the experience of being unemployed, resonates with aspects of hegemonic processes discussed in previous chapters, particularly when considered alongside other comments James made. For example, there is an overriding sense of the separation between work and private lives, which ultimately culminates in a lack of concern from employers about the latter, despite the fact, as James explained, the bank "waited a couple of months to make sure" he and Bibi "weren't going to go nuts". There is also a strong link with the contradictory notion of mobility in global finance – James' use of the word "push" is interesting in light of this, because it reinforces the immediacy and forcefulness with which banks demand and make decisions about all forms of mobility linked with elite banking. Banks' promotional literature evokes a sense of freedom about bankers' ability to develop their own career trajectories (if bankers work hard and do well, they will have choices), including opportunities to travel and work overseas. Yet there seems to be little in what the men shared about their own experiences of working in elite finance to suggest that employees can, in fact, freely engage with these kinds of potential opportunities or, in the case of travel (short business trips or semi-permanent overseas placements), much evidence to infer they necessarily want to engage in them. For example, James relocated with his wife overseas to work in a particular job, but this was prompted by the fact the promotion he originally sought in London (and strongly believed he was getting) was given to a colleague (see Chapter 2). As such, he did not freely search out job opportunities in Australia because that is where he wanted to work. This suggests, instead, a lack of freedom, as well as the fungibility of financial employees (see also Ho 2009) despite banks' claims that employees are all sought after, valued and nurtured for their individual, "unique" qualities. James' alternative enactment of mobility (both career and location) also required him and his wife to make significant changes in their lives. These changes underscore the restrictive form of freedom that mobility in banking seems to rest on: James had to change his employer in order to progress in his career, as well as move halfway around the world – he explained elsewhere how he changed banks because of the limited opportunities he was offered if he stayed where he was in the City (see Chapter 2). Bibi, meanwhile, had to suspend her career completely in order to move with James to Australia – her decision to do so (however freely made) supports the patriarchal practices both of and associated with elite banking.

Mobility practices, as argued already, and which can now be seen to also include the somewhat violent practice of redundancy, constitute a form of institutional control over elite financial workers in the public and private realm and are important components of the processes of hegemony in global finance. In the context of James' remarks about redundancy, other practices governing the notion of mobility in banking have a slightly different connotation yet again to the sense of immediacy combined with opportunity discussed in previous chapters – and this is a sense of immediacy combined with disposability; an institutional form, if you like, of conspicuous consumption. However, James' account also illustrates how these practices of banking-related mobility, including the dispassionate practices of disposability, occur within the broader discourse of competitive individualism. This is significant for it helps legitimise banks' ultimate renunciation of employee well-being.

For example, James explained how he had "wanted to work [in Sydney] for four years and choose when to stop, not be pushed out". He also explained how he was told that his redundancy "had been on the cards for a while". Thus, while James was made redundant during a time of serious financial instability, his account indicates a more deep-rooted inevitability about his dismissal (even though James claimed not to have seen it coming) and hence an underlying impermanence about the whole system as well as a lack of control on the part of employees with respect to determining their own career trajectory. James' account also, however, through its suggestion of inevitability, reflects the language of competitive individualism through which people are positioned as solely responsible for themselves and what happens to them in private and public realms (both their successes and their failures). James' acceptance of his experience, the fact he said he "wouldn't change a thing", legitimises not only his redundancy and the way it occurred but also the whole process of which it is a part: the life cycle of an elite banking career – the recruitments, the rewards and the dismissals – and all the competitive, aggressive and unpredictable practices encountered within it.

Mobility practices in elite banking, whether relating to "success" (promotion) or "failure" (redundancy), can be understood as a largely one-sided process of control. When banks decide an employee is no longer useful, he or she is discarded; the process is sudden and harsh, as the following narrative from James illustrates:

> They shipped us out [to Australia], flew us out, you know. Going out there was brilliant 'cos they do everything for you. But on the way back, it's a little more; it's not in the contract ... So there's a lot of people in a similar position who just didn't envisage that would happen. You don't really plan for something like that. So yeah, I had to do a bit of negotiating. But there are some stories out there which are worse than ours. There's a guy who got made redundant in the first round and he ... he was made redundant when his wife was 8 months pregnant, so they couldn't even fly back home. And I think that's probably part of the reason why I did a little bit better than him, 'cos I think he's gonna, you know, sue the firm. But, yeah, definitely they treated me better on the way out – business class flights and everything's done straight away. They put you up in a really nice hotel and give you a relocation agency to help you find somewhere, and a lump sum in cash for inconvenience costs. Whereas, on the way back, you know, they don't. And it's economy flights, and it took months for our stuff to come through. But at least we got it back [*James later explained that the bank eventually agreed to cover the basic costs of shipping their belongings back to the UK*].

Although James suggested previously that the bank was "quite good about it in a way" because they held off from making him redundant until his son was three months old, it is questionable from James' description whether or not empathy lay at the heart of the bank's decision to wait, or whether the delay was more to do with concern about damage to the bank's reputation from another prospective lawsuit. Either way, however, it does seem there is some potential room for contesting aspects of such a harsh process of redundancy – if enough people, like James and his colleague, question parts of the process and demand more sympathetic, if not humane, treatment, the pressure for change might be greater. Incidentally, James' account also highlights the inequalities in a system which pays off CEOs with vast remuneration packages when they are made redundant but cuts other people off with minimal assistance (see Sassen 2009a).

Elsewhere in his interview, James talked in more detail about the difficulties of finding a job back in London. In doing so, he demonstrated why change, if it is to occur, requires a more fundamental overhaul of the ideology of banking:

> You never really know exactly why you were made redundant, you know. I don't know if maybe I was politically incorrect with a couple of people. Or maybe I was earning too much. Or ... you never really know the real reason. I think that means maybe that when I do get back in,

> I'm just going to make sure there's absolutely, that it's never going to happen again. So play the game a bit better and just do the best I can... Yeah, I'll have to work even harder when I get back in.

As long as employees stick rigidly to the discourse of competitive individualism and the belief that everyone is responsible for their own success or failure and thus deserve their fate (whatever it might be, and despite the fact that, as James suggested, individuals often have no clear idea of what the rules of the game of elite finance are), then change will be difficult. Not only does such adherence to this notion of individualism and the belief that the overarching system is neutral (and natural) support a general lack of empathy for others, it also legitimises the status quo. It is significant that James linked the difficulties he was experiencing finding another job with the financial crisis but did not explicitly link his redundancy to it, choosing instead to blame himself.

When considering how central the practice of redundancy is to hegemonic processes linked with global finance, there are four more points of interest in James' account. First, there is an important contradiction in his explanation, which supports the sense of exclusivity of elite banking and those who succeed in it. This is his suggestion that one should be able to react to or prepare for the unexpected, which is an example of squeezing both avoidable and unavoidable aspects of the game of banking into a rational, naturalising discourse. On the one hand, James suggested that no one ever really knows why they are made redundant, and yet, on the other, he also stated that he was going to make "absolutely sure" that redundancy never happened to him again. It is, of course, precisely this contradiction between certainty and ambiguity regarding the rules of the game of elite finance, however nonsensical they may seem, that helps make it so compelling to play – if everyone knew the rules, then success would not be so exalted and sought after, and winning (even if you win not really ever fully knowing what the rules are) would perhaps not be so satisfying or imbued with the same sense of status. There is then, it seems, a relinquishing of complaining rights by bankers who engage in this rationalisation process.

The second point of interest, which is closely linked with the first, is James' remark that, having experienced redundancy, he will, in future, work even harder than he did before. Earlier in his interview, however, he explained how his working day in Sydney began, on average, at 7am and finished at 10pm. It is thus difficult to comprehend how he could work much harder, especially with a young family to help care for, a marriage to nurture and his own health and well-being to look after (unless of course he was not actually doing much while at work in Sydney, which seems incredibly unlikely). The third point of interest is related to the second. And this is the fact that James' comment about working harder reinforces and legitimises both the separation of work and home, where work commitments are prioritised over physical presence in the family home, and the patriarchal practices associated with this separation, including breadwinning ideals of fatherhood. The fourth, and final, point of interest is James' reference to being politically incorrect, for this seems to suggest that playing the game of finance successfully requires the contestant to be on the right team (and prior to that, to even know which the right team is), which is a clear nod once more to Prins' line of ascent argument.

Redundancy then, both the first-hand experience of it and the threat of experiencing it, appears to play a crucial role in shaping and conferring hegemonic processes in elite banking. It is particularly linked with the seductiveness of the potential rewards that can be reaped from doing well and the dedication and hard work required to do so. This is in terms of both the work the men did in the workplace and the work their wives and other people did to help care for the separated space of the home and family during the men's absence.

The overriding acceptance of and lack of criticism of the process of redundancy, even when the harshness of it is recognised, may seem surprising. Yet the ways in which the men talked about it does seem to provide further evidence of its central role in the structures and practices of elite banking. This connects with Ho's (2009: 226) observation that downsizing is perhaps Wall Street's "most consistent cultural practice", in times of economic prosperity as well as in times of crisis. The crux of the issue for Ho (p. 252), however, was that the pervasiveness of downsizing, combined with the relative ease with which Wall Street bankers were able to find another job and the discourse of the rational market, meant that her respondents showed little empathy for any workers (elite bankers or not) who lost their jobs. The men's narratives above, however, suggest that during a time of crisis at least, there *are* glimmers of empathy around redundancy, although these are ultimately overruled by the rationality discourse. While this illustrates a potential weak point in the process, it also illustrates the strength of the current system.

A compelling game

In the men's references to the 2008 financial crisis, the banking industry as a whole – as well as the individual banks the men worked for – was distanced from the underlying causes of the crisis. This collective disavowal of blame is significant because it further suggests that the system is ultimately still credible, workable and dependable, despite the weaknesses of some individual players (bankers or banks (e.g., Lehman Brothers)) and periods of serious financial crisis. For example, Matt explained that:

> The blame is so broad-based. No one's apportioned it right. It should be taken at a number of levels. Governments hugely encouraged this provision of credit and loans to poor people and said it was a great thing. They hugely enjoyed the tax receipts they got from banks making lots of money. Umm, they totally overlooked regulation, you know – there's very few of these things done that were actually illegal, against

> regulations. So I think it's very rich for governments to blame the bank for lending too much money. There was perfectly good motivation behind it: banks were trying to extend credit broader and more deeply to the population. Allowing people to have more credit means more people have opportunities, so there's good social objective there. But clearly some people were encouraged to buy houses. 'Cos you know, they thought they could afford them and didn't really realise what was going on. So there is abuse at a number of levels. But house-borrowers should have known what they could afford, they're not stupid, these are adults.

Matt's account contains traces of the official morality discourse of banks discussed above. Not only does it acquit the industry in general from blame, but it also positions banks as moral do-gooders "extending their credit further" to those in need. As such, banks are rendered non-accountable for the crisis as well as the difficulties many people were/are still experiencing because of it. Matt's comment additionally suggests that capitalism's fundamental focus on profit maximisation and the link between material worth, opportunity, freedom and social betterment is a universally shared ideology. When combined, these aspects of Matt's narrative are significant, for they endorse the overarching merit of the industry, the power and authority of wealthy City banks and, of course, his own social positioning – his social worthiness as a well-paid City banker – and the structures and practices in his professional and private life that have helped facilitate his success.

James also stood firm in his allegiance to the industry, which is interesting given the lack of institutional loyalty he had experienced in return:

> The average investment banker has got nothing to do with the recession ... I think the general public want things to change – there's this whole uproar with how well bankers have been paid, and I think a lot of that is jealousy, because the average person wants to be in that position. So they'll say, "No! This is outrageous, we need to change the whole system." But it's a typical case of the British press writing these horror stories. They always want to blame someone so, of course, "the bankers – it's all their fault". But the reality is, it isn't the bankers' fault at all, 'cos, you know, it's the Government's fault, and if it's any bankers' fault, it's the Central Bank. They all knew exactly what was going on [with mortgage lending]... As soon as the market starts to turn, that's when we get ourselves into the position we've just been in: you get a recession and everyone starts pointing fingers.

James' account, like that of Matt, connects with the morality discourse of banks, to the extent that banks and their employees, which were positioned as relatively blameless by Matt, were completely blameless according to James. Furthermore, in both James' and Matt's accounts, the crisis was seen as both the consequence and the problem of poor governance and/or other people's deficiency: the greedy Government; the incompetent or condoning Central Bank; the "jealous" general public (or what James termed the "average person" – i.e., presumably non-bankers); or the "stupid house borrowers" that Matt identified. Phrased in this way, bankers and the existing ways of banking, including bankers' unusually high remuneration levels, are not only normalised, but also become the benchmark (moral as well as social) for everyone else to aspire to – the benchmark that everyone else is apparently aspiring to – instead of key components in an unequal, unjust and unworkable system. Furthermore, problems inherent in neoliberal capitalism are also evaded.

In some respects, this sidestepping of responsibility for, if not insouciance about, what occurs in financial markets seems at odds with the ways in which banks position and promote themselves and their employees as experts in finance, financial products and financial markets, as well as the personal business approach and attention to detail they claim to make (see Chapters 2 and 3). And yet it is consistent with the general lack of self-criticism among the men expressed in general (see Chapter 3), and their adherence to the rational market discourse discussed above.

The men also, interestingly, showed particular loyalty to the banks they worked for. This is surprising considering the arbitrary nature of the game of finance and the lack of reciprocal loyalty shown by banks (despite their official claims to do so). It is, however, perhaps reflective of the danger of whistleblowing in the industry. For example, one banker interviewed for a Guardian blog series that ran from 2011 to 2013 (see Luyendijk 2013) mentioned restrictions placed on bankers (especially senior bankers) by banks to talk freely about their jobs especially with regard to anything that might reflect the industry in a negative light. In fact, while I was talking with Matt, he directly checked with me that I was not "an investigative reporter".

While James and Matt showed general support for the whole industry and distanced it from the root causes of the financial crisis, Matt did the same for the individual bank he worked for:

> This institution's probably uncommon in that it, you know, we just weren't at the centre of the mis-selling, a lot of the risk-taking. And that was something that was, err, you know, extremely difficult for us to justify to shareholders for a number of years while it looked like others were being more successful.

Likewise, Paul, Dominic and Graham also absolved the banks they worked for from any blame, using noticeably similar language to Matt:

> I think [this bank's] been quite unfortunate, you know. We've taken a big hit … No one knows what's happening; no one really knows.
>
> (Paul)

> I think it's unfortunate ... [this bank] didn't need any government bailout; the other banks kind of screwed it up for us. And now, kind of Europe, you can't have sovereign defaults and the breakup of the Euro not affect the rest of the world.
>
> (Dominic)

> It's unfortunate how [this bank] got affected actually. We made a few mistakes, but this other bit, that you just can't do anything about, when you're tied to the stock market, that's it – you're just at the mercy of it.
>
> (Graham)

The men's disavowal of blame, whether of the industry or of the individual banks they worked for and thus, by default, themselves, is quite striking. And yet, through this association of the crisis with broader forces positioned as largely out of one's control, both banks and bankers are able to assert and affirm their own and the current financial system's credibility and integrity. The men's professed loyalty to their employers is perhaps, therefore, not so surprising after all. They were, of course, working in the City in an industry that was rewarding them with unusually high remuneration payments. Furthermore, as discussed in previous chapters, their lifestyles were fundamentally dependent on such a level of remuneration and were integrally enmeshed in the practices and structures of banking and family that supported and justified their capability to receive such remuneration levels in the first place. The men's defence of their positioning is to some extent understandable, even if it is not necessarily agreeable.

Given the link between employment and lifestyle, what is surprising in the men's talk about the crisis and redundancy is that concern about sustaining their lifestyle choices if they were to lose their jobs – maintaining the privileges they were buying for themselves and their families (large houses, private education, expensive holidays and so forth) – was not expressed by any of the men; family interests simply did not seem to enter into any of their narratives at all. This does not mean they did not express concern about other associated effects the crisis may yet have or had already had on them. For example, Dominic mentioned a drop in remuneration but did not talk about it in relation to concern about his ability to maintain his current outgoings:

> From a business perspective, everything just revolves around making as much money as possible. Over the last 4 years, we've not made as much money as we have in previous years. So everyone's had to kind of temper their expectations about the job, about what you get paid [*he chuckles*], about bonuses, about everything else, and think more about, "well it's not going to be like it was for the 5 years before that"... It's interesting

'cos I look at it and I think, "Do you bother staying in the industry? Do you go and do something else?"

Paul, meanwhile, expressed a measure of concern about his age (48 years) and the practice of early retirement in elite banking – aspects that he recognised could present themselves more prominently in the turmoil of a financial crisis:

PAUL: [The] problem is, people leave when something like this happens, you know. People my age sort of, decide to retire … they all wander off.

HL: Are you thinking of retiring soon?

PAUL: No, not really [*this seemed to be said with some reluctance*], not really [*Paul's voice became audibly quieter*]. Umm, no, I mean, no. Well, nowadays, at 48, you're probably not even halfway through your life … loads of time left. I might if I had a plan, but I always wanted to work in investment. So, umm, yeah, I don't think now's the time to step out if you don't have the option to step back in. You know, it's a one-way street. No, I'll be clinging on till they throw me out. I certainly don't want to be home all day. But, you know, a lot of people we've got here have never seen a bear market or a recession – a real recession. What we need are people like me who have been through this before. They're basically the people you need 'cos they know not to panic.

Paul's comment is interesting because, while it contests features of hegemonic processes of elite banking that relate to the industry's dynamic image, it also, somewhat ironically, reinforces these same processes. For example, the practice of early retirement, which helps sustain elite banking's youthful and dynamic image (and vice versa of course), is problematised through Paul's suggestion that it can be either a somewhat aimless act ("people wander off") or not always perhaps quite as voluntary as it may appear but instead be part of the constant turnover of employees in the pursuit of development and "progress". Yet rather than explicitly criticise the violent practices of downsizing in the industry (although these are referenced in his comment about ultimately getting "thrown out"), Paul, through his use of the phrase "wanders-off", in effect places the blame on the shoulders of those who leave – the experienced people who, somewhat casually it seems, abandon ship. This is significant, for it further supports the discourse of competitive individualism, which rests on the principle that people are responsible for their own fate. This is further complicated, however, because, as Paul's account also reveals, an additional problematic is that while people do accumulate experience over time this experience is not only devalued within banks' discourse of youthful dynamism but is also devalued precisely by the practice of early retirement (forced or voluntary). It is thus a vicious cycle, whereby the value of youth, linked as it is with innovation, mobility, vitality and market competitiveness, is promoted and practised by banks, and bought into by employees through commonplace practices that include early retirement.

Paul's reference to the "one-way street" of banking further supports this mobility discourse – if you decide to jump ship, then so be it, but it will indicate weakness, and do not expect to get back on because the world of banking waits for no one. Ultimately, Paul's account illustrates the depersonalised and unemotional way in which history and experience is viewed: processes linked with the finance industry, including the ups and downs of banking fortunes (the bear markets and the bull markets), are part of a natural cycle of history and development, which in turn help determine the professional life course of elite City finance workers.

Comments made by James and Dominic echo this narrative:

> I don't want to go through this situation again. And if it happens ten years down the line it's, you know, getting back in probably won't be an option. You know, I'm 31, so I'm a reasonably good age where I've got some experience, and I've still got a lot of years ahead of me. Whereas, if I'm 41, you know, I'm at the next level up, and there aren't that many people who are 40 plus in banking.
>
> (James)

> I talk to someone like my boss, you know, people like that who went through the '87 crash, who went through the '90, '91, '92 recession, who went through the Asian financial crisis, the Russian default, Dot Com Bubble blow-up, small recession again in '02, '03, and then, you know ... You talk to people like that and they think, "Yeah, seen it all before, always comes back". You know, people like that who are, like 50, and been in the industry for 30 years, they're all like, "yeah, this happens". This is a long term one, but ... err... I don't know; it's hard.
>
> (Dominic)

These narratives of redundancy and financial crisis together reveal how crucial and, in many respects, irrational aspects of the elite financial game generate concern: the uncertainty of the rules (James), the aggressive tactics (Graham), the possibility of being forced to stop playing before you want to (Paul and James) and so forth. Yet what is even more significant is the overarching durability of the rationality discourse of elite finance – while the men identified inconsistencies, unworkable practices and irrational aspects embedded in the system, they still held firm to the belief that there is some overarching rationality governing the whole system and that, in spite of all the crises and recessions, the system is right and will always bounce back (see also Ouroussoff 2010: 124; Tucker 2010). Banking and those who win and lose from it are positioned as aspects of an overarching non-human, historical, inevitable system. And, like the system itself, the game of elite finance is seen to go on and on in a never-ending cycle: a game that always (as long as you are playing it of course) offers the potential for reward.

This uncompromising belief in and adherence to the current system and practices of finance and neoliberal capitalism is hugely significant because of the inequalities it rests on and legitimises. As Ho (2009: 274) has observed, elite bankers, while engaging in a high risk–high reward bargain and all the practices that accompany it, not only accept the instability of their jobs but claim this is how it has to be (see also Toynbee and Walker 2008; Massey 2010); and through this process, they also lose sight of the reality of how other people live and what other people earn. Yet while elite bankers may have considerable savings and lines of privilege (professional networks, social networks, academic qualifications and so forth) to fall back on if they lose their jobs, many other people do not have the same security or contacts and thus the requisite means to make alternative choices (Ho 2009; Prins 2009). Bankers' constant exposure to an environment where people are judged on what they are paid, combined with the continuing justification of this system – the belief that making money is the inalienable right of people to pursue happiness, and that anyone could get paid the kind of money elite bankers receive if they worked/had worked hard enough or make/had made the right choices – means poverty easily becomes the mark of failure (Ho 2009: 259). Poverty, in other words, is seen as a consequence of individual laziness or lack of intelligence, or both (Ventura 2012: 4; see also Collier 2010b). Capitalism, as Klein (2009: 1) has remarked, hardens hearts; people "need to believe they are superior to those who are excluded in order to get through the day".

I asked each of the women whether they thought the financial crisis had been stressful for their husband. Cath rather matter-of-factly remarked:

> No, I don't think so particularly. [Dan] never talks about work. He really tries to keep it very separate. You know, when he's here, he's here. When he's there, he's there. I sometimes see him checking his [phone], but not much.

Kara similarly explained that:

> Matt hardly ever talks about work at home really. But he often walks through the door on his [phone] in the evening. And, umm, I think it rarely leaves his head, his work. But I think this is really his escape, you know.

Gwyneth, meanwhile, told me:

> [Paul] hasn't said he's stressed about it. I don't think he is particularly. I think he must be quite good at dealing with stress 'cos he ... well,

> he never, ever talks about his work. He never comes home and says, "This happened today, that happened today". In all the years we've been together, he's never, ever talked about work. So I think, he's probably good at switching off. Although sometimes he can be quiet, so maybe he's stressed. But that's how he shows it really. But he certainly never comes home and says, you know... It's very much, work is one thing, and home is another.

Jess, however, went further to illustrate not only just how the system is so powerful and so seductive, but also how it is self-perpetuating:

> I don't think the financial crisis made [Dominic] stressed, because they actually won clients during it; it actually worked in their favour. So I don't think that really stressed him that much. Although, he did lose a couple of big clients because they went bankrupt – so that's the other side; so that probably was a bit stressful for him. But he would never say he's stressed at work. But I think he does ... you can tell when he gets stressed. [But] he just doesn't see how you can claim that you're stressed at work. He's like, "It's just work", you know, "either you're going through a hard time, or you're going through a good time, but you can't let it get to you too much because in the end, it's just work".

The women's comments are quite poignant in light of the ways in which concerns about humanity, emotion and family are excluded, even from the most brutal of workplace practices. Most significantly, underlying all the men's and women's narratives of redundancy and crisis is not only an acceptance of the system, but the naturalisation of it and the sense that it will inevitably come right in the end – the processes of recruitment and redundancy and the cyclical ups and downs of the fortunes of banking are just how it is. Like it or not, this is elite banking: it may be harsh, but this is how it is; this is how the system has always worked and will always work. There may be some losers but there will also be winners (clients may be lost but they may also be gained; some employees may lose their jobs but others will continue to reap rewards). What this ignores, of course, are the many inconsistencies and ambiguities in the system, as well as the many practices that support them, which result in huge fluctuations and inequalities in fortunes. What is also overlooked, however, in all of these narratives of the crisis, are the ways in which each of these men and women are cogs in the system: the actions they engage in – their practices of work and family, their practices of consumption, their socio-spatial arrangements of work and family – all contribute to the overarching dynamic of the relations and inequalities that define the contemporary moment for them and others: the boom times and the busts.

Conclusion

The 2008 financial crisis, in its severity, was a complex historic moment – a seismic shift in the status quo that challenged the hegemonic order and opened up possibilities to imagine and realise a different future (Hall et al. 2013; see also Harvey 2012; Featherstone 2016). Immediate challenges inevitably had to be faced within and outside the finance industry because of the crisis. Nevertheless, the moment also presented an opportunity to truly adopt and embody a new ethos (Sen 2009: 6) – one centred on the principles of ethical and social responsibility that fully permeates the structures and practices of global finance and their internal and external impacts. Since the crisis, regulations of the finance industry in the UK, Europe and the USA have tightened (although critics have suggested these regulations still fall short of what is necessary – see, for example, Caprio 2013). But while the discourse of banking may have changed, the underlying message with its best of the best storyline still sounds familiar. Indeed, the new ethical responsibility discourse provides a useful means through which to reframe existing processes of hegemony – to reaffirm and re-legitimise the moral and intellectual superiority of wealthy City-based banks and their elite, well-paid workers.

Furthermore, as Adam Tooze (2018) reflects, the basic principles of financial globalisation have not been questioned, and the City remains an important financial centre both locally and globally despite the unsettled and changing nature of national and international political relationships and networks that intertwine with the banking and business world (see also Ho 2009; Bank of England 2018). Evidence that the City's finance industry remains highly valued politically can be seen in the official discourse of Brexit, which continues to privilege the banking elite and their interests, not only in relation to London but to the whole of UK (see UK Government 2017). A high level of self-assurance in the City's finance industry about its own worth and talent, meanwhile, has continued to be actively promoted by key banking figures through a discourse of opportunism (see, for example, a report of a speech by the chairman of HSBC in The Times 2016).

What these observations illustrate therefore, when considered alongside the narratives of redundancy explored in this chapter, is how a period of crisis can sustain and strengthen inequalities and systems and practices of privilege through a process of renegotiation – the hegemonic order might be shaken by a crisis but not necessarily undermined. The significance of what the bankers' narratives have illuminated is not so much the existence of inherent weaknesses in the system but the fact that these weaknesses present a reason or an opportunity to support and refashion *existing* processes of hegemony. While opportunities may present themselves to question, if not rewrite, the rules (for example, through James' first-hand experience of redundancy), this may not lead to any substantial redistribution or re-articulation of power in ways that really are more equitable and just. Rather, despite some disgruntlement among the men, and recognition that some practices are callous and brutal, the system itself was ultimately not held to account by any of the men. Even James, despite his experience, was keen to re-stake his place back in the City. Nevertheless, the fact that weaknesses and moments of contestation do exist is cause to reflect on where and what change could occur. As Marshall Berman (2010) has written: it is "only when you confront the shapes and shadows of the world that it becomes possible to see the world for all it is".

Chapter 6

Conclusion

The City in reflection

This book set out to examine the day-to-day socio-spatial and gendered practices of global finance that help sustain, normalise and naturalise the industry's local and global dominance. It has focused on the banking industry located in the City of London because the City is a centre of acute concentration of institutional and individual wealth and power – a command point for global finance. It is a place of local, national and transnational significance, dominated by the presence of the finance industry, in particular wealthy banks and their well-paid workers. It is a place that has been hailed in government discourse as inclusive and beneficial for all (City of London Corporation 2018), that sits within a city that embraces enormous diversity (Hall et al. 2013). But it is also a context where inequalities and the systems and practices that underpin inequalities are more pronounced, where men continue to dominate the higher echelons of banking and other high-status professions. It is a place where the logic of exclusion and inclusion favours the privileged and normalises their advantage, and where the daily practices of global elites, whether deliberately or incidentally, help shape the space for their own predatory benefit (Sassen 2014).

The book's analysis drew, in particular, on Antonio Gramsci's theory of hegemony (Gramsci 1971), Raewyn Connell's concept hegemonic masculinity (e.g., Connell 2005a; Connell and Messerschmidt 2005) and conceptualisations of space that recognise it as dynamic and relational (e.g., Sassen 2001, 2014; Massey 2010). In exploring the socio-spatial and gendered nature of the City's elite banking sector, this book has focused on the *process* of hegemony. This is in contrast to most previous discussion on the concept of hegemonic masculinity, which has instead tended to consider the *form* of hegemony, with a number of scholars critiquing the concept's essentialising potential and reductionist tendencies (see Introduction). By shifting the focus to the *process* of hegemony, this book has been able to explore the diverse, complex daily "realities" of the institutions and male workers of elite City finance, and to show how hegemony is an ongoing, complex and powerful process, comprising individual, collective and systemic dimensions.

The process of hegemony has been shown to be neither fixed nor static, but in many respects elusive, as Hearn (2006: 45) has suggested. Indeed, the book's focus on the process of hegemony rather than the form has helped illustrate how hegemony gains strength through its very elusiveness (ibid.) but yet is mobilising and concrete in its effects. As such, the book has sought to illustrate how processes of spatial and gendered hegemony linked with global finance, as well as the associated day-to-day social practices of the financial elite, while powerful are not wholly stable, or homogenous or immutable. Rather, these processes are dynamic, overlapping, mobilising and seductive, open to adaptation and change, sustaining power through a variety of intertwined material, economic, political, cultural and discursive dimensions that operate within and between individual, local, national and global levels.

The analysis in the book drew on personal narratives relating to the day-to-day work and family lives of elite male City bankers – men at different stages of their career and life course. These narratives (gathered from both men and women) are situated in a particular historical time – 2008–2013, the aftermath of the 2008 global financial crisis – as well as a particular geographical space – the City of London and its surrounding area. The book's analysis provided insight into how, under particular historical conditions, social relations and practices of the City's banking elite are negotiated and enacted in ways that are both shaped by and help shape and/or contest processes of hegemony linked with global finance.

The book's exploration of data relating to individual male bankers and their wives was combined with analysis of available online promotional material taken from the websites of wealthy City-based banks in 2018. This combination of historical and contemporary data has helped to illustrate both the consistency and adaptability of processes of hegemony, as well as expose elements of hypocrisy and contradiction embedded within them. It has provided insight into the ways in which individual and institutional forms of privilege associated with global finance are both challenged and maintained and how inequalities are legitimised and normalised. The personal and public narratives explored in the book have helped reveal how, in an ongoing circuit of gendered power, the institutional and individual dominance and authority of the global financial elite based in the City of London are constituted, confirmed and conferred through claims to moral and intellectual leadership, supported by forms of political, economic and cultural power.

The narratives of the men and women discussed in this book have helped expose how men working as elite City bankers swirl within a vortex of power and privilege linked with global finance and, in their own, individual ways, help sustain its strength and momentum, whether through willing consent, reluctant compliance or a combination of the two. Bankers' individual spatial arrangements and everyday practices of work and home have been shown to combine with the intricacies of banks' institutional systems and practices of recruitment, retention and reward to shape, support and sustain the common-sense ideology underpinning processes of hegemony linked with global finance and the authority of those who benefit from them.

In an active state of legitimisation and preservation, the gendered local and global spatial dominance and authority of the elite banks and bankers of the City is situated within and justified through the dynamics of naturalised and inevitable large-scale historical change. This bestows on the financial elite, an institutional and individual sense of value and rightful belonging in both business and social spaces and hierarchies. Yet the analysis revealed how this sense of stability combines with one of mobility – an inherent but necessary contradiction embedded within the potent processes of hegemony that enables these processes to not only absorb change but also gain strength through this remoulding. And it is hegemony's very capacity for remoulding and self-empowerment that makes transformational change so difficult to effect.

Exploring the narratives of the men and women has helped illustrate how the high salaries and bonus payments of elite City banking are the fulcrum on which these processes of hegemony rest. They are both the status signifiers and the status (re)producers (Cox 2011). They symbolise success, and provide the justification and the reward for hard work, the legitimisation for notions of individual and institutional worthiness, and sustain the active and seductive force of the patriarchal dividend. They also feed into the constitution of sociocultural worthiness, including a sense of moral superiority, in private and public realms through providing the capability for bankers and their families to make certain choices, including where to live, where to send children to school and what kinds of activities and lifestyle practices to engage in. These choices, in turn, not only reproduce and perpetuate circles of privilege and exclusivity but also, ironically, help justify them. They also, importantly, engender widespread compliance with and general acceptance of the current organisational systems and practices of elite finance, and help mask the fact that economic and social inequalities are not simply a result of different abilities, effort or chance (Jakopovich 2014; Friedman and Laurison 2019). While the men and women in different ways identified and expressed dissatisfaction with the day-to-day workings of global finance and contradictions embedded within, these very inconsistencies were either largely ignored or dismissed in favour of maintaining the status quo or embraced as a reason to actively support it (for example, see James' account of his redundancy in Chapter 5).

Two potential sites of contestation for processes of hegemony linked with global finance were explored, in particular, in this book. The first site was fatherhood, because of changing sociocultural ideals of fatherhood away from breadwinning towards active, hands-on and present caregiving, and the potential for these newer ideals to disrupt certain gendered notions and practices relating to work commitment and career success. The narratives of the men and women explored in this book, however, suggest that these newer fatherhood ideals neither appear to contest processes of hegemony nor compete with traditional ideals of breadwinning. They did not appear to be avoided or rejected or result in dissatisfaction with or especially challenge certain forms of working (see further Longlands and Collier 2018). And nor did the men's or women's narratives signify any kind of straightforward linear change in fatherhood (either from a broader cultural perspective or with respect to individual men) from older, authoritative forms to newer more gender equitable forms (Collier 2013; Madrid 2017). Instead, newer, hands-on fatherhood ideals seemed to have been accepted and absorbed somewhat smoothly into existing hegemonic processes alongside prevailing and seemingly conflicting norms, assumptions and practices relating to both fatherhood and elite banking, thus reproducing and further embedding distinctly gendered assumptions about the nature of commitment to and success in the industry (Longlands and Collier 2018).

When viewed alongside banks' institutional literature – particularly that relating to gender equality policies and well-being initiatives – the personal narratives of the men and women illustrate how the very act of absorption and adaptation reconfigures and reframes family and workplace practices in ways that strengthen existing gender relations and divisions of power in both the private and public realms, without significantly problematising either traditional forms of breadwinning fatherhood or newer caregiving ideals. This helps underscore the challenges and complexity that, as Collier (2016, 2019) has argued, mark the relationship between professional culture and institutional discourses and practices of equality, inclusion and well-being. The men's and women's narratives helped reveal how the identity of being a father can swing between the two alternative ideals of fatherhood, engaging as it does so with the potent neoliberal ideology of meritocracy, hypercompetitive individualism and self-responsibility, such that this double-headed father identity becomes a further badge of honour for already high-status elite City bankers.

The book's analysis helped to show how, regardless of the nuanced and fluctuating dynamics that this composite fatherhood identity comprises for individual men, it signifies both their simultaneous commitment to work and family and their (apparent) ability to successfully combine the two while surviving in the unstable, cutthroat world of elite City banking. And this is significant for it sets the bar for all workers whether inside or outside banking. Narratives of the men and women revealed how the spaces of both work and family are sites of competition in which one can signify, garner and perpetuate individual and intergenerational socio-economic privilege. Moreover, the narratives also helped to show how the men's very positioning *as fathers* lends a crucial moral dimension to processes of hegemony linked with global finance, while the rewards and status associated with City banking in turn help shape and enable the ways in which fatherhood is enacted, embodied and conferred. There is, then, a mutually reinforcing, cyclical and gendered relationship of institutional and individual value operating within and between the private and public spaces of elite City banking.

This is not to oversimplify the reality and suggest that the men and women did not feel some degree of tension or experience different forms of frustration as they negotiated their day-to-day work and family lives; nor is it to suggest that the acts of caregiving the men engaged in were not enriching or positive both for them and their families (see further Elliott 2016). On the contrary, it is to highlight the ability of hegemony not only to reshape but to seduce and control, and to soften, normalise and naturalise relationships of power and their effects – to capitalise on change and moments of disruption without significantly questioning or dismantling the structures of power (Carrigan et al. 1985). As Madrid (2017: 252) has put it, writing on fatherhood among elite corporate men in Chile, it is more than a process of adaptation, but rather a preservation of hierarchies that works as a "bricolage" (Aboim 2010) between old and new, and which presents the illusion of change.

Hands-on, present fatherhood ideals may appear to provide an opportunity for promoting greater gender equality and well-being in both the private and public realm – for resisting and contesting unequal gender relations and divisions of power embedded within current processes of hegemony linked with global finance (see further Elliott 2016). But what this analysis has shown is that realising any kind of meaningful change in this direction is hugely challenging, complex and far from straightforward and requires recognising, understanding and addressing the complex intertwined and underlying structural dynamics and deeply embedded ideologies that militate against change and play out in people's everyday lives (Cornwall 2016; Longlands and Collier 2018).

Education has been explored in this book as a particular terrain through which existing privilege is both signified and transferred within the spaces of both work and family. The analysis has shown how men's and women's narratives of and practices relating to their own and their children's education illustrate and reinforce socio-economic divisions in ways that affirm and justify both the economic, intellectual and moral superiority of wealthy City banks and elite City bankers and their families, and gendered institutional and individual socio-spatial practices linked with processes of inclusion and exclusion. The discussion has illustrated how processes of recruitment associated with particular kinds of applicants to banking – those who received high-status, privileged forms of education – help justify wealthy banks' spatial dominance in the City and their gendered constitution, and legitimise their local and global authority.

This seriously undermines the validity of the enduring discourse around privileged, selective forms of education, which continues to be firmly pedalled in the UK by certain members of the political elite (among others), that increasing access to selective forms of education will somehow contribute to equality and meritocratic processes that facilitate social mobility. It also undermines the associated discourse that upwards social mobility through education – privileged or otherwise – is readily achievable for all, when so often the reality still shows us otherwise, not least because education systems do not operate in a vacuum (see also Maxwell and Aggleton 2016).

Meanwhile, in seeking out and choosing desirable spaces and communities to be educated, live and socialise in, well-paid City bankers and their families contribute to widening socio-spatial inequalities in London and beyond. As the analysis has argued, it is a process which sees these different socio-spatial practices legitimised through a discourse of worthiness that rests on claims to moral and intellectual superiority, and which normalises, justifies and perpetuates not only forms of privilege and belonging but also forms of discrimination and exclusion.

A second particular site of contestation explored in this book was the 2008 financial crisis and the men's associated narratives of redundancy. First-hand experiences of the severity and breadth of the crisis were revealed in the men's narratives. These narratives, along with data explored elsewhere in the book, have helped expose the many ambiguities, inconsistencies and inequalities embedded within the current system and practices of elite City banking and the broader system of neoliberal capitalism that it is both part of and represents – irrespective of periods of crisis (see Ho 2009 for more discussion on representation).

The narratives of redundancy and financial crisis have laid bare some of the brutality and harshness of neoliberal workplace practices in elite City banking and further highlighted the problematic, paradoxical relationship between institutional agendas on equality, inclusion and well-being and a certain kind of neoliberal professional culture (see further Collier 2016, 2019). But they have also revealed the seductive, compelling and enduring nature of hegemony. Despite what seemed to be inconsistent, fuzzy and finite demonstrations of institutional loyalty towards employees on behalf of City-based banks, the men in general and in contrast demonstrated and verbalised significant commitment and loyalty both to the individual bank they worked for and to the finance industry as a whole. Issues of loyalty, or lack thereof, seem bound up in the complex, and somewhat unpredictable processes and practices linked with profit, reward, redundancy and retirement. These, in turn, are intertwined with issues of identity, including notions of worth, dynamism, youthfulness and ageing, which problematise assumptions about meritocracy, agency and choice (see Chapter 5).

Narratives relating to the 2008 financial crisis and redundancy, in a similar fashion to the narratives of fatherhood, reframed *existing* processes of hegemony, reinforcing claims to moral and global leadership of elite banks and bankers. Indeed, the narratives revealed how the crisis itself presented an opportunity for renegotiation and refashioning – a period of remoulding and consolidation which gains energy from the contestation itself. The men's and women's narratives, combined with official banking discourse, helped to illustrate how processes of hegemony are fluid and ever changing, able to be reconfigured and re-conferred in ways that maintain if not strengthen their momentum. For example, the contemporary discourse of ethical responsibility within banking that emerged in response to the 2008 crisis appears to have been absorbed within existing processes of hegemony, refashioning these processes from within in ways that reaffirm, re-legitimise and reinforce the claims to economic, moral and intellectual superiority of global finance and its elite, affluent workers, while once again presenting the illusion of change.

This book has helped to illustrate how processes of hegemony that confer and perpetuate privilege intertwine with one another and are complex and deeply embedded, both obvious and hidden. But while they can sustain and gather energy, they also require nurturing, which gives them an inherent weakness and lays them open to contestation. What this book shows, however, is how contestations, through their very disrupting nature, can be reinvigorating and strengthening, providing the impetus for remoulding, re-conferring and reaffirmation: a buffeting cloak that conceals a lack of meaningful change. The sites of contestation explored in this book – ranging from the external large-scale contestations to those that are individual and small-scale – illustrate the need to look beyond the rhetoric, whether of equality, community, compassion, caring or responsibility, to explore at a more fundamental level whether and what change is occurring, and who or what is or is not benefiting from it.

The old is dying and the new cannot be born[1]

Unterhalter and North (2018: 212) have argued that "notions of hierarchy and transfer will always be inadequate to convey the things they describe". Similarly, using the concept of hegemony to analyse the authority and dominance of global finance can only ever present a partial understanding, and one dependent on my own interpretations and representations. Nonetheless, the discussion in this book has, I hoped, enhanced understanding of the intricacies and complexities of processes relating to global finance that result in and perpetuate inequalities and exclusions, in order that the gendered systems and practices of privilege that benefit the few at the expense of the many do not prevail ad infinitum. We all have much to gain from creating a more just and equitable world.

Taking a step back to reflect on the implications of the book's analysis for the present turbulent moment, when the world seems faced with diverse, interlinked crises of environmental, social, ideological and economic dimensions, marked by an increasing left-right polarisation of politics (Klein 2017; Fraser 2019), therefore, opens up the space to consider two important questions. The first question is whether transforming complex and intertwined systems of privilege from within is possible. Opposing and disrupting processes of hegemony may not be that difficult; transforming them, however, is an enormous challenge, not least because those at the centre control a disproportionate share of economic, political and social resources, which they are likely keen to hold on to, but nevertheless need to be involved in processes of change if they are to be truly transformative.

A process of transformation requires critical analysis of the sort provided in this book of the relationship between men, masculinities, gender, power, accountability and attribution in order to expose and understand the flaws and inequalities embedded in contemporary social arrangements and power relations (Longlands and Collier 2018). For as Hearn (2015, 2004) has argued, the "problem" for equality is a collection of questions about men as much as about masculinities. But a process of transformation also necessitates clearly articulating an alternative *and* believing it to be achievable (Klein 2014; Wilkinson and Pickett 2019). As Lappé (2016: 1) has eloquently written, "we cannot move toward a future we cannot imagine, and we cannot imagine a future we don't believe is possible".

Change, in this sense, requires not only systemic change, but also ideological change – a process of reimagining that learns from the traces of the past and what we know about the present, but offers a clear, alternative vision for the future. This requires, as Naomi Klein (2014: 461) has suggested, "a full-throated debate about values … during which new stories can be told to replace the ones that have failed us", where we start to hear beyond what we currently hear (Butler 2004: 18). Although we must not simply compare contemporary times to radically different historical situations (Achcar 2016), Klein has drawn attention to key moments in history where change towards greater equality has come from below, from grassroots movements that, unafraid of evoking a sense of morality, evolved into a powerful force for transformative change, such as the abolitionist movement and the women's suffrage movement. Indeed, for Klein (2014, 2017), change at a fundamental level requires a mass united movement of resistance against powerful forces that militate against social justice and equality. And given what we know about hegemony, this mass movement must simultaneously tackle political, economic and cultural injustices and structural constraints. Any response to the current moment that aims to bring about change must, in other words, be multifaceted as well as united. But it must also be a movement that dislodges us all from our positions of privilege and authority – whether left, right or somewhere in between (Butler 2004: 18).

Existing processes of hegemony in global finance continue to validate and revere material worth and to position elite banks and bankers as among the worthy few: the few that have worked hard, succeeded and deserve their success; the few that serve the purposes of the many. This gendered positioning of authority may not be done quite so explicitly as it was in the past but it is still there. Indeed, its increasing implicitness gives it strength, helping to further mask the many significant, powerful and enduring lines of ascent intimately related to material worth that enable people, such as the men in this study and their families, to live their lives in the ways they do: their place of birth, family background, schooling and university experiences, who their friends are, who their colleagues are, who their boss happens to be, what clients they manage to secure and so forth. It also masks, or ignores, social, economic and political structures that help determine forms of inclusion and exclusion, advantage and exploitation.

The discourse of worthiness and the structures and conditions that support it, therefore, must fundamentally change in a way that does not simply rehash inequalities to re-advantage and include those who are already privileged while re-excluding those who are already excluded. It must also, for the sake of equality *and* the environment, fundamentally disrupt the valorising of material worth (individual and institutional) and practices of conspicuous and unnecessary consumption as well as the connection of economic prosperity with happiness and well-being (Wilkinson and Pickett 2019).

The overriding recognition that our lives are interrelated with one another is enormously significant and perhaps provides an important starting point for transformation – for refocusing on new stories as well as stories that already exist but have largely been silenced (Klein 2017) in order to transform existing processes of hegemony rather than remould them. For at the centre of the debate about change, whether mobilised at the grassroots level or not, has to be recognition of what Iris Marion Young (2011) has explained as our state of interdependency with one another, with people whom we know but mostly with people we do not. And embedded within this recognition must be awareness that the causal networks and patterns of relations that we are all a part of result in structural injustice, which necessarily means we all share a sense of responsibility for one another. As Young has argued (p. 173), recognising this shared sense of responsibility is "not to assign blame or fault, but rather [to] enjoin a political responsibility to organise collective action for change" with those persons who are more privileged perhaps assuming greater and more specific responsibility.

The second important question, then, is how to engender a more fundamental shared sense of responsibility that rejects the valuing of and preoccupation with competitive individualism and which broadens out beyond the "gated", inward-looking enclaves and confines of the privileged but necessarily engages them. It requires, for one, a sense of responsibility that rests on a far more substantial and cohesive notion of community than that searched out by the men and women in this study. A notion of community, in other words, that does not contribute to but instead helps confront unjust inequalities by breaking down the boundaries around care and compassion, promoting cooperation and a sense of mutual trust, and broadening out our opinions of what constitutes worth and worthiness; a notion of community that is not built on differentiation through separation from and distrust of others but one that embraces diversity and difference and truly values them. It also requires a sense of responsibility that does not view gender equality as a binary or zero-sum game, where one side (men and masculinities) supposedly loses out in favour of enhancing the other (women and femininities), but recognises instead that equality is a fundamental social justice issue that is beneficial to all (Dupuis-Déri 2018; Wilkinson and Pickett 2019).

On the one hand, this may be seen, perhaps, as a challenge for contemporary times, which in contrast seem marked by moments of widespread introspection and right-wing nationalist sentiments, reflected, for example, through the UK referendum vote to leave the European Union (Brexit) and the election of Donald Trump in the USA – two notable events that occurred in the space of a few months in 2016 and left an aftermath characterised by instances of discrimination and bigotry. It is an era that illustrates starkly that what matters is not so much what is true or false but that which is believed (Connell 2019). On the other hand, however, it is precisely such moments and such struggles over meaning that also provide impetus and space for alternative stories to be told and heard (Klein 2017; Achcar 2018).

Connell and Dados (2014) have argued that resistance to neoliberalism requires a more democratic coming together of deeper local social politics across the globe. Hearn (2015: 2), meanwhile, has similarly suggested that "transnational change involves not just doing things differently and building on existing structures, but arises from attempts to create something different across borders" or what Wilkinson and Pickett (2019: 265) have called "a radical alternative". The discussion in this book has shown the enduring power and malleable state of hegemony, but it has also highlighted weaknesses and cracks in the system and revealed how the authority of hegemony can be challenged in small, individual ways. These acts of resistance illustrate what Connell has termed "grounds for optimism" (Connell 2011: 16) because they indicate the capacity for men and women to think about inequalities as contestable and changeable. Such acts can also play a role in shaping the ways the children of the privileged grow up to understand and enact their part in the world, which may help in breaking existing value systems and cycles of privilege. While this is not to overstate the weight of such acts or to oversimplify the challenge, small contestations if mobilised together can be more significant than the sum of their parts.

Spaces where small acts can come together and transcend borders include, for example, the Internet, which is a powerful resource, providing the means for communication, advocacy and activism on a local and global scale (e.g., see Jackson 2018), for listening to different voices and for developing and promoting shared value systems that render forms of inequality problematic. Education systems, meanwhile, and the values endorsed by schools, universities and other sites and spaces of education and knowledge sharing increasingly need to have relevance in transnational arenas (Kenway and Kohl 2013: 286). These cross-cultural spaces of interconnectedness and active knowledge sharing can, of course, reinforce existing hegemonic processes by providing a platform for shaping, promoting and validating forms of discrimination, inequality and exclusion, whether explicitly or not (as I have discussed in this book with respect to education experiences and schooling choices); but they can also transcend geographical, political and social boundaries, promote the ideals of equality and social justice, and help build capacity to resist discriminatory ideologies and destructive, divisive forms of social practice (Connell 2019).

Education – both formal and informal – while not the sole solution to all our ills, of course, must still be recognised as "an important domain for thinking about building a connected society", and every social gathering, whether in a virtual or actual space of meeting, discussion, learning and debate, as an opportunity to build human networks in new ways (Allen 2013: 111). Coming together with others presents the opportunity for telling, listening to and believing in the possibility of different stories, for reimagining and rewriting the future and for mobilising action to transform the unjust processes of hegemony that benefit the few at the expense of the many. As Terry Eagleton (2018: 6) has written:

> It is hard to sustain your faith in change when change seems off the agenda, even if this is when you need to sustain it most of all. [But] … if you do not resist the apparently inevitable, you will never know how inevitable the inevitable was.

Processes of hegemony may be powerful and adaptable, but they are not inevitable and they are never complete – their adaptability and incompleteness mean they have an inherent weakness and can always be contested and transformed.

The old is dying and the new *can* be born.

Note

1 Gramsci 1930, Prison Notebooks, Notebook 3.

References

Aboim, S. (2010). *Plural Masculinities: The Remaking of the Self in Private Life*. Farnham: Ashgate.

Achcar, G. (2016). *Morbid Symptoms: Relapse in the Arab Uprising*. Stanford, CA: Stanford University Press.

Achcar, G. (2018). 'Morbid symptoms: what did Gramsci mean and how does it apply to our time?', *International Socialist Review, 108*, online at: www.isreview.org/issue/108/morbid-symptoms (accessed 08.02.19).

Acker, J. (2004). 'Gender, capitalism and globalization', *Critical Sociology, 30*(1): 17–41.

Allen, D. (2013). 'A connected society: social connectedness has a key part to play in the search for equality', *Soundings: A Journal of Politics and Culture, 53*: 103–113.

Anders, J. (2015). *Private Pay Progression*. London: Sutton Trust.

Apple, M.W. (2004). *Ideology and Curriculum* (Third Edition). London: RoutledgeFalmer.

Asthana, A. and Campbell, D. (2017). 'Theresa May paves way for new generation of grammar schools', *The Guardian*, online at: www.theguardian.com/uk-news/2017/mar/06/theresa-may-paves-way-for-new-generation-of-grammar-schools (accessed 20.10.18).

Ball, S.J. (2003). *Class Strategies and the Education Market: The Middle Class and Social Advantage*. Abingdon: Routledge.

Bank of England. (2018). 'Global economic and financial market developments', *Inflation Report, May 2018*, online at: www.bankofengland.co.uk/inflation-report/2018/may-2018/global-economic-and-financial-market-developments (accessed 15.08.18).

Barclays. (2015). *The Barclays Way: How We Do Business*, online at: www.home.barclays/content/dam/barclayspublic/docs/AboutUs/Purpose-Values/BAR_TheBarclaysWay%20cropped%2023_07_2015.pdf (accessed 20.10.18).

——— (2018a). *About Us: Around the World*, online at: www.home.barclays/about-barclays/around-the-world.html (accessed 19.06.18).

——— (2018b). *About Us: Our History*, online at: www.home.barclays/about-barclays/history.html (accessed 19.06.18).

Bauman, Z. (1998). *Globalization: The Human Consequences*. New York: Columbia University Press.

Beasley, C. (2008). 'Rethinking hegemonic masculinity in a globalizing world'. *Men and Masculinities, 11*(1): 86–103.

Beck, U. (1999). *World Risk Society.* Cambridge: Polity Press.

Berman, M. (2010). *All That Is Solid Melts into Air: The Experience of Modernity* (New Edition). London: Verso.

Blommaert, J. and Dong, J. (2010). *Ethnographic Fieldwork: A Beginner's Guide.* Bristol: Multilingual Matters.

Burgess, S., Crawford, C. and Macmillan, L. (2017). 'Assessing the role of grammar schools in promoting social mobility', *Department of Quantitative Social Science, Working Paper No. 17-09.* London: UCL Institute of Education, UCL.

Butler, J. (2004). *Precarious Life: The Powers of Mourning and Violence.* London: Verso.

Butler, T. and Lees, L. (2006). 'Super gentrification in Barnsbury, London: globalization and gentrifying global elites at the neighbourhood level', *Transaction of the Institute of British Geographers, 31*(4): 467–487.

Caprio (Jr.), G. (2013). 'Financial regulation after the crisis: how did we get here, and how do we get out?' *LSE Financial Markets Group Special Paper Series, Special Paper 226.* London: LSE.

Carrigan, T., Connell, R.W. and Lee, J. (1985). 'Toward a new sociology of masculinity', *Theory and Society, 14*: 551–604.

Castellani, B. and Hafferty, F.W. (2009). *Sociology and Complexity Science: A New Field of Inquiry.* New York: Springer.

Caterino, B. and Hansen, P. (2009). 'Macpherson, Habermas and the demands of democratic theory', *Studies in Political Economy, Special Issue: Finance and Democracy, 83*: 85–110.

Cerra, V. and Saxena, S.C. (2017). *Booms, Crises, and Recoveries: A New Paradigm of the Business Cycle and Its Policy Implications*, IMF Working Paper 17/250. Washington, DC: International Monetary Fund.

Charmaz, K. (2006). *Constructing Grounded Theory: A Practical Guide Through Qualitative Analysis.* London: Sage Publications.

Chase, S.E. (2008). 'Narrative inquiry: multiple lenses, approaches, voices', in N.K. Denzin and Y.S. Lincoln (eds.), *Collecting and Interpreting Qualitative Materials* (Third Edition). London: Sage Publications.

Chinwala, Y. (2016). *Women in UK Financial Services 2016: Putting the Gaghia Review and HM Treasury's Women in Finance Charter in Context.* London: New Financial.

City of London Corporation. (2018). 'City history', in *Things to do: Visit the City: Explore our History*, online at: www.cityoflondon.gov.uk/things-to-do/visit-the-city/our-history/Pages/default.aspx (accessed 27.10.18).

Clark, A. (2009). 'How did Bernard Madoff's victims fall for his $65bn scam?' *The Guardian*, online at: www.theguardian.com/business/2009/apr/02/bernard-madoff-fraud-victims-sec (accessed 15.10.18).

Coffey, A. (1999). *The Ethnographic Self: Fieldwork and the Representation.* London: Sage Publications.

Collier, R. (2010a). 'Masculinities, law and personal life: towards a new framework for understanding men, law and gender', *Harvard Journal of Law and Gender, 33*: 431–475.

——— (2010b). *Men, Law and Gender: Essays on the 'Man' of Law*, Abingdon: Routledge.

——— (2012). 'Good fathers, successful lawyers: transnational business masculinities and the legal profession', in J. Hearn and A. Biricik (eds.), *GEXcel Work in Progress Report Volume XVI*, online at: www.genderexcel.org (accessed 15.10.18).

——— (2013). 'Rethinking men and masculinities in the contemporary legal profession: the example of fatherhood, transnational business masculinities and work-life balance in large law firms', *Nevada Law Journal, 13*: 101–130.

——— (2015). 'Naming men *as men* in corporate legal practice: gender and the idea of 'virtually 4/7 commitment' in law', *Fordham Law Review, 83*: 2347–2406.

——— (2016). 'Wellbeing in the legal profession: reflections on recent developments', *International Journal of the Legal Profession, 23*(1): 41–60.

——— (2019). 'How do we tackle the legal profession's mental health problem?', *Legal Cheek*, online at: https://www.legalcheek.com/2019/04/how-do-we-tackle-the-legal-professions-mental-health-problem/ (accessed 01.06.19)

Collini, S. (2013). 'Sold out', *London Review of Books, 35*(20): 3–12.

Connell, R.W. (1995). *Masculinities*. Berkeley: University of California Press.

——— (2000). *The Men and the Boys*. Cambridge: Polity Press.

——— (2005a). *Masculinities* (Second Edition). Cambridge: Polity Press.

——— (2005b). 'Globalisation, imperialism and masculinities', in M.S. Kimmel, J. Hearn and R.W. Connell (eds.), *Handbook of Studies of Masculinities*. London: Sage Publications.

——— (2007). *Southern Theory*. Cambridge: Polity Press.

——— (2008). 'A thousand miles from kind: men, masculinities and modern institutions', *The Journal of Men's Studies, 16*(3): 237–252.

——— (2009). *Gender* (Second Edition). Cambridge: Polity Press.

——— (2010). 'Lives of the businessmen: reflections on life-history method and contemporary hegemonic masculinity', *Österreichische Zeitschrift für Soziologie, 35*(2): 54–71.

——— (2011). *Confronting Equality: Gender, Knowledge and Global Change*. Sydney: Allen & Unwin.

——— (2012). 'Inside the glass tower: the construction of masculinities in finance capital', in P. McDonald and E. Jeanes (eds.), *Men, Wage Work and Family*. New York: Routledge.

——— (2013a). 'The neoliberal cascade and education: an essay on the market agenda and its consequences', *Critical Studies in Education, 54*(2): 99–112.

——— (2013b). 'Why do market 'reforms' persistently increase inequality?', *Discourse: Studies in the Cultural Politics of Education, 34*(2): 279–285.

——— (2014). 'Global tides: market and gender dynamics on a world scale', *Social Currents, 1*(1): 5–12.

——— (2019). *The Good University: What Universities Actually Do and Why It's Time for Radical Change*. Clayton, VIC: Monash University Publishing.

Connell, R.W. and Dados, N. (2014). 'Where in the world does neoliberalism come from? The market agenda in southern perspective', *Theory and Society, 43*(2): 117–138.

Connell, R.W., Hearn, J. and Kimmel, M.S. (2005). 'Introduction', in M.S. Kimmel, J. Hearn and R.W. Connell (eds.), *Handbook of Studies of Masculinities*. London: Sage Publications.

Connell, R.W. and Messerschmidt, J.W. (2005). 'Hegemonic masculinity: rethinking the concept', *Gender & Society, 19*(6): 829–859.

Connell, R.W. and Wood, J. (2005). 'Globalisation and business masculinities', *Men and Masculinities, 7*(4): 829–859.

Conti, J.A. and O'Neil, M. (2007). 'Studying power: qualitative methods and the global elite', *Qualitative Research, 7*(1): 63–82.

Cornwall, A. (2016). 'Introduction: masculinities under neoliberalism', in A. Cornwall, F.G. Karioris, and N. Lindisfarne (eds.), *Masculinities under Neoliberalism.* London: Zed Books Ltd.

Cox, K.R. (2011). 'Commentary: from the new urban politics to the "new" metropolitan politics', *Urban Studies, 48*(12): 2661–2671.

Credit Suisse. (2010). *Code of Conduct*, online at: www.credit-suisse.com/media/assets/corporate/docs/about-us/governance/standard-and-policies/code-of-conduct-en.pdf (accessed 20.10.18).

——— (2018). *Corporate: Corporate Responsibility*, online at: www.credit-suisse.com/corporate/en/responsibility.html (accessed 20.10.18).

Datta, K., McIlwaine, C., Evans, Y., Herbert, J., May, J. and Wills, J. (2007). From coping strategies to tactics: London's low-pay economy and migrant labour. *British Journal of Industrial Relations*, *45*(2), 404–432.

David, M.E. (2014). *Feminism, Gender and Universities: Politics, Passion and Pedagogies (Research into Higher Education).* Abingdon: Routledge.

de Vries, R. (2014). *Earning by Degrees: Differences in the Career Outcomes of UK Graduates.* London: Sutton Trust.

Deloitte. (2013). 'Culture in banking: under the microscope', in *The Deloitte Bank Survey 2013*, online at: https://www2.deloitte.com/content/dam/Deloitte/uk/Documents/financial-services/deloitte-uk-culture-in-banking.pdf (accessed 01.06.19).

Denscombe, M. (2014). *The Good Research Guide: For Small Scale Social Research Projects.* Maidenhead: McGraw-Hill Education.

Dermott, E. (2008). *Intimate Fatherhood: A Sociological Analysis.* Abingdon: Routledge.

Deutsche Bank. (2018a). *Company: Who We Are: Our Strategy*, online at: www.db.com/company/en/our-strategy.htm (accessed 20.06.18).

——— (2018b). *About Us: Our People: Our Location: Role Search*, online at: www.db.com/careers/en/prof/role-search/role-search-overview.html (accessed 20.06.18).

——— (2018c). *Students & Graduates: About Us: Diversity & Inclusion*, online at: www.db.com/careers/en/grad/about/diversity-inclusion.html (accessed 20.06.18).

——— (2018d). *Responsibility: Strategy: Corporate Culture and Corporate Values*, online at: www.db.com/cr/en/concrete-cultural-change.htm?kid=werte.inter.redirect (accessed 20.10.18).

Donaldson, M. (1993). 'What is hegemonic masculinity?' *Theory and Society, Special Issue: Masculinities, 22*(5): 643–657.

Donaldson, M. and Poynting, S. (2007). *Ruling Class Men: Money, Sex, Power.* Oxford: Peter Lang.

Druckman, D. (2005). *Doing Research.* London: Sage Publications.

Dupuis-Déri, F. (2018). *La Crise de la Masculinité: Autopsie d'un Mythe Tenace.* Montreal: Les Édition du remue-ménage.

Eagleton, T. (2018). *Why Marx Was Right.* New Haven, CT: Yale University Press.

Edwards, J. (2015). 'UK banks have axed 186,111 jobs since the 2008 crisis', in *Business Insider UK: Finance*, online at: http://uk.businessinsider.com/uk-banks-cut-jobs-since-2008-2015-7 (accessed 20.10.18).

Elliott, K. (2016). Caring masculinities: theorizing an emerging concept', *Men and Masculinities, 19*(3): 240–259.

Fairclough, N. and Wodak, R. (1997). 'Critical discourse analysis', in T.A. Van Dijk (ed.), *Discourse Studies: A Multidisciplinary Introduction*, 2. London: Sage Publications.

Featherstone, D. (2016). 'Contested spaces of hegemony: left alliances after the crisis', *Soundings: A Journal of Politics and Culture, 63*: 8–24.

Featherstone, D.J. (2012). 'Gramsci in action: space, politics and the making of solidaritie', in M. Ekers, G. Hart, S. Kipfer and A. Loftus (eds.), *Gramsci: Space, Nature, Politics*. Oxford: Wiley-Blackwell.

Featherstone, M. (1995). *Undoing Culture: Globalization, Postmodernism and Identity*. London: Sage Publications.

Flyvbjerg, B. (2006). 'Five misunderstandings about case-study research', *Qualitative Inquiry, 12*(2): 219–245.

Francis, B. and Hutchings, M. (2013). *Parent Power? Using Money and Information to Boost Children's Chances of Educational Success*. London: The Sutton Trust.

Fraser, N. (2019). *The Old Is Dying and the New Cannot Be Born: From Progressive Neoliberalism to Trump and Beyond*. London: Verso.

Friedman, S. and Laurison, D. (2019). *The Glass Ceiling: Why It Pays to Be Privileged*. Bristol: Policy Press.

Giddens, A. (2002). *Runaway World: How Globalisation Is Reshaping Our Lives* (Second Edition). London: Profile Books.

Gilding, M. (2010). 'Motives of the rich and powerful in doing interviews with social scientists', *International Sociology, 25*(6): 755–777.

Giroux, H. (2007). 'Beyond neoliberal common sense: cultural politics and public pedagogy in dark times', *JAC, 27*(1/2): 11–61.

——— (2011). 'From Benetton to Murdoch: the culture of money, shock and schlock', *Truthout*, online at: www.truth-out.org/opinion/item/2331:from-benetton-to-murdoch-the-culture-of-money-shock-and-schlock (accessed 20.10.18).

Glass, R. (1964). *London: Aspects of Change*. London: MacGibbon and Kee.

Goldman Sachs. (2018a). *Who We Are: At a Glance*, online at: www.goldmansachs.com/who-we-are/at-a-glance/index.html (accessed 19.06.18).

——— (2018b). *Who We Are: Business Principles and Standards*, online at: www.goldmansachs.com/who-we-are/business-standards/business-principles/ (accessed 19.06.18).

——— (2018c). *Who We Are: Diversity and Inclusion: Fostering Inclusion*, online at: www.goldmansachs.com/who-we-are/diversity-and-inclusion/fostering-inclusion/index.html (accessed 20.06.18).

——— (2018d). *Who We Are: Business Principles and Standards: Business Principles*, online at: www.goldmansachs.com/who-we-are/business-standards/business-principles/index.html (accessed 20.06.18).

——— (2018e). *Careers: Explore*, online at: www.goldmansachs.com/careers/students/explore/index.html (accessed 20.06.18).

——— (2018f). *Careers: Professionals*, online at: www.goldmansachs.com/careers/professionals/index.html (accessed 27.06.18).

——— (2018g). *Who We Are: People and Culture*, online at: www.goldmansachs.com/who-we-are/people-and-culture/index.html (accessed 27.6.18).

——— (2018h). 'Our shared responsibility to our clients, colleagues and communities', *Code of Business Conduct and Ethics*, online at: www.goldmansachs.com/investor-relations/corporate-governance/corporate-governance-documents/revise-code-of-conduct.pdf (accessed 20.10.18).

Grafton-Green, P. (2017). 'Brexit: pulling out of European single market "Serious for City of London"', *Evening Standard*, online at: www.standard.co.uk/news/london/pulling-out-of-european-single-market-serious-for-city-of-london-a3443121.html (accessed: 19.05.2017).

Gramsci, A. (1971). *Selections from the Prison Notebooks* (Q. Hoare and G. Nowell-Smith, eds.). London: Lawrence and Wishart Limited.

Gutmann, M. (1996). *The Meanings of Macho: Being a Man in Mexico City*. Berkley: University of California Press.

Hall, S., Massey, D. and Rustin, M. (2013). 'After neoliberalism: analysing the present', *Soundings: A Journal of Politics and Culture, 53*: 8–22.

Hanieh, A. (2009). 'Hierarchies of a global market: the south and the economic crisis', *Studies in Political Economy, Special Issue: Finance and Democracy, 83*: 61–84.

Hardt, M. and Negri, A. (2000). *Empire*. Cambridge, MA: Harvard University Press.

Harvey, D. (2006). *Spaces of Global Capitalism: Towards a Theory of Uneven Geographic Development*. London and New York: Verso Books.

——— (2010). *The Enigma of Capital*. Oxford: Oxford University Press.

——— (2011). 'Rebels on the street: the party of Wall Street meets its nemesis', online at: http://davidharvey.org/2011/10/rebels-on-the-street-the-party-of-wall-street-meets-its-nemesis/ (accessed 15.10.18).

——— (2012). *Rebel Cities: From the Right to the City to the Urban Revolution*. London: Verso.

Headworth, S., Nelson, R.L. Dinovitzer, R. and Wilkins, D.B. (eds.) (2016). *Diversity in Practice: Race, Gender and Class in Legal and Professional Careers*. Cambridge: Cambridge University Press.

Hearn, J. (2004). 'From hegemonic masculinity to the hegemony of men', *Feminist Theory, 5*(1): 49–72.

——— (2006). 'From masculinities back to men: tracing diverse psychological, social and political threads', *The Psychology of Women Section Review, 8*(1): 38–52.

——— (2009). 'Deconstructing the hegemony of men and masculinities – presentation of the research theme', *GEXcel Work in Progress Report Volume V*, online at: www.genderexcel.org (accessed 15.10.18).

——— (2012), 'A multi-faceted power analysis of men's violence to known women: from hegemonic masculinity to the hegemony of men', *The Sociological Review, 60*(4): 589–610.

——— (2014). 'Men, masculinities and the material(-)discursive', *NORMA: The International Journal for Masculinity Studies, 9*(1): 6–24.

——— (2015). *Men of the World: Genders, Globalizations, Transnational Times*. London: Sage.

Hearn, J., Blagojević, M. and Harrison, K. (eds.) (2013). *Rethinking Transnational Men: Beyond, Between and Within Nations*. Abingdon: Routledge.

Hearn, J. and Parkin, W. (2001). *Gender, Sexuality and Violence in Organizations*. London: Sage Publications.

Hearn, J. and Piekarri, R. (2005). 'Gendered leaderships and leaderships on gender policy: national context, corporate structures and chief human resources managers in transnational corporations'. *Leadership, 1*(4): 429–454.

Hecht, K. (2017). *A Relational Analysis of Top Incomes and Wealth: Economic Evaluation, Relative (Dis)advantage and the Service to Capital.* Working paper 11. London: London School of Economics and Political Science (LSE) International Inequalities Institute.

Held, V. (2006). *The Ethics of Care: Personal, Political and Global.* Oxford: Oxford University Press.

Hell, I. (2010). 'Masters of the universe redesign the world at Davos', *The Independent*, 24 January, online at: www.independent.co.uk/news/business/news/masters-of-the-universe-redesign-the-world-at-davos-1876926.html (accessed 15.10.18).

Hills, J., Brewer, M., Jenkins, S., Lister, R., Lupton, R., Machin, S., Mills, C., Modood, T., Rees, T. and Ridell, S. (2010). 'An anatomy of economic inequality in the UK: Report of the National Equality Panel', *CASE Reports*, casereport60, Centre for Analysis of Social Exclusion, London School of Economics (LSE).

HM Treasury and Virgin Money. (2016). *Empowering Productivity: Harnessing the Talents of Women in Financial Services*, online at: https://uk.virginmoney.com/virgin/assets/pdf/Virgin-Money-Empowering-Productivity-Report.pdf (accessed 15.10.18).

Ho, K. (2009). *Liquidated: An Ethnography of Wall Street.* Durham, NC: Duke University Press.

Holgersson, C. (2006). 'Homosocialitet som könsordnande process', *Nordic Journal for Masculinity Studies, 1*(1): 24–41.

Holter, Ø.G. (2009). 'Power and structure in studies of men and masculinities', *NORMA, 4*(2): 132–150.

Hopkins, P. and Noble, G. (2009). 'Masculinities in place: situated identities, relations and intersectionality', *Social and Cultural Geography, 10*(8): 811–819.

House of Commons (HoC). (2006). 'The schools white paper: higher standards, better school for all', *Education and Skills Committee – First Report of Session 2005–06, Volume 1.* Published on 25 January 2006 by authority of the House of Commons, London: The Stationary Office Limited.

——— (2009). 'Banking crisis: reforming corporate governance and pay in the city', *Treasury – Ninth Report, Session 2008–09.* Published on 12 May 2009 by authority of the House of Commons, London: The Stationary Office Limited.

——— (2010). 'Women in the city', *Treasury – Tenth Report, Session 2009–10.* Published on 3 April 2010 by authority of the House of Commons. London: The Stationary Office Limited.

——— (2018). 'Women in finance', *Treasury Committee – Fifteenth Report of Session 2017–19.* Published on 6 June 2018 by authority of the House of Commons. London: The Stationary Office Limited.

Hughes, E.A. and Wassall, A. (2013). 'UK bank assets to rise above 900% of GDP by 2050', *FT Adviser*, online at: www.ftadviser.com/2013/10/25/regulation/regulators/uk-bank-assets-to-rise-above-of-gdp-by-kpRxnbUURbleuMGUDrcDOP/article.html (accessed 15.10.18).

Izurieta, A. and Wade, R.H. (2010). 'Robert Wade on the global financial crisis', *Development and Change, 40*(6): 1153–1190.

Jackson, S. (2018). 'Young feminists, feminisms and digital media', *Feminism & Psychology, Special Issue: Feminisms and Social Media, 28*(1): 32–49.

Jakopovich, D. (2014). 'The concept of class', *Cambridge Studies in Social Research No. 14*. Cambridge: Social Science Research Group, University of Cambridge.

Jamieson, L. (2011). 'Intimacy as a concept: explaining social change in the context of globalisation or another form of ethnocentricism?', *Sociological Research Online, 16*(4): 15.

Jerrim, J. (2013). *Family Background and Access to 'High Status' Universities*. London: Sutton Trust.

Jones, O. (2014). *The Establishment: And How They Get Away With It*. London: Penguin Books.

J.P. Morgan. (2018a). *About Us*, online at: www.jpmorgan.com/global/about (accessed 19.06.18).

——— (2018b). *Career: Global: Why Us*, online at: https://careers.jpmorgan.com/careers/global/en/why-us (accessed 20.06.18).

——— (2018c). *About Us: People and Culture*, online at: www.jpmorganchase.com/corporate/About-JPMC/ab-people-culture.htm (accessed 27.06.18).

——— (2018d). *About Us: Business Principles*, online at: www.jpmorganchase.com/corporate/About-JPMC/ab-business-principles-operational-excellence.htm (accessed 27.06.18).

——— (2018e). *About Us*, online at: www.jpmorgan.com/country/PE/EN/jpmorgan/about (accessed 20.10.18).

Kehily, M.J. and Thomson, R. (2011). 'Figuring families: generation, situation and narrative in contemporary mothering', *Sociological Research Online, 16*(4): 16.

Kenway, J. and Koh, A. (2013). 'The elite school as 'cognitive machine' and 'social paradise': developing transnational capitals for the national 'field of power', *Journal of Sociology, 49*(3): 272–290.

Kezar, A. (2003). 'Transformational elite interviews: principles and problems', *Qualitative Inquiry, 9*(3): 395–415.

Klein, N. (2007). *The Shock Doctrine*. London: Penguin Books.

——— (2009). *Capitalism, Sarah Palin-Style*, online at: http://www.naomiklein.org/articles/2009/07/capitalism-sarah-palin-style (accessed 01.04.19).

——— (2014). *This Changes Everything: Capitalism vs. the Climate*. London: Penguin Books.

——— (2017). *No Is Not Enough: Defeating the New Shock Politics*. London: Penguin Books.

Kowelle, J. and Davies, R. (2016). 'Number of city bankers earning above €1m rises to nearly 3,000', *The Guardian*, online at: www.theguardian.com/business/2016/mar/30/rise-number-city-financiers-uk-earning-more-than-1m (accessed 15.10.18).

Laclau, E. and Mouffe, C. (1985). *Hegemony and Socialist Strategy: Towards a Radical Democratic Politics*. London: Verso.

Lanchester, J. (2016). 'Brexit blues', *London Review of Books, 38*(15), 3–6.

Lappé, F.M. (2016 (reprint)). 'Food farming and democracy', in R. Clark (ed.), *Our Sustainable Table: Essays*. Berkeley, CA: Counterpoint Press.

Letherby, G. (2003). *Feminist Research in Theory and Practice*. Buckingham: Open University Press.

Longlands, H. and Collier, R. (2018). 'Interrogating transnational masculinities, fatherhood and the institutions of men – rethinking gender equality in global finance and large international law firms', in J. Hearn, E. Vasquez del Aguila and M. Hughson (eds.), *Unsustainable Institutions of Men: Transnational Dispersed Centres, Gender Power, Contradictions*. Abingdon: Routledge.

Luyendijk, J. (2013). 'Banking blog: going native in the World of Finance', *The Guardian*, online at: www.theguardian.com/commentisfree/joris-luyendijk-banking-blog (accessed 20.10.18).

Madrid, S. (2013). 'Getting into the lives of ruling class men: conceptual problems. Methodological solutions', in B. Pini and B. Pease (eds.), *Men, Masculinities and Methodologies*. London: Palgrave.

——— (2017). 'The good night kiss: fatherhood among corporate managers and the reconfiguration of hegemonic masculinity in Chile', *Norma: International Journal for Masculinity Studies, 12*(3–4): 240–255.

Manfredi, S., Jarboe, N. and Clayton-Hathway, K. (2016). *Changing Places: Women on Boards*. Oxford: Oxford Brookes University, Centre for Diversity Policy Research and Practice.

Massey, D. (2005). *For Space*. London: Sage Publications Ltd.

——— (2010). *World City* (First Edition 2007, Reprinted in 2010 with New Preface: 'After the Crash'). Cambridge: Polity.

Maxwell, C. and Aggleton, P. (2010). 'The bubble of privilege. Young, privately educated women talk about social class', *British Journal of Sociology of Education, 31*(1): 3–15.

——— (eds.) (2016). *Elite Education: International Perspectives*. Abingdon: Routledge.

McDowell, L. (2010). 'Capital culture revisited: sex, testosterone and the city', *International Journal of Urban and Regional Research, 34*(3): 652–658.

McDowell, L., Perrons, D., Fagan, C., Ray, K. and Ward, K. (2005). 'The contradictions and intersections of class and gender in a global city: placing working women's lives on the research agenda', *Environment and Planning A, 37*(3): 441–461.

McNamee, S.J. and Miller, R.K. (2009). *The Meritocracy Myth* (Second Edition). Lanham, MD: Rowman & Littlefield Publishers.

Messerschmidt, J.W. (2010). *Hegemonic Masculinities and Camouflaged Politics: Unmasking the Bush Dynasty and Its War Against Iraq*. London: Paradigm Publishers.

——— (2012). 'Engendering gendered knowledge: assessing the academic appropriation of hegemonic masculinity', *Men and Masculinities, 15*(1): 56–76.

Messner, M.A. (1992). *Power at Play: Sports and the Problem of Masculinity*. Boston, MA: Beacon Press.

Meyer, J.W. (2000). 'Globalization: sources and effects on national states and societies', *International Sociology, 15*(2): 233–248.

Miller, T. (2011). *Making Sense of Fatherhood: Gender, Caring and Work*. Cambridge: Cambridge University Press.

Morgan Stanley. (2015). *Your Benefits 2016: UK Benefits Programme*, online at: https://morganstanley.tbs.aon.com/Morganstanley/media/default/8403446_A5_Gatefold_Programme_2016_588x210_SCREEN.PDF (accessed 29.10.18).

——— (2018a). *About Us: We Believe Capital Can Work to Benefit All of Society*, online at: www.morganstanley.com/about-us (accessed 19.06.18).

——— (2018b). *About Us: Supplier Diversity*, online at: www.morganstanley.com/about-us/supplier-diversity (accessed 20.06.18).

——— (2018c). *About Us: Diversity and Inclusion*, online at: www.morganstanley.com/about-us/diversity (accessed 20.06.18).

——— (2018d). *About Us: Our Core Values*, online at: www.morganstanley.com/about-us/morgan-stanley-core-values (accessed 20.20.18).

Nadar, L. (1972). 'Up the anthropologist: perspectives gained from studying up', in D.H. Hynes (ed.), *Reinventing Anthropology*. New York: Pantheon.

Navidi, S. (2017). *Superhubs: How the Financial Elite and Their Networks Rule Our World*. London: Nicholas Brealey Publishing.

Nyström, A.-S., Jackson, C. and Salminen Karlsson, M. (2018). 'What counts as success? Constructions of achievement in higher education programmes', *Research Papers in Education*, 1–18.

Odendahl, T. and Shaw, A.M. (2002). 'Interviewing elites', in J.F. Gubrium and J.A. Holstein (eds.), *Handbook of Interview Research: Context & Method*. Thousand Oaks, CA: Sage Publications.

Ohmae, K. (2005). *The Next Global Stage: Challenges and Opportunities in our Borderless World*. Upper Saddle River, NJ: Prentice Hall.

Olchawski, J. (2016). *Parents, Work and Care: Striking the Balance*. London: Fawcett Society.

Olssen, M. and Peters, M.A. (2005). 'Neoliberalism, higher education and the knowledge economy: from the free market to knowledge capitalism', *Journal of Education Policy, 20*(3): 313–345.

Ouroussoff, A. (2010). *Wall Street at War: The Secret Struggle for the Global Economy*. Cambridge: Polity.

Perrons, D. (2005). 'Gender mainstreaming and gender equality in the new (market) economy: an analysis of contradictions', *Social Politics, 12*(3): 389–411.

——— (2010). 'Gender, work and market recognition: understanding and challenging 'market' values', *Renewal, 18*(1–2): 34–42.

——— (2015). 'Gender inequality in times of inequality, crisis and austerity: towards gender sensitive macroeconomic policies', in F. Bettio and S. Sansonetti (eds.), *Visions for Gender Equality*. Luxembourg: Gender Equality, European Commission – Directorate-General for Justice.

Perrons, D., Lacey, N., Phillips, A., Wearing, S., Ashtiany, S., Biressi, A., Carter, C., Chakrabarti, S., Chinkin, C., Couldry, N., Criado-Perez, C., DeLargy, P., Dobbs, L., Harris, S., Himmelweit, S., Jenkins, K., Kabeer, N., Lovenduski, J., Manning, A., Murray, R., Negra, D., Neitzert, E., Orgad, S., Plomien, A., Sen, P., Spicer, H. and Starmer, K. (2016). *Confronting Gender Inequality: Findings from the LSE Commission on Gender, Inequality and Power*. London: London School of Economics and Political Science, Gender Institute.

Piketty, T. (2014). *Capital in the Twenty-First Century*. Cambridge, MA: The Belknap Press of Harvard University Press.

Poster, W. (2013). 'Subversions of techno-masculinity: Indian ICT professionals in the global economy', in J. Hearn, M. Blagojević and K. Harrison (eds.), *Rethinking Transnational Men: Beyond, between and Within Nations*. Abingdon: Routledge.

Power, S., Edwards, T., Whitty, G. and Wigfall, V. (2003). *Education in the Middle Classes*. Buckingham: Open University Press.

Prins, N. (2009). *It Takes a Pillage*. Hoboken, NJ: John Wiley & Sons, Inc.

Ramazanoğlu, C. and Holland, J. (2002). *Feminist Methodology: Challenges and Choices*. London: Sage Publications.

Reay, D., Hollingworth, S., Williams, K., Crozier, G., Jamieson, F., James, D. and Beedell, P. (2007). '"A darker shade of pale?" Whiteness, the middle classes and multi-ethnic inner city schooling', *Sociology, 41*(6): 1041–1060.

Reis, C. (2002). *The Private and Public Lives of Men Managers in a European Multinational Company: A Feminist Cross-Cultural Analysis between England, Germany and Portugal.* PhD Thesis, Institute of Education, University of London.

Reuters. (2017). 'Daily FX trade more like $3 trillion than 5 – CLS', *Reuters: Fund News*, online at: www.reuters.com/article/global-forex-volumes/daily-fx-trade-more-like-3-trillion-than-5-cls-idUSL5N1GK1F5 (accessed 20.10.18).

Rouse, C.E. and Barrow, L. (2009). 'School vouchers and student achievement: recent evidence and remaining questions', *Annual Review of Economics, 1*: 17–42.

Rushe, D. (2011). 'Financial turmoil even hits the masters of the universe: Goldman Sachs' Blankfein and JP Morgan's Dimon suffer millions of dollars of paper losses', *The Guardian*, online at: www.theguardian.com/business/2011/aug/11/financial-turmoil-even-hits-masters-of-the-universe (accessed 15.10.18).

Sandel, M.J. (2010). *Justice: What's the Right Thing to Do?* New York: Farrar, Straus and Giroux.

——— (2012). *What Money Can't Buy: The Moral Limits of Markets.* London: Penguin Books Ltd.

Sands, D. (2013). 'The changing labour market: delivering for women, delivering for growth'. A report prepared by *The Fawcett Society*, online at: www.fawcettsociety.org.uk/the-changing-labour-market-delivering-for-women-delivering-for-growth (accessed 20.10.18).

Sassen, S. (2001). *The Global City: New York, London, Tokyo* (Second Edition). Princeton, NJ: Princeton University Press.

——— (2002). 'Locating cities on global circuits', *Environment and Urbanization, 14*(1): 13–30, special issue on Globalization and Cities.

——— (2009a). 'Too big to save: the end of financial capitalism', online at: www.opendemocracy.net/article/too-big-to-save-the-end-of-financial-capitalism-0 (accessed 15.10.18).

——— (2009b). 'Global cities and survival circuits', in J. Radway, K.K. Gaines, B. Shank and P. Von Eschen (eds.), *American Studies: An Anthology*. Oxford: Blackwell-Wiley.

——— (2013). 'When territory deborders territoriality', *Territory, Politics, Governance, 1*(1): 21–45.

——— (2014). *Expulsions: Brutality and Complexity in the Global Economy.* London: The Belknap Press of Harvard University Press.

Savage, M. (2000). *Class Analysis and Social Transformation.* Buckingham: Open University Press.

Sealy, R., Doldor, E., Singh, V. and Vinnicombe, S. (2011). *Women on Boards: 6 Month Monitoring Report* (Cranfield School of Management), Cranfield: Cranfield University School of Management.

Sealy, R., Doldor, E. and Vinnicombe, S. (2016). 'Women on boards: taking stock of where we are'. *The Female FTSE Board Report 2016.* Cranfield University School of Management, Cranfield.

Sealy, R. and Vinnicombe, S. (2013). 'The female FTSE Board Report, 2013'. *Cranfield International Centre for Women Leaders, Cranfield School of Management.* Cranfield University School of Management, Cranfield.

Sen, A. (2009). 'Capitalism beyond the crisis', *New York Review of Books, 56*(5), online at: www.nybooks.com/articles/22490 (accessed 15.10.18).

Sennett, R. (1998). *The Corrosion of Character: The Personal Consequences of Work in the New Capitalism*. New York: WW Norton & Company, Inc.

Siraj-Blatchford, I., Mayo, A., Melhuish, E., Taggart, B., Sammons, P. and Sylva, K. (2011). 'Performing against the odds: developmental trajectories of children in the EPPSE 3–16 study'. *Department for Education Research Brief 128*. Department for Education, UK Government, London.

Stedman Jones, D. (2012). *Masters of the Universe: Hayek, Friedman, and the Birth of Neoliberal Politics*. Princeton, NJ: Princeton University Press.

Swift, A. (2003). *How Not to Be a Hypocrite: School Choice for the Morally Perplexed Parent*. Abingdon: Routledge.

TheCityUK. (2017). *Key Facts: About the UK as an International Financial Centre 2017*. London: TheCityUK.

——— (2018). *UK Fund Management*. London: TheCityUK.

The Times. (2016). 'HSBC chairman on Brexit: "We have to turn the challenges into opportunities"', online at: www.thetimes.co.uk/static/exporting-for-growth/hsbc-chairman-on-brexit-we-have-to-turn-the-challenges-into-opportunities/ (accessed 20.10.18).

Tienari, J., Vaara, E. and Meriläinen, S. (2010). 'Becoming an international man: top manager masculinities in the making of a multinational corporation', *Equal Opportunities International, 29*(1): 38–52.

Tooze, A. (2018). *Crashed: How a Decade of Financial Crises Changed the World*. London: Allen Lane.

Toynbee, P. and Walker, D. (2008). *Unjust Rewards: Exposing Greed and Inequality in Britain Today*. London: Granta Books.

Treanor, J. (2010). 'Investigation launched into soaring executive pay', *The Guardian*, online at: www.guardian.co.uk/business/2010/nov/09/executive-pay-inquiry-launched (accessed 19.10.18).

——— (2012). 'Taxpayers' £66bn in RBS and Lloyds at risk, say MPs', online at: www.theguardian.com/business/2012/nov/16/taxpayers-share-rbs-loyds-at-risk (accessed 15.10.18).

——— (2015). 'Lloyds pays boss £11.5m and resumes dividend after seven years', *The Guardian*, online at: www.theguardian.com/business/2017/jan/10/hard-brexit-threatens-global-financial-system-city-chiefs-tell-mps (accessed 20.10.18).

——— (2017). 'Hard Brexit threatens global financial system, City chiefs tell MPs', *The Guardian*, online at: www.theguardian.com/business/2015/feb/27/lloyds-pays-antonio-horta-osorio-11m-resumes-dividend-after-six-years (accessed 20.10.18).

Treanor, J. and Farrell, S. (2016). 'Lloyds Banking Group to cut 1,755 jobs and close 29 branches', *The Guardian*, online at: www.theguardian.com/business/2016/feb/03/lloyds-announces-job-cuts-branch-closures (accessed 15.10.18).

Tucker, J. 2010. 'Financial crises: A culture of complacency', *Journal of Organizational Transformation and Social Change*, 7(1): 7–23.

UBS. (2018a). Careers: Why UBS? www.ubs.com/global/en/about_ubs/careers/why-ubs.html (accessed 27.06.18).

——— (2018b). *Investment Bank: About Us: Who We Are*, online at: www.ubs.com/global/en/investment-bank/about-us/who-we-are.html (accessed 27.06.18).

——— (2018c). *Global Topics*, online at: www.ubs.com/global/en.html (accessed 27.06.18).

UK Government. (2017). *Government Response to the House of Lords European Union Committee Report, 'Brexit: Financial Services'*, online at: www.parliament.uk/business/committees/committees-a-z/lords-select/eu-financial-affairs-subcommittee/news-parliament-2015/financial-services-government-response/ (accessed 19.05.2017).

Unterhalter, E. (2007). *Gender, Schooling and Global Social Justice*. Abingdon: Routledge.

Unterhalter, E. and North, A. (2018). *Education, Poverty and Global Goals for Gender Equality: How People Make Policy Happen*. Abingdon: Routledge.

Van Dijk, T.A. (2011). *Discourse Studies: A Multidisciplinary Introduction* (Second Edition). London: Sage Publications.

Ventura, P. (2012). *Neoliberalism Culture: Living with American Neoliberalism*. Farnham: Ashgate.

Verlaine, J. and Choudhury, A. (2015). Horta-Osario's compensation jumps as Lloyds returns to profit, *Bloomberg*, online at: www.bloomberg.com/news/articles/2015-02-27/horta-osorio-s-compensation-jumps-as-lloyds-returns-to-profit (accessed 20.10.18).

Vincent, C. and Ball, S.J. (2006). *Childcare, Choice and Class Practices: Middle-Class Parents and Their Children*. Abingdon: Routledge.

Whitehead, S.M. (2002). *Men and Masculinities: Key Themes and New Directions*. Cambridge: Polity Press.

Wilkinson R. and Pickett, K. (2010). *The Spirit Level: Why Equality Is Better for Everyone*. London: Penguin Books.

——— (2019). *The Inner Level: How More Equal Societies Reduce Stress, Restore Sanity and Improve Everyone's Well-being*. London: Allen Lane.

Wintour, P. and Elliott, L. (2010). 'Spending review axe falls on the poor', online at: www.theguardian.com/politics/2010/oct/20/spending-cuts-george-osborne-axe (accessed 15.10.18).

Wodak, R. and Meyer, M. (2009). 'Critical discourse analysis: history, agenda, theory and methodology', in R. Wodak and M. Meyer (eds.), *Methods for Critical Discourse Analysis*. London: Sage Publications.

Wolfe, T. (1987). *Bonfire of the Vanities*. London: Vintage Books.

Wright, E.O. (1985). *Classes*. London: Verso.

Young, I.M. (2011). *Responsibility for Justice*. Oxford: Oxford University Press.

Zhang, Z. (2001). 'Mediating time: The "rice bowl of youth" in *fin de siècle* Urban China', in A. Appadurai (ed.), *Globalization*. Durham, NC: Duke University Press.

Index

Note: Page numbers followed by "n" denote endnotes.

For Product Safety Concerns and Information please contact our EU representative GPSR@taylorandfrancis.com
Taylor & Francis Verlag GmbH, Kaufingerstraße 24, 80331 München, Germany

www.ingramcontent.com/pod-product-compliance
Ingram Content Group UK Ltd.
Pitfield, Milton Keynes, MK11 3LW, UK
UKHW011015180926
475701UK00004B/747
9780367785055